COMPLEX CASES IN SPORT PSYCHOLOGY

Complex Cases in Sport Psychology offers instructors and students a unique and novel approach to teaching and learning about sport psychology. The book consists of a series of character-driven narratives—set within the context of a university athletic department—which encourage discussion and critical thinking in order to find solutions to issues such as athletes lacking in motivation, introducing mental skills training programs and improving recruitment.

The book begins with a section introducing the teaching cases approach (suggesting further reading and methods for its delivery), the university setting and the issues this context provides for the sport psychologist, and the cast of characters involved. It goes on to detail over twenty cases spread across four parts (organizational performance, team performance, individual performance, and injury and recovery), each based around a piece of theory and including clear learning outcomes, tasks and non-prescriptive guidance on reaching a solution.

With online resources which include topical cases, further guidance on the teaching cases approach and an instructor's manual, this is an essential supplementary resource for any instructor looking to provide experiential learning and encourage critical thinking in their sport psychology classrooms. Covering a full range of psychological issues in a relevant sporting context, it is also an important, hands-on guide to counseling for any upper-level student of sport psychology.

John E. Coumbe-Lilley, PhD, CMPC, CSCS, is a Clinical Associate Professor, Department of Kinesiology and Nutrition, University of Illinois at Chicago, USA. He has been providing sport psychology consulting services since 1999 for college, national and Olympic athletes and teams.

COMPLEX CASES IN SPORT PSYCHOLOGY

John E. Coumbe-Lilley

Routledge
Taylor & Francis Group
LONDON AND NEW YORK

First published 2018
by Routledge
2 Park Square, Milton Park, Abingdon, Oxon OX14 4RN

and by Routledge
711 Third Avenue, New York, NY 10017

Routledge is an imprint of the Taylor & Francis Group, an informa business

© 2018 John E. Coumbe-Lilley

The right of John E. Coumbe-Lilley to be identified as author of this work has been asserted by him in accordance with sections 77 and 78 of the Copyright, Designs and Patents Act 1988.

All rights reserved. No part of this book may be reprinted or reproduced or utilised in any form or by any electronic, mechanical, or other means, now known or hereafter invented, including photocopying and recording, or in any information storage or retrieval system, without permission in writing from the publishers.

Trademark notice: Product or corporate names may be trademarks or registered trademarks, and are used only for identification and explanation without intent to infringe.

British Library Cataloguing in Publication Data
A catalogue record for this book is available from the British Library

Library of Congress Cataloging in Publication Data
Names: Coumbe-Lilley, John E., author.
Title: Complex cases in sport psychology / John E. Coumbe-Lilley.
Description: Milton Park, Abingdon, Oxon : New York, NY : Routledge, 2018. | Includes bibliographical references and index.
Identifiers: LCCN 2018000135 | ISBN 9781138897366 (hbk) | ISBN 9781315178882 (ebk) | ISBN 9781138897397 (pbk.)
Subjects: LCSH: Sports--Psychological aspects--Case studies. | College athletes--Psychology--Case studies.
Classification: LCC GV706.4 .C689 2018 | DDC 796.01/9--dc23
LC record available at https://lccn.loc.gov/2018000135

ISBN: 978-1-138-89736-6 (hbk)
ISBN: 978-1-138-89739-7 (pbk)
ISBN: 978-1-315-17888-2 (ebk)

Typeset in Bembo
by Taylor & Francis Books

Visit the online resources: www.routledge.com/9781138897397

For all athletes, coaches, administrators and peers who shared their college sport experiences with me.

CONTENTS

Preface ix
The teaching case method xiii
Cast of characters: chapter(s) xxiii

1 Burnout/self-handicapping 1
2 Coach–athlete relationship 10
3 Seizing an opportunity to play professional soccer 20
4 Anterior cruciate ligament (ACL) injury rehabilitation 29
5 Goal keeping errors during games 37
6 Coach–athlete relationship conflict 49
7 Coming out 58
8 Staying with or leaving a team 65
9 Hand injury 74
10 Coach development 81
11 Transition out of college sport 91
12 Underperformance 102
13 Coach personal development 112
14 Eating disorder 122

15	Binge drinking	131
16	On-court aggression	140
17	Team toughness	150
18	Team building	158
19	Team development	168
20	Sport administrator-directed improvement: part 1	178
21	Sport administrator-directed improvement: part 2	188

Index *198*

PREFACE

I was inspired to write this book for college teachers in my field because of the experiences I had in my classes with students who came alive when they were encouraged to think critically about issues in challenging ways and express their ideas without the fear of being right or wrong. I was first exposed to the method from my own research and reading; then by chance I received an email advertisement from the Harvard T.H. Chan School of Public Health about learning the teaching case method through a public health lens. I attended a three-day session in Cambridge, Massachusetts, before attending the training, and completed a series of pre-reading and exercises all attendees were expected to do (which is a feature of the teaching method). Fifty other professors from around the US and I engaged in long days of learning, practice, discussion and assumption testing. I came away inspired by my peers with a renewed commitment to the approach and to my teaching. My self-awareness as a teacher increased, and my creativity was sparked to write teaching cases for my students based on my consulting experiences. I became even more engaged in my passion for teaching and learning.

These days I frequently write fresh cases and lead teaching case sessions at my own institution in courses with undergraduates and graduates in the fields of sport and exercise psychology, nutrition counseling and teaching in higher education. Teaching cases are grounded in reality, directly connected to rich evidence-based content and real cases found in the popular press. The heart and lungs of a good teaching case is a story that students connect with. It has clarity and the stakes are invariably higher than normal; some risk is present in the case that has to be mitigated. Like many other readers of fiction, I enjoy a good story. But I prefer reading non-fiction even more because I am inspired by ordinary people doing extraordinary things. I am amazed when unexpected situations happen to them or they are involved in challenging moments demanding they face up to them and they continue to strive to reach a goal or find a solution. While the defining characteristics of the individuals, locations, and teams have been obscured, the cases presented in this text communicate real situations and dilemmas challenging the reader to consider how they might approach the issues presented. This book outlines the teaching case method; my belief is that this kind of face-to-face learning is the nexus of classroom learning. It enhances decision-making capabilities of emerging and new professionals and creates strong connections leading to significant learning experiences.

Through my teaching I have used many fantastic text books in sport and exercise psychology. These texts often provide valuable surveys of the field, but have not really helped me in the ways I needed to develop critical thinking and decision making in my students. There are terrific case study texts where leaders in our field provide expert views and pathways guiding us through how they approached specific cases, and the Association of Applied Sport Psychology (AASP) has introduced the online journal *Case Studies in Sport and Exercise Psychology* (*CSSEP*) to disseminate learning and experience from actual cases. These are positive learning opportunities, but none gripping enough to focus the critical attention of my students or recognize the nuances and inconsistencies of the human character, competition and organizational contexts in sport. On one hand they represent what I feel is best about our field, which is knowledge production, sharing and strong scholarly communication. However, I found it challenging to engage the attention of my students in the content and promote independent critical thinking, allowing them to identify the key facts for themselves, make up their own minds about an approach, and then defend their own decisions about how they might handle a specific case. I often feel academic texts identify a problem or an issue but seldom suggest how things can be improved in the real world, and seemingly reduce solutions to a check list of activities to be completed. They rarely touch on the operating assumptions, culture, emotional elements and humanity in a sport situation. By using teaching cases I found an important solution for improving student learning and relating research evidence with the humanity in sport situations found in the field. These connections led me to create richer learning and enjoyable teaching experiences.

In my view, the spirit of discovery and exploration with an expert teacher facilitating the conversation is central to guided learning for discovery. This book is aimed at the creative college teacher who desires a teaching approach capable of capturing their students' attention and who want to challenge themselves and their students to immerse themselves in the field.

I believe we want students in our field and those who dream of becoming sport psychology practitioners to be prepared thoroughly enough to identify the key facts and features they are presented with and make judgments and decisions leading to positive actions. Teaching cases can help prepare new professionals and help accelerate their understanding of the challenges and opportunities they will face in their practice.

What follows below is a guide to help college teachers use this text, and use it as a starting point for their way of applying the teaching case method. The first section of the book explains the teaching case method; then a guide to teaching and assessing the method is provided so that the teacher has a place to start using the approach immediately. The main section of the book provides teachers with cases drawn from my experience as a sport psychology consultant working with college student-athletes, and cases that I was briefed on in detail. All character names, teams and sport affiliations have been changed to avoid direct comparison with any cases, people or sports I have been involved with.

I encourage readers to review the sections about the teaching method and recommendations about how to be an effective teaching case facilitator. An instructor can select the cases in this text in any order they want for their own purposes and the unique qualities of their course and course members. At the end of each case you can find my responses to the case and further reading from contemporary researchers and thought leaders in the field, providing additional perspectives on each case.

During the preparation for writing this guide for college teachers I was asked why I chose not to focus the teaching cases on national team or professional levels of sport performance. The reasons for my decision not to spotlight those performance environments follow here.

There are very few elite athletes in any sport. They have often achieved success and accomplishment because they developed the tools necessary to cope on the way to these levels of competition. There are exceptions and cases at the elite level where the usual and customary mental performance tools like visualization, goal setting and relaxation are used to enhance performance. However, often mental health, emotional wellbeing and mental illness issues arise at the level of elite sport which might affect sport performance for specific athletes and coaches. I feel that an experienced licensed clinical psychologist or similar qualified mental health professional with experience in sport performance is more useful to professional athletes and elite sport organizations than an unlicensed sport psychology professional because of the pressures surrounding elite performance.

I know from having worked at elite levels of competition and not being a licensed clinical mental health provider that I was limited in my scope of practice, and I often referred athletes to properly qualified, trained professionals to provide the necessary services I was not able or licensed to give. I learned early on in my career that an unlicensed individual should "stay in their lane" and know their ethical and legal boundaries and the scope of their role. This text concentrates on student-athletes because it is likely the students of college teachers using this guide might relate more strongly to and recognize the situations more readily than those arising at elite levels of sport competitions like the Olympics or the World Championships. It is also possible that graduate student internships or practicums might occur in a college sport setting.

According to the National College Athletic Association (NCAA, 2017) there are 460,000 student-athletes, and about 65,000 student-athletes compete in other organizations such as the National Athletic Intercollegiate Association (NAIA, 2017). These numbers are dwarfed by the High School Athletics Participatory

Survey for 2014–15 which reports that 7.8 million students engaged in competition (NFHS, 2017). It is possible that emerging sport psychology practitioners developing their knowledge base, expertise, clinical skills and emotional selves are likely to work with teens and young adults as part of their development process. While the United States has significant youth and college sport environments allowing development of teaching cases, it is not the only country where these kinds of teaching cases might develop. For example, the British Universities & Colleges Sport organizing body has 170 universities competing with each other, and approximately 160,018 participants (BUCS, 2017); Canada has U Sports, the national governing body for university-level sport, with approximately 12,000 athletes (U Sports, 2017); Australian University Sport represents over 1 million participants (AUS, 2017); and the European University Sport Association hosted 19 championships in 2016 (EUSA, 2017). These examples of student athlete participation demonstrate that teaching cases concerning this population are helpful for developing understanding in sport psychology students.

Lastly, the issue of why focus on student athletes involves the complexity of the situations I experienced. The life of a student athlete is often defined by time and playing eligibility in student competitions. These aspects are characterized by a series of inevitable and unavoidable sport, personal, social and academic transitions. There is a defined beginning and defined end to a student-athlete's college playing career. Student-athletes tend to be young adults who are forming their ideas and identities. As such, the issues that present themselves in this context can be highly complex and far-reaching, with major and lasting impacts on those involved. It is for all these reasons I chose to draw from my experiences with student-athletes and offer this text as a useful addition to the college educator's toolkit, helping to focus student attention and develop their critical thinking through critical dialog.

References

Australian University Sport(AUS). (2017). About Australian University Sport. Retrieved from www.unisport.com.au/inside-aus/inside-aus

British Universities & Colleges Sport(BUCS). (2017). Active Universities Evaluation Report, Year 3: Summer 2014. Retrieved from www.bucs.org.uk/page.asp?section=17414&sectionTitle=Sport+England

European University Sport Association(EUSA). (2017). About EUSA. Retrieved from www.eusa.eu/eusa/about-eusa

National Association of Intercollegiate Athletics(NAIA). (2017). About the NAIA. Retrieved from www.naia.org/ViewArticle.dbml?DB_OEM_ID=27900&ATCLID=205323019

National College Athletic Association(NCAA). (2017). Sports Sponsorship and Participation Research. Retrieved from www.ncaa.org/about/resources/research/sports-sponsorship-and-participation-research

U Sports. (2017). U-Sports 2016–present. Retrieved from https://usports.ca/en/about/history

THE TEACHING CASE METHOD

The teaching case instructional method is a content-rich, discourse-facilitated process led by a subject matter expert who is skilled at facilitating whole class discussions. This approach is not new; according to Herried (2011), the use of this kind of method started at Harvard University 100 years ago. It began in the Business School and spread to other disciplines in others forms through the twentieth century. These forms included the lecture case told in the form of a story firmly instructor centered, with analysis and wisdom imparted by the professor to the students about the case. Discussion cases were whole class facilitated discussions led with the idea that group dialog would conjure up learning and wisdom. As the decades moved on, small group discussions focused on a teaching case took root and evidence began to show that small cooperative and collaborative groups learned more through the teaching case method compared to other methods. This approach was found to promote diverse opinions and respect for alternative judgments and viewpoints. A supplemental approach is to provide direct cases to individuals to process on their own and return to class with a response for discussion.

For the purposes of this guide I suggest giving the case ahead of time for students to study or having them start with it in class and compare which approach yields the best outcomes in your class. Each course is different because there are different members in it. I experiment with this approach early on in the semester and find which works better and then stay with it.

For the teaching case method to be effective the case presented to students (whether before or during class) should follow the principles Abell (1997) recommends:

1. Ensure the case presents an issue that must be resolved, not just a story. This process requires a decision to be made by the student on what they might do to resolve the issues presented. It is not enough to identify the issues in the

case; the student must decide how a solution might be used to solve the problem posed.
2. The case tackles an important issue in the field. Important issues might include those which are topical and relevant to the contemporary sport environment. Cases can be of a technical, social, personal or organizational nature, or a combination of these elements.
3. The case should encourage discovery by the student of alternative points of view. Cases that cause values, attitudes, beliefs and/or conflicting ideas to be discussed often lead to meaningful learning.
4. Use a case that has a sense of controversy about it. A case which elicits heated intellectual exchanges shows it has content provoking strong responses because it touches on issues students take personal ownership of.
5. Contrast and comparisons should be part of the teaching case method. In order for decisions to be made at the end of the learning process differences should be highlighted, promoting critical thinking through evaluation.
6. Introduce cases with specific details that students might develop generalized applications from. This point is useful because issues presented in a case can provide broader understanding of an issue influencing future dealings with the issue presented.
7. The case should contain data in the form of contextual descriptions, quantifiable information and the predispositions of the individuals in the case. Cases should be contextually relevant to the issue being presented, and the information presented ought to connect with the course content.
8. Cases with recognizable characters add a personal touch for the student. Characters give students a point of view they can look at the issue through. It gives them an opportunity to examine the issues through a different lens and express empathy for an individual too.
9. Cases should be concentrated and concise and no longer than ten pages of double-spaced lines. Tightly written cases that focus the attention of the reader on the key issues are preferred.
10. The case should be easy to read and follow. Jargon-heavy texts get in the way of reader understanding. This does not mean they should be written in a colloquial manner, but they should use language any reader in the course can readily grasp. Cases should simplify the presentation of the issues not dumb them down.

For cases to be effectively examined and discussed in a course, instructors are responsible for assuring students have the necessary content knowledge to respond to the issues presented. Students should be prepared to engage in discussion which might unsettle them a little bit too. Sometimes students from different learning backgrounds and cultures might be taken by surprise by this approach, which requires every student to contribute to the dialog and express their position and justify their decisions. Several ways college teachers can prepare students to participate in dialog is to follow the steps below.

1. Explain the teaching case method.
2. Describe the roles and responsibilities of everyone in the course when the teaching case method is going to be used.
3. Set the ground rules for discussion before it begins, and make sure every student recognizes their responsibility in the learning process.
4. Conduct a micro session to show students how things work.

The role of the instructor

The role of the instructor in the classroom is to facilitate effective discussion with prepared questions that guide the discussion toward consensus and then change direction to create controversy. A contest of ideas should be promoted and encouraged. Weighing and evaluating of evidence should be part of the discussion, and whiteboard work is essential. This teaching method provides a college educator with the opportunity to display a range of content knowledge, teaching skills and expertise. Educators should demonstrate a constructivist teaching style, examining cases through discussion to understand the case presented, weigh up the issues and evaluate the approaches that might be taken. The result of this process should assure students decide a possible course of action to resolve challenges posed in the case. The following sections review important considerations for college teachers who are thinking about but have not yet started using the teaching case method as part of their regular approach to teaching.

Your teaching philosophy

Before you begin using cases take time to clarify what your beliefs are about critical thinking and how you develop it in your students. Fundamentally, the use of the teaching case method engages students to critically evaluate, analyze and determine a course of action based on the evidence presented in the case. In order for them to complete these tasks they should be able to engage in powerful dialog, and conditions should be created that foster significant learning (Fink, 2013). If you are considering using the teaching case method, be clear in your mind what your attitudes and beliefs are about the learning process. It is essential you have the belief that learning is an active behavior, not a set of passive responses students engage in.

Questions are powerful tools

This approach to teaching requires you to develop strong questions to achieve the aims of the learning process. Questions should emphasize the thinking process desired in the student. What, how, when, where, who and why questions lead a form of inquiry. Typically, questions beginning with "what," "how" and "why" tend to be broader and elicit more information from one or more discussion participants. They allow for additional facts, challenges and connections to be made. Closed questions ending with "yes" or "no" answers tend to confirm, validate and qualify a specific point of content matter pertinent to the issue being discussed. Crafting effective questions fosters problem identification, problem solving, analysis, evaluation and decision-making in students through discussion. Questions develop themselves over time through testing and evaluation of the content they yield as demonstrated in the discussion. Questions should focus on ideas and not be directed at people. Questions can be used to start, develop and terminate a discussion. They can be posed from a battery of prepared notes or emerge organically through the discussion, and they can be owned by an individual or shared between group members. Every case presented in this text has a series of questions to help begin a discussion about the case presented. The questions presented at the end of each case are not the only questions that could or should be used. Teachers must judge their class needs for themselves and see the questions provided as a starting point for case examination and discussion.

Communication skills

All language is communication. The nature of teaching with cases necessitates the college teacher being open, warm, collaborative and objective. Facilitation skills are vital for college educators using the teaching case method. Course leaders should demonstrate powerful forms of listening through short reflective statements, paraphrasing and summarizing what students have said. Sometimes, when three or more voices have spoken in a round of discussion about a key point, the teacher enters at a pause in the dialog to capture the content as it was said and writes it down on a whiteboard or flip chart in the words used by the discussants without interpreting, embellishing or noticeably changing the words or their meaning through interpretation.

If ground rules have been set concerning how the group operates, often one rule appearing on many lists is something like "one voice at a time." Use role models to show the behavior the ground rules expect. Avoid interrupting students and breaking their flow; this is often seen as a "power move" by the group, and often felt as such by the individual being cut off. I also recommend avoiding putting road blocks in the way of good discussion like arguing, judging or embarrassing discussants because you feel they are off track, wrong or ill-informed in their judgment of the case. These behaviors often shut students down and diminish their role rather than promoting it as part of the learning process. There will be moments when you might strongly disagree with the content and direction of a discussion, but your place to share your thoughts is most likely at the end of the process when you step into a knowledge transmission role from a facilitative role.

It is important to facilitate in a nimble and agile way, and be open to what is discussed and how is processed. Focus on understanding the intention and meaning in the statements made by contributors to the conversation. Of particular importance is to concentrate when listening to a claim made by an individual without evidence to support it. Using reflective listening to identify the claim and its missing evidence, this process often leads to a question designed to elicit the information supporting the claim made. Working this process allows everyone in the discussion to see the claim and its support and weigh up what they heard for themselves.

Preparing to lead discussions

Facilitating engaging and rich discussion can be challenging even for experienced educators and discussion facilitators. There are several concrete steps which can be taken to make the successful outcome of a teaching case discussion more likely. These include but are not limited to the following tips.

Objectives and process

Make sure before you start the discussion that you and all the participants know the direction it is going in. Set and communicate the session plan and process to students so that they recognize the learning process and know their roles and responsibilities in it.

Preparation activities

Sometimes discussions can deteriorate into unhelpful and uninspiring moments in the classroom. These moments are characterized by some students listening without contributing to the collective discourse. One or two individuals speak their thoughts out loud and go on unless reined in, and the goals of the discussion are often obscured as the instructor focuses on managing the room and not facilitating the discussion. To overcome these occurrences there are several preparatory steps an educator can take to assure a quality discussion.

According to Hollander (2002), concurrently with content knowledge learning, instructors can set expectations for student engagement using three short assignments leading into the teaching case discussion. The first assignment is a one- or two-page reflection responding to the questions:

- What makes a good discussion?
- What kind of discussion do you find most helpful to your learning?
- What makes someone a good discussion contributor?
- What kinds of discussion behaviors are helpful or unhelpful to your learning?

The second assignment is a short goal-setting exercise asking the student to set their learning goals for the upcoming discussion using specific, measurable, attainable, realistic and time-framed (SMART) goal-setting principles. The final assignment is a one- or two-page evaluation of the teaching case discussion asking students to reflect on what happened in the discussion and their role in its quality. Students are asked to outline how they reached their discussion goals and how the discussion helped or hindered their learning of content. These assignments promote thoughtful student reflection and preparation for discussion and allow instructors to learn about their students before the teaching case discussion occurs and make reasonable preparations. They also permit some students to express themselves in ways they might not in whole class discussions (White, 2011).

This approach teaches students their roles and responsibilities for the upcoming discussion and opens up opportunities for learning and, explicitly, everyone's accountability for their behavior during discussions. There is no doubt that this process takes effort and commitment from students and instructors, but the payoff is the rich discourse and the opportunity for multiple levels of learning in knowledge acquisition, application and discussion capabilities.

Ground rules

Ground rules set expectations for how discussions will occur and the expected behaviors of all those participating in the learning process. With novice groups, following a prepared set of rules used in other meetings at the beginning is one strategy to help students get started and learn how the teaching case discussion works. A potentially more powerful process is to have the members co-create the ground rules and post them where everyone can see them as a reminder of their commitment once they understand the learning process. I recommend 8–10 statements, and those most likely to get the behaviors desired for the goals of the learning process. This engages the students in their own learning process and provides a different and sometimes higher level of accountability than a set of ground rules that was prepared.

Time management

Facilitating a discussion takes time, so make sure to communicate to the participants how time is going to be managed and how facilitation will occur given the time constraints. If a case contains complex issues which create uncertainty and ambiguity in the minds of learners, it is likely more time will be needed and interactions will need to be carefully managed. Positive outcomes and effective time management are more likely if preparations have been made before the discussion to set up participants to engage in effective communication to achieve the discussion's goals. This method is ideally facilitated face to face and recommended for between 1½ and 3 hours.

Create an inclusive learning experience

Every individual should have a voice in the class. The conditions for creating an inclusive environment mean assuring that views are respected, that all students represent themselves and that their contributions are noted. Arrange the seating in a semi-circle if possible so that students can see each other's faces easily. Learn students' names and have them learn each other's. Use name tags or table signs to ensure all students are known to each other. This organization of the learning space helps all students voice their position. This means that students who feel a bit inhibited or perhaps anxious about speaking in front of others should be treated respectfully but encouraged to speak from their perspective. Often when rapport and trust have been established between instructor and students, even the most reluctant students will offer a thought in these conditions. Their contribution should be supported, validated and noted.

One way to ensure that everyone participates is to get one contribution from each student before opening up the discussion. Another way is to have students work in pairs; one partner reports the major thought the pair had and the other supports it. This way students team up and the contribution is both shared and individual, and all students can feel like they had a say. It is very important to start a discussion session off well, and respectful inclusion is a strong choice to achieving this objective.

Participation policy

Many college educators have syllabus policies explaining how points are given for participation. When grades are seen to be at stake, this can incentivize poor discussion behavior. Before leading a teaching case discussion make sure a system is in place for noting the type and quality of contribution from a student, and that every student in the class knows this system well ahead of time. Make all policies and assessment connected to discussions clear, transparent and easy to understand. Reduce student confusion concerning these matters through good preparation.

Assessing discussions

Thinking about assessing student performance through discussion might feel like a thankless task; after all, how might a college teacher know where to start with this idea? A simple way of characterizing discussion contributions is to track who speaks: who posed a question; who answered a question; who added to someone else's thought; who used evidence; who disagreed with a peer and provided a counter point; who added a "discussion changer" thought and moved the conversation to a deeper level? Ideally a teaching assistant might track for you, or you might record and review the discussion, and you could have students self-rate against your rating. Providing students know how their participation is being monitored they can participate in discussions with knowing their performance matters.

Another way of assessing the discussion is to elicit a reflective response from the students, identifying how they contributed and their own weighting of their participation against set criteria. Additionally, a reflective statement about what they learned from the discussion provides a double reflection on the learning process and its outcomes.

Finally, assessment can be ongoing and used in sequential fashion too. For example, content might be delivered and a quiz given to check recall; then a teaching case discussion could take place with self-assessment, followed by a final piece of work such as a term paper or presentation of some kind. Whatever the form of assessment chosen, make sure it is accurate and defines criteria standards for students to operate by.

How to get started using teaching cases

Get trained

The Harvard T.H. Chan School of Public Health offers an annual three-day program showing how to write, facilitate and validate teaching cases. I found the training and the faculty outstanding. There are business school faculties in the USA that occasionally lead open workshops on how to use teaching cases. If you have three days and the funding for such a program I highly recommend it. You will leave with the tools necessary to get started immediately. On the other hand, there are lower-cost opportunities, and a range of texts such as *Teaching with cases: A practical guide* (Anderson et al., 2014), articles and YouTube content demonstrating the teaching case method could also be organized and curated into a self-directed learning program.

Write your own

Over an 18-year period I had several long-term and short-term intense commitments with a number of athletes and sport teams. I documented most of my work, answering the key questions of who, what, why, when, where and how in narrative form. I decided to replace the identifying facts and features of the characters but essentially keep the content as it was when it happened. Occasionally I added a "headline" effect from current relevant sports news for my own students. I wrote cases of half a page, 1 page, 2 pages and so on until I reached the recommended 10-page limit.

Progress from short and simple to long and complex

Recognize that you must start short in content and length. The shorter your work, the less detail and complexity there will be; but this is okay because you need practice writing your cases and you need to test your work weekly with your students. Use your classes as a learning lab and listen to the feedback from your students. They will tell you if the case was too easy, too hard or, in some cases, if it made no sense to them. I only release a teaching case into the world if I have used it in various forms two or three times. Then I improve it as I need to, based on feedback from students.

Start off low stakes

Until you have tested your teaching cases and know where they are strong and weak, use low-stakes evaluation approaches until you have refined them and extended their complexity. As complexity and length increase so does the challenge the student faces, and assessment can become more demanding.

Know your content

When you write a case you need to think from both sides, yours and your students'. The case must allow students to call upon the knowledge they have learned in your course and any other information sources pertinent to the case they are challenged by. Write a case with boundaries implied, and the content you want the student to retrieve should be contained inside the boundaries of the narrative. Therefore you must know what you have taught and the reasonable relationships that might be drawn between different units of knowledge. For example, if you write a teaching case with the title "Jimmy's battle with concentration" and it is part of a section you are teaching on mental skills training, your reader would expect the emphasis of the case to be on the concept of concentration and might expect to have questions focused on mental skills training. It is reasonable for the reader to anticipate the nature of the conversation they might have. If a case is being used as a demonstration of applied principles and practices by students at the end of the learning module, it is reasonable for the students to surmise they will apply the knowledge they have learned about mental skills training to this case and present their process, findings and decisions.

Structure the use of the teaching case

I use teaching cases at the end of learning modules. For example, in my class on the psychology of injury—for which I use *The Psychology of Sport Injury and Rehabilitation* (Arvinen-Barrow & Walker, 2013)—I teach 3 × 5-week learning modules comprised of 10 × 75-minute learning sessions. Luckily, the course text has short (half-page) case studies focused on the chapter content which I use to introduce the concept of cases which scaffolds the learning module; then I provide a take-home teaching case for each student to review (direct case method). The third step is to have the students return, pair up and share their views; they then pair up again to make foursomes and discuss their findings, and then the whole class (average size 28–32) comes together and I facilitate the case using the facilitation skills outlined above. I allow the entire class period (75 minutes) for this process to occur.

Case outlines

Each case is designed for use one at a time or in combination with other cases where the same characters are involved. Each case has the same structure:

- Introduction
- Content implications
- Purpose

- Student learning outcomes
- Cast of characters and selected athlete/coach profile
- The case
- Discussion questions
- Author's notes
- Further reading

Instructors are encouraged to follow the guidelines above in the preparation, delivery and assessment of each teaching case.

Do teaching cases work?

It depends on who you ask and whose teaching scholarship and opinions you read. If you ask faculty and students to report on the quality and value of the learning, and their satisfaction with and enjoyment of teaching cases the responses are very positive. But if you want empirical, positivistic, experientially derived findings stating that teaching cases are better than other methods to develop critical thinking, the jury is out. Even though evidence is not equivocal on this point, I prefer this approach to teaching and learning over others because students can make up their own minds about what facts matter to them and how they decide to use them. I can be the guide on the side, and I get to demonstrate my own expertise through this role. I become a learner when I hear the views of my students when they generate an approach to the case I had not considered. I found using the teaching case method a powerful approach to engage my students; they get more out of the course and I enjoy teaching even more.

References

Abell, D. (1997). What makes a good case? *ECCH: The Newsletter of the European Case Clearing House*, Autumn/Fall.

Anderson, E., Schiano, W. T., & Schiano, B. (2014). *Teaching with cases: A practical guide*. Boston, MA: Harvard Business School Press.

Arvinen-Barrow, M., & Walker, N. (Eds.). (2013). *The Psychology of Sport Injury and Rehabilitation*. New York, NY: Routledge.

Fink, D. (2013). *Creating Significant Learning Experiences* (2nd ed.). San Francisco, CA: Jossey-Bass.

Herreid, C. F. (2011). Case study teaching. *New Directions for Teaching and Learning*, 128, 31–40.

Hemmings, B., & Holder, T. (2013). *Applied sport psychology: A case-based approach*. Hoboken, NJ: Wiley.

Hollander, J. A. (2002). Learning to discuss: Strategies for improving the quality of class discussion. *Teaching Sociology*, 30(3), 317–327.

National Federation of State High School Associations (NFHS). (2017). Participation Statistics. Retrieved from www.nfhs.org/ParticipationStatics/ParticipationStatics.aspx

White, J. W. (2011). Resistance to classroom participation: Minority students, academic discourse, cultural conflicts, and issues of representation in whole class discussions. *Journal of Language, Identity & Education*, 10(4), 250–265.

CAST OF CHARACTERS: CHAPTER(S)

Becky Washington, Head Coach, Women's Basketball: 16
Carolyn Banks, Shawndra Banks's Mother: 11
Celia "Cissy" Drew, Assistant Athletic Director and Women's Sport Administrator: 2, 10, 12, 18, 19, 20, 21
Cindy Varga, Viktor Varga's wife: 19
David Dean, Athletic Trainer, Swimming and Diving: 14
Diana Davis, Women's Swimming: 1
Dominique Xavier, Women's Basketball: 16
Drake Payton, Men's Soccer: 15
Esmerelda Diaz, Women's Tennis: 2
Isabel Schmid, Women's Tennis: 7
Jaime Varedo, Goal Keeping Coach, Men's Soccer: 5, 6, 17
Jake Johnson, Assistant Coach, Men's Basketball: 12
Javier Aguilar, Sport Psychology Consultant: 1, 2, 3, 6, 8, 9, 11, 13, 16, 18
Jenny Johnston, Athletic Trainer: 9
Jenny Yang, Women's Diving: 14
Lily "Sparksy" Sparks, Athletic Trainer: 1, 4
Louisa Young, Women's Tennis: 2
Mark Champion, Men's Soccer: 6
Mark Redmond, Men's Soccer: 3
Marty Kelly, Assistant Head Coach, Men's Soccer: 5, 17
Micah Rowland, Women's Soccer: 4
Michelle Ball, Graduate Intern, Counseling Center: 15
Michelle Court, Athletic Director: 17
Mike "Thompo" Thompson, Assistant Head Coach, Strength and Conditioning: 4, 14
Mike Beck, Men's Basketball: 8

Mike Brillo, Co-Captain, Men's Soccer: 17
Mike Landing. Head Coach, Men's Basketball: 12
Otto Reinwagner. Rob Reinwagner's Father: 5
Quang Tham, Career Adviser: 11
Rob Reinwagner, Men's Soccer: 5
Robin Marriot, Head Coach, Men's Soccer: 3, 5, 6, 10, 5, 17, 20, 21
Sara Cooper, Women's Tennis: 7
Shawndra Banks, Women's Basketball: 11
Sime Radic, Men's Water Polo: 9
Tina Morrison, Head Coach Women's Tennis: 2, 10, 18, 20, 21
Vikto Varga, Head Coach, Men's Water Polo: 9, 13, 19, 20, 21
Vivian Moreno, Sport Psychology Consultant: 12, 20, 21
Yannis Papadopoulos, Coach, Men's Basketball: 12

1

BURNOUT/SELF-HANDICAPPING

Introduction

Swimming at the US National Collegiate Athletic Association (NCAA) level often involves two training sessions per day most days of the week. Student-athletes often carry a minimum full-time course load, with many overloading their academic schedule in the off-season transitioning into the competitive season. The day for a swimmer can begin around 4:30am and finish around 9pm or later depending on their academic schedule. Most weekends are spent swimming and catching up with school work. Training and academic demands are constant and unyielding. High volume of effort, overloaded intensity and lack of recovery time and a feeling of helplessness often leads to burnout in student-athletes. In this case, the athlete uses injury as a way of 'self-handicapping' to cope with burnout. This is a complex case with two things presented at one time, making for rich discussion.

Content implications

This case is rich in opportunities to discuss the causes, symptoms and treatments for burnout. It is recommended that this discussion take place against the backdrop of academic performance too. An interesting conversation about self-handicapping and how it works to preserve and promote an athlete's attitude and self-appraisal might be had, given that it can promote a positive appraisal in the mind of the athlete. Additionally, when injury is used as a cause of athlete behavior, the way in which self-handicapping might be addressed by a sport psychology practitioner is also up for debate. Finally, the teaming of sport medicine and sport psychology professionals might be explored through this case too. The benefits and limits of these kinds of working relationships might be instructive for students to think through how they might approach a similar situation in their future work.

Purpose

The purpose of this case study is to help students think through the circumstances they might face working with an athlete intending to play professional sport following a successful college career.

Student learning outcomes

At this end of this case study learning opportunity, students should be able to:

1. Identify the issues causing burnout and self-handicapping
2. Discuss interventions helping student-athletes cope with burnout
3. Consider how working with an athletic trainer might help resolve self-handicapping behaviors in a student-athlete
4. Discuss how a sport psychology practitioner might be effective when a student-athlete presents two or more issues at once

Cast of characters in order of appearance

Javier Aguilar, Sport Psychology Consultant.
Diana Davis, Women's Swimming.
Lily "Sparksy" Sparks, Athletic Trainer.

Athlete profile: Diana Davis, women's swimming

Diana Davis is a sophomore swimmer specializing in sprints of 50m, 100m and 200m in front crawl, and she swims the first leg for the 4 × 100m relay team. She was recruited to The U because of her rise up the state rankings in her junior and senior years. She matured and became a dominant age group swimmer. Diana was widely recruited by college swimming programs on the east and west coast but wanted to stay close to home and study business and communications, like many other student-athletes did at The U. She was an excellent student and saw herself running her own business or working in media communications one day.

At the end of her freshman year Diana experienced difficulties she had not faced at high school. The swimmers she competed against from schools all over the Midwest region and in her conference were strong, tough and capable of producing their top performances whenever it seemed they needed to. Diana, on the other hand, could not replicate the consistent performances she had had in high school. During her freshman year she found the training sessions grueling and long. She often arrived at competitions tired from training and from studying, and felt unable to produce her best performances on demand like she used to. She enjoyed swimming and studying but was feeling like she was on a treadmill with no end in sight, until an injury developed.

In the final six weeks before the conference championships, Diana started to feel pain and soreness in her left shoulder. At first the pain was barely noticeable, and she was able to swim through it and use ice and legal medicines to reduce the pain and swelling around her shoulder. When the pain grew too much, her training became incomplete and she would tell the team's athletic trainer and her assistant coach she had to rest. She learned that resting and not finishing her sets gave her more energy, so she decided to train hard on some days and not on others; on the days she was tired she told the coach and the trainer she felt pain. She also began to tell her team mates about her injury and found this was a useful way to explain away her performances, get the rest she needed to swim in competition and do her studies. The tradeoff seemed to work, especially as her times were as good as in her senior year at high school but just not good enough to challenge for high positions at college meets. She maintained her position on the team, kept swimming and disguised her actual status. However, when her shoulder healed, Diana still reported pain and discomfort. The trainer, coach and Diana discussed her condition and they agreed she would compete, but her focus was on full recovery for her second year.

After the swim season stopped and practice intensity dropped Diana's commitment increased; her times were more consistent but she was careful not to show she was fully fit and healthy, and made sure everyone on her team knew it. Diana trained quite hard during the summer vacation; she was very careful with her diet as she tapered her training. As long as she kept the same times as the preceding year she believed she would be on the team and could study and rest as she needed to.

When Diana returned to The U after the summer break the coaching staff adapted the training program to shorter and explosive sessions, twice a day on a block schedule. Diana knew how to act in front of her coaches and team mates to be part of the team, but she found this training even more challenging compared to her first year and decided to claim pain had returned to her shoulder. The trainer was not convinced and the communicated their beliefs to the coach, who referred Diana to Javier Aguilar, The U's sport psychology consultant. Their first meeting happened in October. It was brief and based on introductions. They agreed to meet again in November as the swimming season was ramping up.

The case

Diana met Javier in her coach's office overlooking the swimming pool. Her coach had left for a meeting after the late afternoon session and would be gone for the whole time she was going to be using the room. She agreed to meet with Javier for 30 minutes after the session to pick up after a 15-minute meeting they had had several weeks before. They sat down opposite each next to a large window, allowing them both to look out if they wanted to.

JAVIER: "How's things Diana?"
DIANA: "Okay, school's kicking my butt, but I'll be okay."
JAVIER: "Good. What's the best thing for us to talk about to help you out today?"
DIANA: "Nothing really."

4 Burnout/self-handicapping

JAVIER: "Okay. Nothing's on your mind then?"
DIANA: "No."
JAVIER: "How's your shoulder?"
DIANA: "It's really sore. Like worse than when I saw you before."
JAVIER: "Really? That sounds awful."
DIANA: "Yeah. It's really bad."
JAVIER: "I hope you don't mind, I talked to Sparksy. I don't know much about swimming injuries, and I like to know what they can be like so I asked her about your injury. It's confidential. Nobody else knows; just you, me, her and the coach."
DIANA: "Why did you do that? You didn't tell me you were going to do that. I didn't give you permission to do that."
JAVIER: "I just wanted to understand. See it from my viewpoint if you can. I don't know you well, I wasn't a swimmer, and sometimes I need more information. When we met at first we really introduced ourselves and that was it. I wanted to be even more helpful in this meeting."
DIANA: "Well I guess so ... but can you ask me before doing something like that again?"
JAVIER: "Sure. After I learned about your surgery I was curious. How come you haven't had surgery? You've had pain for months."
DIANA: "It's not that bad."
JAVIER: "What do you mean not that bad? You've missed a lot of training and I see your times haven't improved. Does it bother you?"
DIANA: "Yes it bothers me, but as long as I can swim and I'm on the team it's okay."
JAVIER: "Sparksy will be joining us shortly too."
DIANA: "What! Why?"
JAVIER: "Sometimes I've found it very helpful for athletes to work as a team with their people who support them. Sparksy and me have worked with the women's soccer team and men's basketball team when injuries have come up. We find it good for the players to see we are working together."
DIANA: "But why would you do that? I thought you all worked separately. This is the second thing you've done I didn't give you permission to do."
JAVIER: "I know you didn't give me permission. I'm sorry about this. I thought it would be best because we don't have a lot of time."
DIANA: "It's because of my injury my times are what they are. You can understand that pain gets in the way of swimming can't you?"
JAVIER: "Oh yes. I imagine it can be very difficult for a swimmer."
DIANA: "It is. All my team mates and my coach know the hell I've been through to just keep swimming. Even though I'm in pain I do the things they expect me to do to be a good team member."
JAVIER: "No doubt you do. I was just wondering how much disappointment you must have felt though, going through all those weeks and months of not being able to improve. It must have been terrible for you. I know you're a good

swimmer, it must tear you up to see others doing well and you kind of keeping steady."

DIANA: "It's not so bad. I get on with it. I get on with my school work. I focus on getting good grades. Of course I'd like to be better, but it just isn't possible right now. I mean, I'm in pain so I say the best thing is for me to get on and do what I can, and that's school work."

JAVIER: "Yeah, school work is important. I wonder how tired you are too. I mean I hear that injures can really knock you out and take a toll on a swimmer, with those long days and two times per day practice. It's like your life isn't your own. I mean it's so difficult to get anything done when you're that tired."

DIANA: "Yeah you're right. I mean it's all of that. But my tiredness isn't so bad because the pain means I cut back on my swimming so I get rest, and I'm physically okay so I can study more. The most important thing is that my coach sees me trying, sees me putting the effort in and knows I'll swim when I have to."

Javier turned from looking at Diana and saw Sparksy walking down the poolside towards them. She entered the office and pulled up a seat. They sat in a triangle shape.

DIANA: "Hey Sparksy. I found out you were coming just now."

SPARKSY: "Yup, I have 5–10 minutes before I get back to the training room. Has Javier told you why I'm here?"

DIANA: "No."

SPARKSY: "Okay, so the reason I'm here is because I'm not sure you are in as much pain as you say you are, and I wonder if somethin' else is going on with you that you want to talk to me or Javier about."

DIANA: "Why do you think that?"

SPARKSY: "Well it's like this. Your shoulder does not need surgery; we had the X-rays last season. I've done all the tests I know how to do and I see you doing all the things coach asks you to do, but I notice when things get hard your pain comes on. It's almost like your shoulder thinks for you. Like it's sayin' "here we go" and even before the session gets tough you're out of the water. So I'm wonderin' what's going on. Then I see you talkin' and hear you tellin' people about your injury and how bad it is, and then I hear you tellin' the same people about how much school work you've got goin', and I'm wonderin' what's goin' on with you. You know, when somethin' seems right but isn't, that's the feelin' I got here. I'm bringin' it up because I think you're a good person and you have athletic potential, and I'm concerned I might be missin' somethin'."

Diana felt a surge of emotional intensity. Her eyes welled up and tears lined her face. Sparksy put her hand on Diana's knee to comfort her.

SPARKSY: "It's okay. We know somethin's goin' on with you. You can tell us if you want to, but you don't have to. We all know that."

Diana took a breath and her tears receded.

DIANA: "How long have you known?"
SPARKSY: "For sure, since the beginning of this semester. You're physically strong and capable, and nothin' was bad enough to make you quit like you did in trainin'."
DIANA: "I just can't manage it all."
JAVIER: "What do you mean?"
DIANA: "Last year I got so tired. I just couldn't do both. I couldn't do school and swimming. I was physically drained all the time. There's so many deadlines for school. I feel my only time off was when I said I was in pain. The only time I felt good was when my swimming was less and I rested and slept and two a day practices went away. I was kind of hating swimming for the first time; every day was the same, but I've always been on a swim team and I want to be on this one. So I just did what I needed to in front of the coaches and my team mates. That doesn't make me a bad person does it?"
JAVIER: "No it doesn't. But it does say something has to change."
SPARKSY: "How bad is your pain?"
DIANA: "You already know."
SPARKSY: "You're not in pain are you?"
DIANA: "No, not really. Sometimes I feel sore but like pain after a hard session, not like it was when it first happened for real. Does the coach know what you think?"
SPARKSY: "No. Me and Javier talked, but I wanted to hear from you before I said anythin' to the coach."
DIANA: "What are you going to do?"
SPARKSY: "Well, it depends on you. Coach knows we're all meeting. He knows me and Javier have worked with athletes before about a bunch of things. Coach doesn't know details. But he will if we don't get this sorted out."
DIANA: "Okay, what do I have to do? I don't want to get into trouble."
JAVIER: "We don't want to get you into trouble."
SPARKSY: "Tell us a bit about what's going on with you."
DIANA: "School's important to me. I try every session to make every one think I'm a good team mate. I do what the coaches say and I do my best. I try to be what I think they want to see in me, because I do like swimming. I maybe don't love it like I used to, but I like it a lot and I want to do it, but not as much as I want to be good at my studies. I'm not going to be a national ranked swimmer. They're too good, but I can be a good enough swimmer here."
JAVIER: "So it's really about your studies?"
DIANA: "Yes"

SPARKSY: "But it's also about you being one thing and not lettin' on to everyone about what's really goin' on. You want to be part of the team, but it sounds like you just want to be in it not striving to win and compete at the top level, is that it."

DIANA: "When you say it like that, it sounds terrible. I like being part of the team."

SPARKSY: "Yeah no doubt, but is it fair to your coaches and team mates you actin' like this?"

DIANA: "I don't think of it is fair or unfair. When I swim I do my best ... You're not going to tell anyone are you?"

JAVIER: "No, we're not."

SPARKSY: "Okay Diana. How do you think we should act with this information?"

DIANA: "What do you want me to do?"

SPARKSY: "Oh no, this is on you, not on us."

DIANA: "I don't know."

JAVIER: "It sounds like fatigue and tiredness are the biggest factors, and you're worried about your grades."

DIANA: "Yes."

JAVIER: "How would you feel about Sparksy and you having a conversation with your coaches about your training loads and your goals for school?"

DIANA: "What would that do?"

SPARKSY: "Do you think you're the first student-athlete who has ever had this problem?"

DIANA: "I guess not."

SPARKSY: "That's right. Athletes get burned out all the time. Students need good grades, that's a no-brainer. But it isn't right you actin' like this and making people think somethin' that's not true. You need to be honest with others and yourself."

JAVIER: "I'll arrange the meeting with you, Sparksy and your coaches, okay?"

DIANA: "What will you tell them?"

JAVIER: "I'll tell them something like we talked, and Sparksy and you have a plan to get the most out of yourself and a way to balance your studies. Your coaches are understanding people. They're tough coaches but they were student-athletes themselves and know what getting good grades means. Besides, both of them have graduate degrees too. They know the value of school as much as they know swimming."

DIANA: "But what if anyone finds out what I have done?"

SPARKSY: "If you won't tell, we won't tell. It's up to you. My job is to get you healthy and in the water. But I want you to do well and feel like this is a good place for you to be too."

DIANA: "When will you set the meeting for?"

JAVIER: "This time next week. I won't be there. Sparksy knows how to handle this with you. You need to talk together and plan for the meeting. I'll talk with Sparksy about the meeting next week too. We won't say what we learned

from you today. What's important is getting on track for the future, not what you've done in the past."
SPARKSY: "That's right."

Discussion questions

1. What do you think the issues are in this case?
2. How do you feel about the way the sport psychology practitioner and athletic trainer behaved in this case?
3. How might you address issues around burnout and self-handicapping?
4. What interventions might you recommend to Sparksy and Diana in this case?
5. How might you have handled this situation differently if you were the sport psychology practitioner?

Author's notes

I prefer a gentle approach when complex issues like the ones in this case are presented. When burnout and conflicting priorities are presented I tend to prefer to focus on coping from the point at which the issue has been presented. It does not serve the student-athlete to focus on what they have done so much as what they can do now to cope. I like to work with the student-athlete to define the issue in their own terms and then have them develop a list of opportunities they might take advantage of to cope better with their situation. Once the list is developed, I work with them to explore and determine the solutions to the short-term issue and get them on track to consider longer-term solutions. I like to use short-term goal setting and planning with student-athletes to anticipate future challenges and how they might be dealt with. I take a pragmatic approach to future planning to focus on progress not perfection in how coping occurs, particularly at the beginning of the process.

When burnout is presented it might be more physiological than cognitive-emotional, or the other way around, or it might be a blended experience tipping back and forth. I typically take a bio-physiological view first because a change and reduction in training and competition load can yield positive mental and emotional benefits quicker than a counseling session. I prefer to advocate for physical recovery first. I think this preference comes from my own competitive sport experience. For student-athletes balancing the demands of training, competition and studies, the availability of unstructured time to study and rest is vital to their freedom and experiencing some balance in their lives, particularly when practicing twice a day as many sports do at different times in their annual schedule.

Self-handicapping can be a way for an athlete to protect themselves and preserve their identity and self-esteem in a competitive environment. In this case, the student-athlete used the opportunity to manage and impress other people's perceptions of them to achieve a personal goal outside of the team's competitive aims. I do not necessarily see this is a negative thing, but it is not always a positive choice by the student-athlete either. I prefer to learn how much the student-athlete wants to improve, if they have the tools to do so and their willingness to pay the price in terms of effort and persistence to achieve improved performance. If they do not and I am responsible for providing feedback to the coach about their position, I have no issue telling the coach this is the case. However, I only do this if I have the student-athlete's permission. If I do not, I work with the student-athlete to enhance their intrinsic motivation, explore ways to increase their feelings of competence, and work to identify the opportunities for a positive sport experience in spite of the level of competition negatively affecting their self-appraisal and ego.

Further reading

Coudevylle, G. R., Ginis, K. A. M., & Famose, J. P. (2008). Determinants of self-handicapping strategies in sport and their effects on athletic performance. *Social Behavior and Personality: An International Journal*, 36(3), 391–398.

Gustafsson, H., Kenttä, G., & Hassmén, P. (2011). Athlete burnout: An integrated model and future research directions. *International Review of Sport and Exercise Psychology*, 4(1), 3–24.

Kellmann, M. (Ed.). (2002). *Enhancing recovery: Preventing underperformance in athletes*. Champaign, IL: Human Kinetics.

Lemyre, P. N., Hall, H. K., & Roberts, G. C. (2008). A social cognitive approach to burnout in elite athletes. *Scandinavian Journal of Medicine & Science in Sports*, 18(2), 221–234.

2
COACH–ATHLETE RELATIONSHIP

Introduction

Interpersonal conflict is usual in human interactions. Difficult moments between coach and athlete are normal in sport too. This case challenges students to consider a range of behaviors, types and modes of communication, and provocative interpersonal moments directly related to an incident which took place in training. Students are challenged to decide what to focus on first and what to work on over time with the player and coach involved in the case.

Content implications

This case might be used for discussions about coach leadership, conflict-resolution, coach development, goal setting, and the use of power and status in sport relationships. From a relational point of view, instructors might discuss how peripheral figures to an incident have a strong influence on how a case might be managed too.

Purpose

The purpose of this case study is to help students consider how to work with a player and coach following a training incident in which the coach and player displayed conflicting expectations and communication styles and patterns.

Student learning outcomes

At this end of this case study learning opportunity, students should be able to:

1. Identify the issues causing interpersonal conflict
2. Select psychosocial interventions to mediate interpersonal conflict

3. Discuss coach communication and leadership
4. Discuss how a sport psychology practitioner might be effective in this kind of scenario.

Cast of characters in order of appearance

Louisa Young, Women's Tennis.
Tina Morrison, Women's Tennis Coach.
Esmerelda Diaz, Women's Tennis.
Cissy Drew, Assistant Athletic Director and Women's Sport Administrator.
Javier Aguilar, Sport Psychology Consultant.

Athlete profile: Louisa Young, women's tennis

Louisa Young is a 20-year-old freshman playing on The U's women's tennis team. She is originally from Canterbury, England. She was ranked 20 in Britain and achieved a world ranking of 945. Louisa was recruited to The U through one of the sport agents who represent the institution in Europe to prospective recruits. The head coach, Tina Morrison, had not met Louisa before she arrived on campus, but she had watched videos, read about her matches and talked to peers about her. She felt Louisa was going to be an asset to the team because of her attitude and experience.

The agent had told her that Louisa was a confident and determined individual and she would have no trouble settling into The U's ways. Since she was 16 years old Louisa played frequently in International Tennis Federation tournaments in Europe, national sponsored events in England and many county tournaments. Her ambition had been to represent Great Britain as part of the Federation Cup team, but after her first year out of high school and first year proper on her own trying to balance playing, training and teaching tennis lessons to make ends meet she felt she did not have what it took to achieve her ambition.

Louisa was able to make this decision with her dad (Martin), who was also her coach. Louisa's mother (Alexandra) was a high-powered partner in a law firm and her father was a teacher. Her parents had met playing mixed doubles at the local tennis club when they were teenagers, and got married after they both graduated from college at the age of 22. Louisa was born six years later. They shared parenting duties, but as Alexandra's career blossomed it was clear Martin would need to step in to take the weight off looking after Louisa. Martin became a physical education and math teacher immediately after college and retired after 20 years of teaching to support Louisa and Alexandra at home doing part-time math tutoring with local students. He and Alexandra had stayed out of Louisa's tennis development and promoted the local tennis pro, growing Louisa's love for the game.

When Louisa was 13 the local pro left to take another position. Louisa had shown great promise, but there was no coach in place at the club and Martin stepped in. Louisa's game continued to improve mainly because she and Martin would collaborate on how she would improve, and he stressed that learning and improvement could be fun at the same time. He never wanted their involvement in tennis to come between them. As Louisa matured, her relationships with her parents continued to strengthen, and she frequently referred to them as her best friends. She did well at school and could have decided to stay in England and attend college, but she felt she needed a change. She enjoyed the experience she gained through tennis, but once she saw for herself that her standard would likely not improve enough to get into the top tier of British women she voiced the ambition to try something else.

Martin reached out to The U's agent. He knew about The U, its location and the women's tennis program. He felt it would be a good fit for Louisa because he read the coach was consistent and, from what he read, she had some of the qualities he saw in his wife Alexandra. It seemed like an ideal fit. Louisa arrived on campus and settled into her college dorm with her team mate Esmerelda Diaz (who was also a freshman) from Naperville, a suburb of Chicago. It was The U's policy to place each team in a dorm with regular students to make sure they interacted with individuals outside of their team and keep them grounded in student life.

Louisa loved the first week of college. Even though she was an only child, she was well adjusted and she found the antics of her dorm mates fun and refreshing. She felt like she had made the right choice after the first week on campus. She and Esmerelda met Tina Morrison early in the first week of the semester. Louisa then completed a student-athlete orientation, had her first conditioning sessions and began the first week of her classes in her exercise science major. The week ended with a welcome party hosted by the faculty in her major. Louisa called home and raved about her decision to attend The U.

The case

Tina stood on the court staring at Louisa on the other side of the court. The coach gripped her tennis racket like Thor holding his mighty hammer and pausing before smashing it into the ground. She felt this moment with her willful British recruit coming since the end of the fourth week of the semester.

TINA: "I have told you several times today Louisa. Play as I tell you to, not as you think you should!"

Players on the two courts either side of the center court where Tina and Louisa stopped playing. Louisa was aware her team mates were watching this. Louisa knew this moment had been coming since the end of the first month of training, and she was not going to back down from Tina.

LOUISA: "I know what you have been telling me, Tina. But it's not working for me … why would I keep doing things that don't work for me? It make no sense."

TINA: "It does make sense, and stop calling me Tina. I'm your coach not your friend. You call me 'Coach T' or just 'Coach.' We all know you can play well. I want you to play better. You know, your Dad and me have a lot in common. I'm sure he would agree with me that you can improve in these areas."

Tina let the grip on her racket go as she felt her authority returning. Louisa listened and looked into her racket as her fingers plucked at the strings of the sponsor's logo framed by the racket's head.

LOUISA: "Sure Tina. If that's what you think."

Tina looked incredulously at her player as she strode around the net towards her. The players around held their rackets limply at their sides and watched in silence to see what would happen. None of them dared move or breathe. The tension was almost too much for Esmerelda. She walked to the side of her court and quietly sat down with her racket at her feet, drying her hands with a towel. Tina closed to within five paces of Louisa.

TINA: "I used to ride horses. You ever ridden a horse? Horses take some getting used to. Each one has their own personality, but eventually you break 'em and they come around. Some take longer than others. My Dad bought me riding lessons and I learned how to ride and train horses. You look like a stubborn horse to me. One who has power and energy but is too willful to let anyone ride it. You try and put a saddle on a horse and it might buck. Is that what you're doing here Louisa, bucking me?"

Louisa had never been spoken to like this before, especially by a coach and on The U's outdoor courts in public view with team mates looking on.

LOUISA: "What, so you're making me out to be some animal you can train, are you? Is that how you see tennis players, is it? You know my dad used to say you educate players and you train animals. You see us girls like horses in your stables do you? What kind of coach are you to say this to me? Just because I have a preference ..."

Tears began to well up in her eyes and her hands were numb from holding the racket too firmly.

LOUISA: "This is wrong. You're wrong. You don't treat people like this."

Tina drew a breath and was about to speak when Louisa walked past her to her bag and started to pack up her belongings.

TINA: "Where are you going!?"

LOUISA: "I'm done here. I'm going to see the women's sport administrator. You're not allowed to treat me like this. We aren't even in season and you're acting like I have problems with my game. Why don't you see me play competitively first before you try making me do things differently? You're not a coach. You're a bully."

Tina realized the power of those words. Scenes flashed back in her mind to the days she played on two national championship winning teams. She played sixth on her team and always felt like the coach was pushing her around, demanding more than she could give and always threatening to leave her out of the lineup despite her winning points for the team. She had felt isolated and bullied at times by her coach. But, on the other hand, she respected the coach because she won trophies and championships. Many times over the years she had thought the wins were worth the aggravation with the coach.

Louisa had dried her eyes and was leaving the court not, but yet fully organized for her walk to see the women's sport administrator.

TINA: "You don't leave until I tell you to leave!"
LOUISA: "You're not the boss of me Tina. I am. I did quite well in Europe without you thank you very much. You can take your tennis coaching and you can …"

Louisa wrinkled her nose, smiled and turned away. Tina felt herself go blood red with embarrassment, and barked at Louisa's team mates:

TINA: "Well, what are you looking at? Finish the drills I set for you!"

Practice finished without further incident. Esmerelda had one of her better sessions because she felt like she played with more freedom. Since moving to The U she had found it hard to regain her form from her senior year of high school. She reached the state finals but was unable to place. Although she was a solid player, she knew she was not a top player. She expected to play at fifth or sixth on the team roster when the season came around. She was happy with that because at least she felt she would contribute to the team. Unlike Louisa, she did not have an athletic scholarship; instead she and her family had got grants, loans and other funds together to pay for The U's tuition. Esmerelda studied Spanish and English literature, and hoped to become an immigration lawyer at the end of her academic career. As Esmerelda zipped up her tracksuit top and reached down for the loop of her equipment bag Tina approached her.

TINA: "Ezzi, did you see how Louisa was with me?"
ESMERALDA: "Yes."
TINA: "Okay, so when you get back to the dorm or whenever you see Louisa next I want you to talk to her and see if you can calm her down and make her see I

do things for her best interests, just like I do things for everyone's best interests on the team."

Tina looked at Esmerelda and hoped for affirmation, but instead Esmerelda put her bag on her shoulder.

ESMERELDA: "Okay Coach, I'll talk to her but what can I do? I feel like Louisa will get mad at me and I don't want to upset her."
TINA: "You mean you won't do what I asked you to do?"
LOUISA: "No. I mean she's my team mate and my friend and I feel like she'll get upset with me and see me against her."
TINA: "So you mean you won't take my side on things."
ESMERELDA: "It's not that I don't want to take your side. I feel like she should talk to you. I mean, she's my roommate too and we have to be together all the time. I don't have classes with her but I see and speak to her more than I see or speak to anyone else here."
TINA: "I thought when I recruited you that you and I were going to get along, but I'm feeling like there might be trouble ahead for us."
ESMERELDA: "Coach, I don't want any trouble. I just feel bad talking to Louisa about this."
TINA: "Look, it's okay. I get where you're coming from. You can tell Louisa I told you to talk to her. Tell her to text or call when she's ready to talk to me. I don't want to put you in a bad position but, you know, sometimes when a friend speaks to you, you listen more. Will you do this for me?"
ESMERELDA: "Okay Coach, I'll talk to her."
TINA: "You're a good team mate Ezzi. I knew I could rely on you."

Tina raised her hand for a high five and Esmerelda patted her hand back.

TINA: "I'll see you tomorrow at practice Ezzi."

Tina turned and walked away across the court to inspect the playing area. Esmerelda stood quietly staring at her bag still at her feet with its looping bag handle lying limply in her hand. She thought to herself, "I don't want to do this." She pulled up the loop which took bag's weight, hoisted it over her right shoulder and walked off toward the dorm and her conversation with Louisa.

Louisa was already showered and changed into her regular street clothes when Esmerelda entered the room. Louisa seemed perky and upbeat.

LOUISA: "Hello roommate, do you want to get some lunch with me?"

Esmerelda put her bag down and paused. Louisa looked at Esmerelda and saw something was not right. She looked sad and low.

LOUISA: "What's happened?"
ESMERELDA: "Tina spoke to me. She wanted me to tell you to calm down and give her a call or text her to make things right."
LOUISA: "Oh."
ESMERELDA: "Yeah, the way she spoke to me kind of made me feel like if I didn't talk to you about it I might get punished in some way."
LOUISA: "What?"
ESMERELDA: "Yeah, she kind of threatened me … I didn't know she could be like that."

Louisa crossed the room to Esmerelda and gave her a hug. Even though the two had only been sharing a dorm for a month, they got along really well. Esmerelda called herself Louisa's "culture guide" and Louisa labeled herself Esmerelda's "big sister." Their relationship developed quickly.

LOUISA: "Let's have lunch after you shower. I texted Cissy Drew. She said I can meet her anytime this morning, so I'll go over and tell her about what happened this morning. How about you meet me at the dorm café in an hour? It's 11am now so see you at 12pm. I've got class from 2 to 5pm."
ESMERELDA: "Sure. I'll see you then."

Louisa grabbed her cell phone and jacket and, as she opened the door to leave, she turned to her roommate.

LOUISA: "By the way, there's no chance Tina's getting a call or text from me today. If my mum was here she'd say 'Make her wait,' and that's what I'll do."

She closed the door quietly and began her walk to Cissy Drew's office. Cissy was coming out of the sport medicine clinic and saw Louisa walking down the hall towards her.

CISSY: "Hi Louisa, you came straight over."
LOUISA: "Hi Cissy. Sure, I think you'll want to hear about what happened between me and Tina now."
CISSY: "Okay, let's talk in my office; this corridor echoes."

Cissy sat opposite Louisa with her office door closed. Louisa told her what happened that morning between her and Tina.

CISSY: "Well Louisa, this is tough situation. She is your coach after all."
LOUISA: "I know but she can be so disrespectful and demeaning. Nobody ever spoke to me like that … I'm not a kid and I am coachable. I could not have done what I have done in my tennis career without being adaptable, but it feels like only her way works … Sometimes I don't know what my Dad saw in her."

Cissy paused and suggested she would speak to Tina and that Louisa should go on with her day and she would call her later. Louisa left Cissy's office to meet Esmerelda for lunch. Cissy texted Tina: "You free for lunch? Let's talk."

TINA: "Louisa?"
CISSY: "Yes. She was just here."
TINA: "Oh God. Drama! Another Brit with attitude."
CISSY: "See you at Café Renoir at Center U at 12:30pm."
TINA: "Sure. You buying?"
CISSY: "Sure."

This was not the first time Cissy and Tina would be talking about a recruit she had had public confrontations with. The last time was four years earlier. Tina had been at The U for four years before she started recruiting European players. In her fifth year she started to recruit Spanish and Italian players, then the next year she recruited a transfer student from California by way of a coach she played under in college. While she liked winning the conference championship, Tina wanted to progress deeper in the national playoff tournament. On one hand she found the personal responsibility the European players showed attractive, but on the other hand she found them difficult to coach. She found she would have to break them of their attitude to fit in with her way of doing things. But she could not figure out why her teams could not progress. She noticed the players had no energy and seemed burned out by the championship phase of the season. She questioned the strength and conditioning coach because she thought they were causing the players to overwork, but that did not seem to be the issue.

Cissy met Tina at the café. It was busy but they managed to find a table in the corner out of earshot of eavesdroppers. The pair exchanged pleasantries before Tina asked Cissy about the meeting with Louisa.

CISSY: "She called you a bully."
TINA: "She did? Nothing much happened. She refused to do the drills and I called her out on it. All the other girls were doing them; she should be doing them too."
CISSY: "That's not exactly how Louisa explained things to me. She told me you talked to Esmerelda too."
TINA: "Louisa is highly strung … you know, she's a Brit and they think they can be like however they want."
CISSY: "Tina, let's not go there again."
TINA: "What do you mean?"
CISSY: "How sure are you that you are not repeating history again?"
TINA: "Come on Cissy, that was years ago. I was just going through a rough patch back then. Anyway, we won didn't we?"
CISSY: "Yes. The team won, but you and I have talked about a pattern of behavior emerging based on the feedback from the student-athlete exit interviews.

Your graduating players often talk about how you are sometimes too edgy and too in their business."

TINA: "Yes, but they also say I am a great coach and I get results."

CISSY: "Yes they do, and they make it clear it is not fun playing for you."

TINA: "Well my college coach was not fun to play for and we won. I mean that's why I was hired right? To win ... yeah ... you remember Cissy you hired me!"

CISSY: "Tina I am not your enemy. You have recruited a good player and a potential team captain when you got Louisa to come here. I am asking you to repair the relationship damage quickly and do not risk a formal complaint being made about your behavior."

TINA: "What?"

CISSY: "Louisa will play for you, but be gentle. She respects your ability but not how you deal with her."

TINA: "Who is the coach here?"

CISSY: "You are ... and there are different ways to handle students. I am asking you to take it easy in your dealings with her but do not drop your standards. Make her a partner."

TINA: "Are you serious?"

CISSY: "Yes Tina I am ... I am going to text Louisa now and tell her you and I spoke over lunch. I want you to contact her later to get on track and repair the relationship."

Tina stared at Cissy and raised her eyebrows. Cissy made a half smile and got up from their table, taking her lunch with her. She could not wait to send the text to Louisa.

TINA: "Talked to Cissy. Nice job. Got me in trouble! Talk later. Don't talk to anyone else about this. You need to be on my page."

LOUISA: "I'm talking to Javier next."

TINA: "Don't do that."

LOUISA: "It's done."

TINA: "Why?"

LOUISA: "Because I need to."

Tina did not respond to the final text. She finished her lunch and sat thinking about the next steps with Louisa.

Discussion questions

1. What is the role of the sport psychology practitioner in this case?
2. How might you approach Tina about her coaching behavior?
3. How might you facilitate a meeting between Tina and Louisa?
4. How might you coach Louisa to communicate with Tina?
5. How might you address this situation with Cissy, Tina and Louisa present?

Author's notes

If I heard a version of what happened from Tina and Louisa within 48 hours of the training incident occurring I might work with them both separately and together to communicate so that each has the space and time to consider how to work to repair and restore their relationship. They have things in common, and it seems like they want things to work out. I feel a bolder step is to have the coach and the player in a meeting with me too.

By working with them separately it might give me an opportunity to address their individual needs, and then bring them together to express their positions and views respectfully in a deescalated manner. I would ask them to identify and focus on demonstrating one or two strong behavioral choices between each other to establish trust, respect and acceptance in their interactions. Tennis requires a lot of one-on-one interaction between coach and player and a respectful, effective relationship provides the foundation for the two individuals to build to the next phase of the relationship, which would be goal setting.

To bring them closer together, I would engage in joint and shared goal setting for their on- and off-court relationship. I would use their shared energy for tennis to set process and performance goals that they agree to work on together. I would set a 6–10-day time frame for the goals to be worked on, and then arrange another meeting to check and assess progress. I would take this approach because tennis is what brought them together and is therefore the place to start making progress.

I would set aside other issues like coach leadership, interpersonal conflict, recruitment practices and player development to concentrate on what I perceived to be the main issue:. following up in a situation like this to maintain accountability and close the loop on feedback so that player and coach can learn from the experience and move on to new and better ways of being with each other.

Further reading

Giacobbi, P., Roper, E., Whitney, J., & Butryn, T. (2002). College coaches' views about the development of successful athletes: A descriptive exploratory investigation. *Journal of Sport Behavior*, 25(2), 164.

Jowett, S. (2003). When the "honeymoon" is over: A case study of a coach-athlete dyad in crisis. *Sport Psychologist*, 17(4), 444–460.

Lafrenière, M., Jowett, S., Vallerand, R., & Carbonneau, N. (2011). Passion for coaching and the quality of the coach–athlete relationship: The mediating role of coaching behaviors. *Psychology of Sport and Exercise*, 12(2), 144–152.

LaVoi, N. (2007). Interpersonal communication and conflict in the coach–athlete relationship. In S. Jowett & D. Lavallee (Eds.). *Social Psychology in Sport* (pp. 29–40). Champaign, IL: Human Kinetics.

3

SEIZING AN OPPORTUNITY TO PLAY PROFESSIONAL SOCCER

Introduction

This case introduces students to a common issue in National College Athletic Association (NCAA) sports: the transition of elite student athletes close to the top level of their sport from college to professional sport. This kind of situation tends to affect student athletes who play a sport connected to a professional league in the USA such as Major League Soccer (MLS) and its affiliates, the National Football League (NFL), Major League Baseball, the National Basketball Association (NBA) and the Women's National Basketball Association (WNBA).

Content implications

Students might discuss content concerning: life and career transitions; injury rehabilitation and recovery; interposal communication; coach–athlete relationships; and the role and scope of sport psychology practitioners working with student-athletes attempting to transition to a professional sport environment.

Purpose

The purpose of this case study is to help students think through the circumstances they might face working with an athlete intending to play professional sport following a successful college career.

Student learning outcomes

At this end of this case study learning opportunity, students should be able to:

1. Identify the factors affecting the athlete's decision-making

2. Recognize the challenges and opportunities facing athletes in a try-out situation
3. Demonstrate a critical understanding of the ways a sport psychology consultant might approach an individual experiencing these challenges
4. Demonstrate an understanding of the range of knowledge, skills and capabilities a sport psychology practitioner might apply in complex cases
5. Demonstrate an understanding of the possible conflicts between sport psychology practitioners, coaches and athletes

Cast of characters in order of appearance

Mark Redmond, Men's Soccer.
Javier Aguilar, Sport Psychology Consultant.
Robin Marriot, Head Coach, Men's Soccer.

Athlete profile: Mark Redmond, men's soccer

Mark Redmond is The U's men's starting goal keeper. He has been a four-year starting player for the team, and his accomplishments include being the All-Conference first team goal keeper in his first three years. Mark was recruited from a local youth soccer club. His parents live 50 minutes from campus, but Mark lives close to campus. He is a business and communication major intending to graduate on time in four years. He is an excellent student with a grade point average of 3.8. On the surface Mark balanced completing his studies, soccer and his relationship with his long-time girlfriend, Anna. But tensions had arisen between them in Mark's senior year.

He and Anna had been together since their junior year in high school. She attended The U and graduated the previous year with a degree in education and was certified to teach at elementary school level. She started her first teaching job for the Wilcox School district in the adjoining town to Lake Beyond the Hills. After initial difficulties, things improved for Anna and she found her feet. Anna considered her and Mark a long-term couple, and thoughts about marriage and children after Mark graduated had been on her mind.

Mark was in a no-fault accident in training early in the soccer season. He had fallen heavily on his shoulder and upper back, injuring himself so much he missed the remainder of the season and a sophomore replacement took his place. However Mark did heal in time to be on the bench in the Conference Championship game. His younger replacement was very good, and while Mark was disappointed not to play, he supported the young goal keeper. Mark's behavior did not go unnoticed, and his team voted him player's player of the season for the way he handled himself during his injury and recovery. However this honor did not console him because his season had been upended because of the injury and his dreams were like fractured ice waiting to crack and melt away.

During the fall season he expected to be on top form and intended to work on relationships he had with soccer coaches in the MLS, or at least in the second-tier

22 An opportunity to play professional soccer

North American Soccer League (NASL). His childhood dream had been to play professional soccer. He worked hard to make U23 teams, player development league teams and summer camp talent identification programs. He traveled to the Midwest and central region as far as Florida and Texas to show top coaches he could perform well and had what it took to be a professional goal keeper. Mark was single-minded in his determination, but his injury was a setback.

Over the Christmas break Mark communicated with a number of coaches. He felt confident and upbeat, and looked forward to the MLS draft positively. He talked with Javier Aguilar, the team sport psychology consultant, and expressed how good he was feeling and wondered which club would come for him and where he might be living. The MLS draft came and went. No club came in for Mark, and tensions between him and Anna intensified. He made a call to Javier.

The case

Javier and Mark met in Robin Marriot's office. Mark was comfortable meeting Javier on campus. They had a good working relationship and would text and talk on the phone whenever Mark wanted to communicate. They sat together at the round table, knowing Robin would join them when he was free from an earlier meeting.

MARK: "Thanks for coming this afternoon. I know you don't normally do morning meetings on campus."
JAVIER: "It's okay, this was a good day and I planned a break for myself this afternoon."
MARK: "Nice."
JAVIER: "So, it's unusual for us to meet up in the morning. What's up?"
MARK: "Robin got me a trial with Orange Metro in California. They are in the North American Soccer League and they have at least one spot, and I just have to beat one guy out to get the spot."
ROBIN: "Wow! Congratulations Mark. That's great news. The last time we talked you were feeling like things were not going to go well for you, maybe you missed your chance."

Their hands met in a high five above the table and they both grinned broadly.

MARK: "Yeah I know. This was not how I hoped things would go, but I got this chance and that's all that matters."
JAVIER: "Okay, so I am happy for you, but I am wondering what made you ask for this meeting today?"

Mark's face settled and looked subdued. He had been alert and sitting upright, but now he slumped and seemed down.

MARK: "It's Anna. I've not told her yet, and when I do I think she's going to be mad with me … and I have to travel to California on my own. It's the first time I will have ever been on my own away from my family and Anna, and I just talked to Anna about maybe doing graduate school too."

Javier blew out a big breath, raised his eyebrows and leaned back in his chair.

JAVIER: "Okay, so why are we in Robin's office talking about this?"

Javier was not upset, he was curious. These kinds of conversations normally took place off campus. But not today.

MARK: "Robin has experience of players in this kind of situation before. I know you have a good relationship with him and with me, and you are the only two people I know who understand me and I trust to help me with this situation. I feel torn and I don't know how to do all the things that I need to do. The only time I have traveled is for soccer, and one of my parents or Anna always seemed to be around. "

JAVIER: "So you're feeling stretched, you're worried you won't cope and Anna doesn't know about this. In fact you might have confused her a bit with other things you discussed with her."

MARK: "Exactly. And I need to register for classes this semester to finish my degree, but I need to get online courses or courses that are hybrid, otherwise I'm not going to be able to do this trial … luckily I only need to take 12 credit hours, but all of this is going on while I'm on this trial. I feel overwhelmed about all this stuff."

As Mark finished, Robin opened the office door.

MARK: "Hi Coach."

Robin reached out his hand to meet Javier's.

ROBIN: "Hello Javier. Good to see you."
JAVIER: "You too Robin."

Robin sat down, with the three at equal distances from each other around the table.

ROBIN: "How much do you know about Mark's situation?"
JAVIER: "Quite a bit. We just talked and he gave me the news that Orange Metro would give him a go."

ROBIN: "I have a friend there who knew Mark from a game he saw him play in Florida. It was me that thought it would be good for us all to meet. It seems like this situation could be complicated, especially with Anna and school. I can handle the course load with the academic advisers for Mark. Something can be figured out, but Anna and all the independent living stuff I thought you could help Mark with."

Mark nodded as if judging a legal case and made no sound, and Javier composed himself.

JAVIER: "Do you think that we should be discussing Anna as if she is a problem?"
ROBIN: "It's not that she's a problem, but she is an important factor here. I know she's important to Mark, isn't she Mark?"

The head coach looked to Mark for affirmation.

MARK: "Anna is not a problem. The problem is I don't know how to talk to her about this. Things are serious between us. You know we've been together for a long time and I know she has ideas of us getting married after I graduate."

Robin cut in before Javier could say anything.

ROBIN: "Mark, you've got to get your head straight here. I got you this opportunity. You need to step up and take it, take this opportunity. There's plenty of girls, but you only play professionally once. You know what I mean?"

Mark looked hurt, and Javier saw this too.

JAVIER: "Okay Robin, I know you want Mark to do well and you are motivated for him to have this opportunity and seize the moment, but let's take a moment to unpack everything that is in front of us."

Javier looked at Mark and Robin earnestly.

JAVIER: "Mark you have an opportunity to follow your dream and you have to get your courses sorted out; you have to organize your travel; you have to talk to Anna; you have several transitions in front of you, and you have to make decisions about what you want and recognize the effects on people you around that you care about. You also have limited experience doing anything like this … when is your trial?"

The room was silent. Mark stared at Javier.

MARK: "It's in two weeks ... well, I mean in 15 days."
JAVIER: "Look, I think this is best dealt with off campus. Can I be frank with you?"
MARK: "Sure"
JAVIER: "I feel you and Anna should come to my office and talk."
MARK: "But what about the trial?"
JAVIER: "This is what I mean, Mark, about making decisions. What are your priorities and what are you prepared to commit to? I feel like you want your relationship with Anna to work out, you want school to work out, and you want your soccer life to work out. You want it all to work out and you want it all to be resolved in the next two weeks ... I mean 15 days."
ROBIN: "Mark's got a point Javier. You know trials for professional clubs don't come around that often, and after the season he's had this could be the last chance he has to ever make it to the pro level."
JAVIER: "I get that Robin. But these are three areas of stress that relate to each other. If we include the injury it's four areas. All impact each other. Stress from personal relationships can affect concentration and impact performance. Graduating from college and transitioning into something else is inevitable and brings additional stress too; then there's living alone during the trial period. How long will this trial last?"
MARK: "Three weeks."

They all paused, thinking to themselves about what they heard.

JAVIER: "Okay, let's do this. Mark, you speak to Anna and call me later today and tell me if both of you can come by tomorrow evening to discuss this."
MARK: "Should I tell Anna what this is about?"
JAVIER: "Yes. Don't surprise her. Be fair to her."
ROBIN: "But won't that make things worse? Shouldn't she be told only when she gets with you? I mean she could get mad and things could get out of hand before we even get to your office?"
JAVIER: "Robin, Anna is not a problem and it is not terrible if she is upset. If you put yourself in her position she might have a right to be upset."
ROBIN: "Well if it was me I would not be thinking about how my girlfriend felt. I'd get right on this opportunity. My wife has always known soccer comes first most of the time. She understands what's important to me."

Javier eyed Robin and wondered if he should recognize what he heard with a response. Instead he chose to address Mark.

JAVIER: "Call me later Mark. Schedule a meet up after Anna finishes teaching, sometime between 5:30 and 8:00pm tomorrow, okay?"

MARK: "But what if she can't make it?"
JAVIER: "Encourage her Rob. Convince her that this is very important to both of you."

Robin thought the meeting was concluding and pushed his chair back from the table.

JAVIER: "Wait a minute Robin. I know you played professionally. What planning have you done to help Mark prepare for the trial so far?"
ROBIN: "Not much. We talked yesterday a little bit. I was hoping you would take care of those things. You know, work on his mental game plan, that kind of thing."
JAVIER: "I can do that, but what would help me is if you explained to Mark what he needs to do practically to get himself out of California, what to expect, how to conduct himself and how to keep his focus."
ROBIN: "You mean you want me to do your job?"
JAVIER: "No, that's not what I am saying. What I'm telling you to do is share your experience – experience I don't have – and help Mark be successful. After all, you recruited him and you have seen him through his career here. This is about being practical right now. Things can be organized and managed, but we need to take time with the people side of things … I mean Robin, how much does his success reflect on you and this program?"

Robin understood what Javier was telling him. He turned to Mark.

ROBIN: "What do you have going on this afternoon Mark?"
MARK: "I have to register for courses, we have practice and then I'm free at 4:00pm."
ROBIN: "Okay, let's meet then. Give the meeting 30–40 minutes."

Javier got up from his seat.

JAVIER: "Okay guys, let's call it a day. Mark I'll see you tomorrow. Would you mind if Coach and I had a minute to ourselves?"
MARK: "Sure. I'll see you later Coach."

Mark left the office and closed the door quietly behind him. Robin was standing up now.

JAVIER: "Robin, can I ask you to do something?"
ROBIN: "Sure. As long as it's not your job."

Javier smiled.

JAVIER: "No, no more than I would try to do yours. Mark is a young man with a lot of promise. He is not you, and pushing your values on him is not the strongest choice for him. Guide him and let him come to his own conclusions. I know these opportunities don't come along often and it's his dream, but see him as a whole person, not just a player."

ROBIN: "Are you done? Did you just tell me how to do my job? Do you think I don't know what I'm doing? You're well off in your thinking Javier."

JAVIER: "Sorry Robin. I call it as I see it. We've worked together for a while. I hoped you might be comfortable with an open dialog. Perhaps you're not."

ROBIN: "I am. But don't go sticking your nose into something you don't know much about. You're a counselor. Stick to that. I'll stick to coaching."

JAVIER: "Okay Robin."

Javier reached out to Robin and the two shook hands. Javier turned and left the office, leaving the door open behind him.

Discussion questions

1. What is going on in this case?
2. What kind of conflicts exist in this case?
3. How would you work with Mark and any other individual in this situation?
4. What interventions might be applied for the athlete's benefit in this case?
5. How might you evaluate the effectiveness of your consultation?

Author's notes

I feel this is a tricky case with many angles to consider. For example, Mark has to contend with his own ambition to play professional soccer; achieve long-held goals; process a long-term personal relationship with his girlfriend; register for courses and balance his academic choices against his needs; and manage the tension he might experience being around others like Javier and Robin. These issues have to be considered in the context of a pressing (possibly) once-in-a-lifetime opportunity in front of him beginning in 15 days.

The first thing I would do is to set a 15-day short-term goal and task achievement schedule with Mark and Robin. If I am involved in a situation like this I tend only to think in immediate and proximal terms and deal with things on a day-to-day (or even shorter) basis. Next, I would most likely focus on identifying the barriers to goal achievement and work with Mark to prioritize them, from most difficult to easiest to address. Once we had done this, I would invite Mark to decide which challenges he wanted to take on next. I would expect us work on how to remove those obstacles in a timely fashion, focusing more on solutions and less on attitude, beliefs and so on. I would make sure Robin and I have open and ongoing communication and recruit him on the soccer side of things to help Mark prepare in ways that would make him successful. Given the organizational context,

I have to be mindful of a positive and enduring relationship with a coach. I need to be authentic and consistent in my approach with a coach, but also mindful of the long-term nature of college sports compared to the short-term, ephemeral nature of professional sports.

If Mark wanted my assistance to process his approach to engaging Anna in his decision making I would do that one-on-one with him. Unlike Javier, I would not invite Mark to attend a collaborative session with Anna because this might raise too much tension during an already challenging period. I would focus on Mark's decision-making and behavior. In a tight situation like this I would expect to check in every two or three days to monitor the process and make myself available, and expect this to increase to four–five days after the first week. However, if Mark decided that he and Anna wanted to discuss things with me, and work to reach an understanding that would help them progress in their relationship, I would meet with them. I would take a collaborative and cooperative approach to learn what they wanted and needed from our collaboration. I would ask them to set an outcome goal for the session and work backwards from this goal. Given the time frame, I would focus on problem solving and solution finding, and engage Anna as deeply as she is prepared to go in the conversation and ensure Mark is with us all the way. My sense is that without Anna being satisfied with the outcome, Mark will feel badly too. Therefore, arriving at the outcome in a way they can both live with would be my intention.

Further reading

Anderson, A. G., Mahoney, C., Miles, A., & Robinson, P. (2002). Evaluating the effectiveness of applied sport psychology practice: Making the case for a case study approach. *Sport Psychologist*, 16(4), 432–453.

Bourke, A. (2003). The dream of being a professional soccer player: Insights on career development options of young Irish players. *Journal of Sport and Social Issues*, 27(4), 399–419.

Frankl, D. (2013). Narrative research addressing the challenges of a career in professional sports. *JTRM in Kinesiology*, December, 1–12.

Lubker, J. R., Visek, A. J., Geer, J. R., & WatsonII, J. C. (2008). Characteristics of an effective sport psychology consultant: Perspectives from athletes and consultants. *Journal of Sport Behavior*, 31(2), 147.

4

ANTERIOR CRUCIATE LIGAMENT (ACL) INJURY REHABILITATION

Introduction

This case demonstrates the experience of a women's soccer player recovering from an anterior cruciate ligament (ACL) injury. The student-athlete will be working with a strength and conditioning coach and an athletic trainer to implement an imagery and visualization program. It is not uncommon for sport medicine professionals to have training in and awareness of the fundamentals of mental skills such as visualization, relaxation and goal setting. The role of sport psychology practitioner is seen as a guide on the side providing feedback and direction to the individuals implementing the program.

Content implications

A facilitated discussion could go in a number of directions: for example, on the scope of sport medicine professionals conducting mental skills training and any overlap with the role of sport psychology practitioners. Discussions concerning the role of sport psychology practitioners helping student athletes cope with the challenges of long-term (6–12-month) physical rehabilitation after significant injury and surgery might lead to examination of the canon of sport psychology applications and perspectives on the diversity of therapeutic approaches such as rational emotive behavioral therapy, cognitive appraisal models, relapse prevention, and narrative- and solution-focused approaches.

Purpose

The purpose of this case study is to help students think through how they might approach working with an athlete returning from an ACL injury.

Student learning outcomes

At this end of this case study learning opportunity, students should be able to:

1. Demonstrate application of principles and approaches to an imagery intervention.

Cast of characters in order of appearance

Lily "Sparksy" Sparks, Athletic Trainer.
Mike "Thompo" Thompson, Strength and Conditioning Coach.
Micah Rowland, Women's Soccer.

Athlete profile: Micah Rowland, women's soccer

Micah is a 22-year-old senior soccer player. Her competitive goal is to play in the women's professional league after college, with the hope of making the national team for the next Olympic Games. Last year, Micah's sophomore year, she sprained the medial collateral ligament (MCL) of her left knee and had surgery to repair the damage. The injury was caused in a tackle. Micah had been dispossessed of the ball by her opposite number and got frustrated at her performance. The very next play her opponent gained possession Micah accelerated into the tackle and came off second best. Just after the injury Micah was overheard saying to a team mate: "I was mad at the tackle she just made on me and I was like ... bitch you're gonna get it! I just zoned in her look what happened." The surgery caused Micah to be redshirted in her junior year, which meant she had to see out that season and retain a year of NCAA eligibility. This was a bitter blow to Micah because she beat out a senior for the same position.

At the time of her successful selection onto the team this was very satisfying because her girlfriend had said "I need some space. Let's take a break," which upset Micah; and, on top of that, she was not doing well in her core business classes. This was disappointing Micah because if soccer did not pay off she knew she needed a backup plan, and she thought she was good at selling and marketing. This was her belief, but she had no proof she was good at it outside of class projects. Even though this injury came at a bad time, Micah had successfully recovered from injuries before, but this was the first surgery she had experienced.

During a rehab session after receiving approval to return to training Micah met with her conditioning coach, and during the warm-up she said to him:

> Mike, I'm not sure my coaches know what's going in with me. I mean, they seem to treat me like I'm too precious ... they don't seem to have a clue about my injury. I mean I've come back from injury before; why won't they just let me play?

The case

Lily Sparks looked up from her latest inspirational quote book as Thompo popped his head around the door to her office.

THOMPO: "Ready?"
SPARKSY: "Sure."

> Sparksy turned the book over and stood up. As they walked down the corridor to the women's soccer team meeting room, Sparksy confided in Thompo.

SPARKSY: "Mike, let's see how Micah responds to what we ask her to do. Her attitude will be key to us expanding her training program. She's her own worst enemy. We're trying to nurture her and we know she's not happy with us. But, if she's going to try to go for the next level, she's got to be 100 percent ready physically and mentally. It's our job to help her get there, whether she likes it or not!"

> Thompo listened quietly. His listening skills and non-judgmental attitude were why he was favored and trusted by athletes and coaches to incorporate mental skills training with athletes.
> Micah was waiting in the team room. She was seated at a desk with an iPad next to a text book, and it seemed like she was making notes. She looked up and smiled.

MICAH: "Hey Sparksy … Thompo, how are you doing today?"

> Micah's reaction to Thompo and Sparksy made them feel relieved. Outwardly they were smiling, but in their minds they both said "Phew!"

THOMPO: "Micah, we feel we've got an opportunity to help your progress back to play."
MICAH: "Okay. So what does that mean?"
SPARKSY: "We both know your lateral movement could improve, and you're frustrated at the rate of progress. We feel if we introduce an imagery training program into your regular training it's going to help you return to playing quicker. How does that sound to you?"
MICAH: "That's fine Sparksy, but I don't know anything about imagery. I don't think I've ever done it. Is there time? I mean, is it just one more thing to do, or is it really going to help me achieve my goals?"

> Sparksy looked blankly at her then turned to Thompo for help. He looked at Micah and spoke softly.

THOMPO: "Micah, we want you to reach the next level. There is a form of imagery that has been in professional rugby we feel you could make use of. It is a fresh approach and would make your rehabilitation efforts unique. It could make the difference for you. We need you to feel more confident in your lateral movement. We see you wincing and slowing down after you turn or cut sharply. You're in the return to sport phase and we feel you do have imagery abilities. We know you can see yourself being successful, and we feel the outcomes you will achieve from this form of imagery are going to put you in a position to achieve the next level. Will you give it a go?"

Up until recently Micah felt her coaches did not care and were just treating her "preciously" for no strong reason (in her mind). Although Thompo had told her this, she felt like Sparksy really had her well-being in mind when she spoke to her, too.

MICAH: "If this means I get stopped being treated like I can't do anything or can't get back to competition I'm open to it, but not if this is about pushing me off and making me sit out even more."
SPARKSY: "No, this is not about pushing you off, it's about getting you back and trying something innovative to help you progress back faster. We've tried other things and we think this might be helpful."

Micah gazed up at the ceiling and then looked around her, seeing pictures and messages players posted over the years to remember past players, motivate the current team and encourage recruits to join the team. She was feeling a little sorry for herself.

MICAH: "Okay Sparksy. I'll give it a go. What do I have to do?"
THOMPO: "Come down to the Strength Room. We'll get you started with a bit of education, a bit of practice and we'll follow the best practice guidelines together so we both know what we should be doing when you're training."
MICAH: "How long's this going to take?"
THOMPO: "Don't worry about that, it will be manageable."
MICAH: "Wait … how much time is this going to take? Is Coach going to know about this? … How will I know if I'm getting better?"

Thompo's eyes grew wide. He sensed this was not going to be an easy sell to an experienced athlete.

THOMPO: "We'll do it in six 30-minute sessions over the next two weeks, but you have to practice every day and do what I tell you to do."

Micah's eyes narrowed. She did not like the idea of having to do what she was told, especially with something she knew nothing about.

SPARKSY: "Yes, Coach will know, but not the specifics and the proof will be in your confidence, the quality of your movement and the way you cope with training ... It's all good. Coach wants you back too."

Micah thought on the invitation for a moment.

MICAH: "Alright. When do I come and meet you?"
THOMPO: "Can you come down after practice today, say for ... 30 minutes to go over an introduction?"
MICAH: "Sorry, I can't do that. I have to study. How about tomorrow morning?"
THOMPO: "Sure, come tomorrow around 7am, okay?"
MICAH: "For real!"
THOMPO: "Yeah for real. I'll be there."
MICAH: "This better be good Thompo."

Thompo gave Micah a high five and left with Sparksy to return to her office to talk through what just happened. Sparksy opened her door, they both walked in and Thompo closed the door quietly behind him. "That went better than expected," he said.

THOMPO: "It could have been worse"
SPARKSY: "How sure are you this will work?"
THOMPO: "Yeah, I am sure. If she does what she is supposed to do she can turn this around."
SPARKSY: "Okay, this is your deal Thompo. Let me know how it goes tomorrow with Micah."
THOMPO: "Sure. I'll text you, okay?"
SPARKSY: "Sure."
THOMPO: "You look miserable Sparksy. Cheer up."

The coach left the room, looking over his shoulder.

THOMPO: "See you tomorrow Sparksy."

Micah arrived at 7am sharp and met Thompo in his office in the Strength Room.

THOMPO: "Well done Micah! Good to see you. Come on in."

Micah went in and sat down in one of the two chairs in front of Thompo desk. Thompo then sat down opposite her.

THOMPO: "Okay, so how much do you know about the idea of imagery?"

MICAH: "Nothing at all. I mean I heard about it in a sport psychology class I took in sophomore year, but I don't really remember what it was about ... is it the same as visualization?"

THOMPO: "Yeah kind of, what do you know about that?"

MICAH: "It means you see yourself playing in the future, and you do it before you go to bed."

THOMPO: "Do you do anything like that before you go to sleep?"

MICAH: "Nah ... I try not to think before I got to bed. It gets me in my head."

THOMPO: "Okay, well imagery is supposed to help you gain consistency and control over your play. You achieve this by practicing seeing yourself move from through your own eyes and from a third point of view like a video camera watching you play. It's basically visually rehearsing seeing yourself play well over and over again so that when you go back and train and play you have already done it hundreds of times without kicking a ball."

There was a quiet silence. Nobody else was training. Micah furrowed her brow.

MICAH: "This stuff works?"

Thompo, feeling like he had to work harder to convince Micah of the benefits, reached out to pick up two papers off his desk: a frequently asked question sheet about imagery to educate athletes; and an imagery self-assessment sheet he had downloaded from the Internet to use with athletes to determine their imagery capabilities.

THOMPO: "Yeah it works. I've read loads of athletes have used it."

MICAH: "Okay, so what do you want me to do?"

THOMPO: gave Micah the assessment sheet.

THOMPO: "Here's a pen, go ahead and complete the self-assessment. Then give it back to me so I can check it out and read this sheet answering all your questions. Once you've done that we're going to do a practice exercise based on your self-assessment to help train your imagery skills, okay?"

MICAH: "Sure ... how come you know about this stuff?"

THOMPO: "I went to a weekend workshop a couple of years ago. The presenter was a psychologist who used it with their athletes, and it made a lot of sense to me. I've used it with a couple of men's soccer players and a few of the basketball players, you know, men's and women's."

Micah put her head down and worked through the imagery assessment. Once she finished it she gave the forms to Thompo.

MICAH: "So, are you talking to the sport psych guy we have here about me?"

THOMPO: "Yeah. I told him all about you and your stuff."

MICAH: "What did he say?"
THOMPO: "He said he would answer my questions about goal setting and visualization, pretty much anything else I brought up to him too. But I told him, I got this, and I know what I am doing."

Discussion questions

1. What factors are influencing the athlete's rehabilitation from injury in this case?
2. What might you expect to observe when Thompo and Micah meet for the first imagery training session?
3. How would you advise Thompo to implement an imagery program with Micah?
4. How would you implement an imagery program with Micah?
5. What kind of cognitive behavioral strategies might also be used by a sport medicine professional in a rehabilitation program to keep Micah on track?
6. What role might a sport psychology practitioner have in this case?

Authors notes

Micah is frustrated with her situation, and I empathize with her desire to return to play. She is determined to play and seems to see beyond her current status. However, I am not convinced by Thompo and Sparksy's approach to working with Micah. I feel an opportunity might be missed here; for example, given the nature of the injury, I feel that a meeting with Micah including a member of her medical team (not mentioned in this case, perhaps the athletic trainer), Sparksy and Thompo to show Micah the progress she has made to date and the typical outcomes an athlete at her stage of recovery can expect if they do too much too soon in their recovery from this type of injury would be useful. By using data to lead the conversation I feel Micah's vision for herself might be influenced so that she might look at her situation with realism and optimism at the same time.

Second, I would prefer to be contacted to check over the imagery education Thompo was thinking about providing. I have no problem with sport medicine professionals integrating mental skills training into their work but, on the other hand, there are forms of imagery training that be better for this case. For example, performance imagery, movement imagery, healing imagery and rehab imagery have different purposes and slightly different processes too. Additionally, I would want to match the imagery training with ball and movement work, and perhaps integrate video images taken with a cell phone for immediate feedback. I feel this athlete might be better served by a holistic counseling approach.

What do I think my role might be in this case? I see my role in this case as facilitation, guidance and support to the individuals who choose to take responsibility for this process. I do not see a direct role for me with this athlete. There are already important people Micah values supporting her at this time. I think it is important to stay out of some situations because too many people involved makes things unnecessarily complicated and messy, particularly when the athlete has a strong and purposeful goal in their vision. Too many voices might become a distraction to the purpose of the intervention Thompo is intending.

Further reading

Reese, L. M. S., Pittsinger, R., & Yang, J. (2012). Effectiveness of psychological intervention following sport injury. *Journal of Sport and Health Science*, 1(2), 71–79.

Wierike, S. C. M., Sluis, A., Akker-Scheek, I., Elferink-Gemser, M. T., & Visscher, C. (2013). Psychosocial factors influencing the recovery of athletes with anterior cruciate ligament injury: A systematic review. *Scandinavian Journal of Medicine & Science in Sports*, 23(5), 527–540.

Wiese-Bjornstal, D. M. (2010). Psychology and socioculture affect injury risk, response, and recovery in high-intensity athletes: A consensus statement. *Scandinavian Journal of Medicine & Science in Sports*, 20(s2), 103–111.

Williams, J. M., & Andersen, M. B. (1998). Psychosocial antecedents of sport injury: Review and critique of the stress and injury model. *Journal of Applied Sport Psychology*, 10(1), 5–25.

5
GOAL KEEPING ERRORS DURING GAMES

Introduction

This case concerns a younger and less experienced goal keeper replacing an older, more experienced goal keeper who is injured because of a no-fault accident in training. The replacement keeper is capable of performing at college level but has not been satisfactorily prepared to play in competition. There are various tensions in the relationships between the young goal keeper, his team mates and the goal keeping coach. There is also tension between team coaches. In the first two games the replacement goal keeper showed courage and made several saves, but he also made notable errors. His family is supportive but physically distant.

Content implications

This case offers a range of challenges to sport psychology students. These include coach–player interactions, coach–coach interactions, team mate interactions, replacing an injured player in your position, coaching methodology and development, concentration during competition, situational decision-making during competition, stress management, use of technology in coaching practice, interpersonal relationships, goal setting, self-talk, and visualization.

This case is time sensitive. The team needs performance improvement from the goal keeper and the defensive unit to be enhanced in several days of development. There are a number of contextual factors. The level of insertion and scope of the role of the sport psychology practitioner is ambiguous too. Instructors are encouraged to have students consider the risks and benefits of their approach to handling this case.

Purpose

The purpose of this case is to challenge students to consider the needs of the athlete and contend with the context they are operating in so that they might develop a nuanced eye to the key issues within their scope of practice they might help the athlete cope with.

Student learning outcomes

At this end of this case study learning opportunity, students should be able to:

1. Identify the contributing factors to the challenges Rob (the goal keeper) faces
2. Recognize the internal and external influences on Rob's experience
3. Demonstrate a critical understanding of the ways a sport psychology consultant might approach an individual experiencing these challenges
4. Demonstrate an understanding of the role and scope of responsibilities of a sport psychology consultant in this situation
5. Demonstrate an understanding of the possible solutions to reduce the negative impact on Rob's performance and enhance his play.

Cast of characters in order of appearance

Otto Reinwagner, Rob's Father.
Rob Reinwagner, Men's Soccer.
Jaime Varedo, Goal Keeping Coach, Men's Soccer.
Robin Marriot, Head Coach, Men's Soccer.
Marty Kelly, Assistant Head Coach, Men's Soccer.

Athlete profile: Rob Reinwagner, men's soccer

Rob Reinwagner is 20 years old, 6 feet 2 inches, and 180 lbs. He is now the starting goal keeper and a sophomore who intends to major in finance and one day go into financial planning or banking. His grade point average is 3.2 and he hopes by the end of the year to raise it to 3.4. He was an in-state recruit who won honors as the goal keeper and captain of his high school team who won back-to-back state championships in his junior and senior years of varsity completion. He played at the regional Olympic Development level following a semester studying in England, and playing for the youth academy of a professional club in the second tier of competition. He was a popular captain known for being steady and easy to get along with, and leading by example.

Rob was recruited as a back-up to Mark Redmond, a prospect for the Major League Soccer (MLS) draft in his senior year (see Chapter 3), when the previous back-up keeper transferred to another college to get more playing time. Rob sat on the bench for his whole freshman year and played very little competitive soccer. He knew he would be learning how to get along with new team mates and that he would have to build trust with the defensive unit in particular. The U's defense was miserly and was marshalled masterfully at center back by the captain, Luis Gonzalez, with Mark in goal for every game. Luis and Mark were recruited at the same time and roomed together on campus and when the team played away matches. Their relationship was very close and it transferred to the field, where they gave confidence and belief to others in the team's defensive capabilities.

Mark and Rob got along well. Mark made Rob feel welcome and made a point of making him feel comfortable. They were friendly without being too close. They trained well together and tested each other's capabilities. Two days before the fifth game of the 19-game regular season Mark Redmond fell awkwardly during a training exercise. Nobody was to blame, and the fall happened without contact from any player. He landed heavily on his shoulder and the diagnosis was a shoulder separation requiring a minimum of 6–8 weeks of treatment. Mark would miss the rest of the season and the playoffs. Rob got his chance to start.

Rob had taken a mature approach to his time as a back-up. He focused on learning on and off the field. He made friends on the team and confided regularly in his father, Otto, and his mother, Hilda. His parents were second-generation Germans who had settled in the Milwaukee area of Wisconsin. His best friend on the team was another sophomore, Steven Garret, a center midfield player who had been recruited from the same high school as Rob. Steven was getting playing time and contesting for a starting place.

When Mark Redmond got injured Rob knew he might get playing time. He did not want Mark to be injured, but at the same time he wanted to play and knew this was his moment. He had waited 16 months to get the starting opportunity and show what he could do. Team morale was low because Mark was out of action for the rest of the season. The defensive unit had no experience playing in front of Rob in competitive play. Luis Gonzalez was both disappointed and curious about how things were going to go.

The case

Otto answered his son's call on his cell phone.

OTTO: "Hello there."
ROB: "Did you see the game last night? ... I didn't do too good."
OTTO: "I saw the game on the Internet. The online stream was really clear. You did not do too bad ... you've done worse before ... I remember when you were seven years old and ..."
ROB: "Dad!"
OTTO: "Okay, okay, I'm just loosening things up."
ROB: "Ha, okay ... I'm not feeling great Dad. It wasn't the start I wanted ... that first goal was definitely my fault and the third one I was at least 50–50 to blame too."

OTTO: "Wow! You better quit now! It sounds like you'll never cope at this level. It's the end of your world and you've never had this happen to you before."
ROB: "Dad come on, you don't have to make a joke of it."
OTTO: "Exactly! It was your first time with this team and it did not happen like you wanted. Okay, it's not the first time this has happened, so learn from it and move on."

Rob was silent.

OTTO: "Okay, what happened Rob? It looked like you were not confident. It's not like you. What happened?"
ROB: "It started the day before in training. I've only had one training session with the defense; the captain and Mark were best friends. The coach wanted us to play a high backline pressing into their half and wanted me playing high out from the goal. We haven't trained like this before, and even though we haven't played together before he expected me to play the same way Mark did … I made some errors in positioning … you know I'm not used to the speed of play and the habits of the guys in defense. Then we practiced set plays, especially dealing with crosses. We knew we were playing Mumford and we expected them to play with their big striker on his own but they didn't. They played with two big central strikers, and one was a center half who seemed to make contact with me anytime he could. It was fine in training. I felt good but when the game came it went bad."
OTTO: "It was your first game, what did your coaches and team mates expect? You've been playing the bench since you arrived."
ROB: "I'm supposed to be a good goal keeper. I mean I'm supposed to be solid and I'm supposed to be Mark's replacement when he graduates. Based on what I did yesterday the team might doubt me."
OTTO: "Come on, you don't think that do you?"
ROB: "Dad, we don't lose. You know our record—we're a very strong team. Losing to Mumford was a bad result for us. Coach was pissed."
OTTO: "How was your goal keeping coach after the game?"
ROB: "He surprised me. He was pretty chill. He helped me through the one training session and he was supportive. It felt like he knew what I was experiencing … you were right Dad. I didn't feel confident … look, I got to go. I'll call you after practice tonight."

Jaime Varedo finished picking up the cones marking the training area for the goal keepers. He always picked them up walking in the direction of the locker rooms. Putting the last cone in the equipment bag, he carried it over to the training goal located in front of the entrance to the locker rooms and far enough away that nobody would hear the conversation he was going to have with Rob.

JAIME: "So how was practice today Rob?"

ROB: "Good, I felt a bit better, you know, like I was in the right place and at the right time."
JAIME: "Yeah, you seemed a bit more comfortable today."
ROB: "Yeah, Luis talked with me more. I thought he was really mad at me for the third goal. Now I've seen it on the video I see I hesitated coming out and made him adjust. Mark wouldn't have done that."
JAIME: "Well he wasn't playing. You were ... How confident were you in yourself by the time the third goal happened?"

Rob drew in a deep breath and let it out slowly.

ROB: "Not much. I mean, the first goal was a disaster. I knew they were going to test me, but when the ball came into the box I got lost behind the fake striker and our defender and didn't see the run to the near post. It was a free header. I didn't read the play. It was a rookie mistake. The second goal there was nothing I could do. It was a solid finish, and the third goal ... I didn't communicate. I waited for Luis to take control of the situation, and when I saw he didn't like I expected he would it was too late."
JAIME: "Pretty good Rob. I see it the same way. It seems like you lost concentration and lost your presence. Did you feel like you couldn't focus?"
ROB: "To be honest, I couldn't even think. At the end of the game I just wanted to get off the field and into the locker room. I felt like I let everyone down. It wasn't the first game of my career I wanted."
JAIME: "Uh huh ... you know we're playing Barrow in three days right, and you know these are our biggest rivals in conference. The only thing worse than losing in the conference finals is losing to Barrow in the regular season. We have two training sessions between then and now and you have to get comfortable and confident, and be composed under pressure. They are going to bomb you with crosses. You thought Mumford were physical? Barrow won't mind taking a couple of yellow cards to get you in your head. They will have seen the game tape; they will know Mark's out and they will know you're going to be our starter. So we are going to train like you've never trained before with us. You need to be ready to battle on Friday night under the lights."

Otto answered Rob's call on his cell phone: "Hello there."

ROB: "Did you see the game tonight? ... It was worse than the first one."
OTTO: "Are you doing okay? That was a tough game. It's been a long time since your Mom and me have seen you play in a game like that. I mean, come on, how that boy was not red carded for the challenge on you at the near post was unbelievable. If anyone thinks you don't have guts ... they are crazy. I'm proud of you. But your Mom's worried about you."
ROB: "Tell her I'm okay."

OTTO: "Anyway, why do you think this was worse than before?"
ROB: "I dropped a couple of balls and I felt the defense sinking back because they didn't trust me. Luis even told me to punch the ball out if I wasn't going to catch it."
OTTO: "The goals had nothing to do with you."
ROB: "I know, but I've let in five goals in two games and that's much worse than when Mark was in goal."
OTTO: "You did not lose. It was a good tie. In the end you got a result."
ROB: "Dad it was Barrow. It's like war between us and them. We hate them and they hate us. I don't know why but that's the way it is. Winning is expected here ... especially against them!"
OTTO: "How was your goal keeping coach?"
ROB: "He was pretty chill but it seemed like I disappointed him."
OTTO: "Did he talk to you?"
ROB: "Not really. He just said 'good job' after the game."
OTTO: "Are you doing okay?"
ROB: "Yeah, I'm fine. I'll call you in a couple of days. We have a recovery day tomorrow and then two more days before our next game against Charles College in another conference game."

The men's soccer team was given the day off after the Barrow match to recover, catch up with homework and just relax. The loss of Mark had taken a toll on the team. The defense was leaking goals and while the team liked Rob, there was wonder and mistrust of Rob's abilities in the team, and the coaches knew it.

Robin Marriot, Marty Kelly and Jaime Varedo watched the final seconds of the recording of the previous day's 2–2 tie against Barrow. They sat around the table in Robin's office on the second floor of the Unity Performance Center overlooking the soccer field. It was 10am and the team would be in classes or in the athletic room recovering under the supervision of the trainers, so they would be nowhere near Marriot's office. The three coaches stared at each other around the table.

ROBIN: "That was tough viewing ... I know Rob's a good kid. He's been good since he joined us. I didn't see this coming."
MARTY: "I've been saying for a while that we needed to get him involved more. I think this is on us. He had no game time prior to this and we put him in with very little preparation. He showed toughness yesterday. I mean Barrow really went after him and the referee did not help him. He hung in there and he did make a couple of big saves, and he did try to do the things we asked him to do."
JAIME: "He is weak. He loses concentration at important moments. He seems not have learned from training or by watching Mark and the boys. Whether he had game time or not he should have been ready to step in. That's why we recruited him."

MARTY: "Whoa, steady Jaime. You're supposed to be his goal keeping coach. Does he know you feel this way about him?"
JAIME: "No. I don't think he could take the honesty."
MARTY: "Honesty? You're brutal! Instead of running him down how are we going to help him get through this, because he is all we have got and we need to help him along here. Sometimes Jaime I don't know what's in your mind."
JAIME: "I have standards and he needs to reach them."
MARTY: "So your view is that Rob needs to be ready to go without preparation ... would we do that with an outfield player?"
JAIME: "He knows what's expected of him. I am disappointed, but I can make him better. I can get him to where we need. I have a good idea of what to do to get him where we need him to be."

Marty and Rob looked at each other and looked back at Jaime. Robin fixed his eyes on Jaime.

ROBIN: "You should talk to Rob ... start right and warm up your relationship."
JAIME: "Coach the warm and fuzzies is not what I am good at. I am a coach for the field, that's where I do my best work."
MARTY: "You mean you don't want to meet up with him to build your relationship? I'll meet with him. At some point you have got to develop yourself Jaime and have these conversations, whether you like it or not. It's part of coaching to have relationships. We're in a hole, and this can't wait. I'll meet with Rob later but the next meeting, that one happens between you Jaime and Rob. I'll tell Rob you had a prior family commitment. You handle it and you take responsibility for this part of yours and Rob's development."

At the same time as the coaches were meeting Rob was walking across campus from his dorms to class. He thought over the previous day's game and began to ruminate on the questions he thought about before he went to sleep: What's going on with me? Why am I making these mistakes? How am I going to fix this? Why am I playing badly? How are Luis and the boys going to treat me after this? What does Jaime really think about things? What a nightmare. He arrived at his class and opened his lap top to take notes. The class was over before he realized it had even started. Over and over again the errors of the last two games kept playing in his mind. He could not picture anything positive in his play, and Luis's words during the game echoed in his mind.

On his way from class he checked his cell phone for emails and saw Marty Kelly had sent him a message. It read: "Hi Rob, head up! Stop by the coaches' office to talk after you're done in the training room this afternoon." Rob smiled. Marty was the coach most players talked to about things. Rob liked him too because he reminded him of his dad a bit.

It was 5pm when Rob knocked on the door to the coaches' office. On recovery days coaches normally started around 7:30am and finished around 3:30pm.

MARTY: "Come in Rob."

Marty got up, walked over to the door and shook Rob's hand. Marty was old school and always respectful.

MARTY: "Come and visit with me."

Marty pointed to the table he had sat at with the other coaches in the morning. Rob sat in the chair Robin Marriot had used in the morning, with the best view of the soccer fields, and placed his rucksack by the side of the chair. Marty sat across from Rob with a lap top on the table where they could both view it well from their seats.

MARTY: "How's things going Rob?"
ROB: "Okay. How's things with you Coach?"
MARTY: "Fine. I wondered if we could talk about how you're feeling after the last two games? I feel they might have been tough for you."
ROB: "It hasn't been easy for me. I mean, I keep thinking about what the things I haven't done and how my team mates see me. It's all I kept thinking about today. I couldn't concentrate in class."
MARTY: "Okay, so you're feeling low about how you played."
ROB: "Yeah."
MARTY: "I'd like to understand a bit about what's going so that we might be able to step in before the next game."
ROB: "Okay."
MARTY: "Let's watch a few clips and talk me through what you see going on."
ROB: "Sure."

Rob had done some video analysis in pre-season with Jaime before, but none concerning real game time. Normally he was coached on the field and Jaime worked with Mark on his own. Marty opened the lap top and showed Rob how to control the video clips. He invited Rob to show him the clips he wanted to talk about. Rob scrolled through the video and picked out all his errors. Rob looked up—it was 5:45pm.

ROB: "Do you need to go Coach?"
MARTY: "No. I'm good until 6:30pm, then I'll go home for some dinner ... you know Rob you have not shown me anything you did well. All I heard was how you did not to do this or that. You know where you made mistakes but you have not said how you might not make those same mistakes again. It sounds like you're stuck on what you did not do."

Rob leaned back and quietly sat in the chair adjacent to Marty and looked out of the window to the goals he usually trained in. They sat quietly for a moment. Marty broke the silence.

MARTY: "What's on your mind Rob?"
ROB: "It's hard … Mark's a great keeper and he's good person. I was sad for him he got injured and kind of happy that I got the chance to play, but it's been difficult … I've had no game time and me and the defense don't know each other. We've had no time to get to know each other."
MARTY: "I know Rob, that's on us a bit."
ROB: "How come Jaime's not here and it's you Marty? He's supposed to be my coach. I work with him most of the time … I don't know what he wants from me. We train hard but Mark is his favorite."
MARTY: "What do you mean 'favorite'?"
ROB: "I mean he treats me like I'm second and I feel like sometimes I'm just there to be Mark's workout partner. Mark doesn't make a big deal about it … anyway where's Jaime?"
MARTY: "He had a personal commitment; he couldn't be here. I'll call him tomorrow morning and we'll talk before training."

Rob nodded and reached into his bag for his water bottle. He took a sip and saw the clock above the office door showing there was 20 minutes remaining. Marty noticed Rob looking at the clock.

MARTY: "Rob you're our number one goal keeper now. Mark's out for a while and you're going to play a lot. We need you to have confidence, but I think I'm hearing you're not confident and you don't have faith in your training. Is that right?"
ROB: "Yeah."
MARTY: "Listen, the field training we can organize better for you."
ROB: "What about Luis?"
MARTY: "What about Luis? … What's the issue with Luis?"
ROB: "I don't think he trusts me."
MARTY: "Why do you say that?"
ROB: "He told me to punch. He doesn't have confidence in me. He's not mean, but you know. You can tell when someone doubts you and he's someone you don't want to have doubt in you."

The exchange created tension in the room. Marty felt like he was dealing with things not of his making, and Rob was feeling like this was the first time he had expressed how he was feeling but he was nervous he spoke out of turn.

MARTY: "We can deal with the field stuff Rob. Some of these other things I don't know too much about. Would you be willing to chat with Javier Aguilar about how you're feeling about a few things?"
ROB: "You mean the sport psych guy?"
MARTY: "Yeah, he's a good guy, he knows his soccer. He's a big Boca Juniors fan."

ROB: "He's Argentinian?"
MARTY: "Yeah, he came here for school and married an American."
ROB: "What do sport psych people do?"
MARTY: "That's a question for him."
ROB: "But I'm not sick. My dad says people who see psychologists are not well. I don't feel unwell."
MARTY: "He's not that kind of psychologist. He can help you work through things so you can play well."
ROB: "Who else on the team works with him?" Marty felt stuck because nobody worked with Javier this season and he could not recall a case of a goal keeper working with Javier.

Discussion questions

1. What are the main issues presented in this case?
2. Which issues might you deal with first?
3. How might you address coach behavior?
4. What strategies might you use to work with Rob to enhance his performance?

Author's notes

This is difficult case for a number of reasons. Rob has been successful in high school but now, so many months on from that part of his playing career, he faces several disadvantages and challenges, including: limited playing time; replacing an injured team stalwart; possible interpersonal conflict; lapses in concentration during the game and missing important aspects affecting his play; hesitancy; an emerging negative mindset; the possibility of some social isolation; and working with a coach who is in at least two minds about the player. Additionally, the case reveals there might be a somewhat fractious relationship between the assistant head coach and the goal keeping coach. It is possible that one of them needs coaching themselves and an attitude adjustment to working with Rob. There are so many issues to sort through in this case it is difficult to know which one to go with. Finally, Rob has not worked with a sport psychology consultant before.

On the other hand, Rob has supportive but physically distant parents. He has one team mate he was recruited with and is connected to, and the assistant head coach who expresses a desire to understand and help the Rob through this difficult time. Rob showed physical courage and bravery in the recent game that seems to have earned respect from his team mates. He has not become a poor goal keeper over the period of time the case takes place. He showed self-awareness about the underlying causes of his performance, which suggests he sees possible solutions. However, he is unaware of his goal keeping coach's mindset towards his level of readiness.

If I was presented with this case, knowing there was a game upcoming I would recommend using debrief (Hogg, 2002) and rapid technique correction (Hanin et al., 2004) processes. I used these in situations where rapid improvement was required in a short time and found they matched my preference for a consultative/coaching style of work. They make use of Socratic and systematic learning of the athlete's perception of what works well and what does not work well, what can change and how the change might result in improvement. Secondly, rapid technique correction means working with the coach and the athlete on the field, facilitating the use of feedback from coach to athlete and the receptivity of the athlete to the coach's pointers. The use of video analysis and the application of a communication style that focuses on achieving the explicit shared objectives of athlete and coach in a relational context are the ways I would approach this case. This case has an experienced player and an experienced coach. They have been successful and they know how to do things well. I prefer in this case to concentrate on them amplifying their combined strengths for the good of the athlete and the team's performance.

I recognize this work is not easy. I cannot change Jaime's attitude or mind, but I can facilitate the communication between him and the athlete and the use of technology. I can be a buffer between athlete and coach. I can help the partnership set goals for the coach and the player to achieve on a session to session basis. These might include goals for the defensive unit too. The time constraint indicates the focus should be on one goal per session and one primary objective for the next game. My preference would be for Luis, Robin, Jaime and Rob to be in this discussion. I would keep Marty off to the side because he had been the conduit, and I feel his external view might be useful later in the process. I found it useful to have a third party acting as an observer. It will not be me because I will be facilitating the meeting, and someone must observe what happens. Marty has insight and awareness; he also stepped up to support Rob by staying late after the usual work day to see him when he did not have to.

In order to achieve the objectives of this approach I need Robin Marriot to commit to the process, and I need him to give me enough authority and latitude to work the process through. Given there has been little interaction between the team, as a sport psychology consultant I recognize I have one opportunity to show my value here. The way I work with coaches and players and comport myself might determine how much more support I will be called on to provide to the team in the future. These are fine margins.

There are a number of items I could work on, like goal setting, mental skills training and so on, but in my view these are longer-term solutions to the issues at hand. Goals would be generated. I would set up the process, the input would come from the participants, and then we would go do it. The time for surveying and implementing a mental skills program is pre-season with top-up or booster sessions during the season. But there is no foundation to act from in this case; therefore for me to go in this direction would be a weak choice based on my preferences and skill set.

My experience has demonstrated that performance improvement is possible in a short time. When a capable athlete and a qualified and competent coach relate and focus on achieving objectives together, utilizing the available resources, they can transform the athlete's performance from an old way into a new way. Therefore I prefer to work in ways where coaches and athletes connect deeply and focus on the performance aspects of play. This case indicates that the coach and the player want to improve quickly, so I perceive my role as dealing first with the on-field performance and allowing the other issues to unfold once the primary objective of my work is achieved.

Further reading

Hanin, Y., Malvela, M., & Hanina, M. (2004). Rapid correction of start technique in an Olympic-level swimmer: A case study using old way/new way. *Journal of Swimming Research*, 16, 11–17.

Hogg, J. M. (2002). Debriefing: a means to increasing recovery and subsequent performance. In M. Kellman (Ed.), *Enhancing recovery: Preventing underperformance in athletes* (pp. 181–198). Champaign, IL: Human Kinetics.

Jones, R. L., & Wallace, M. (2005). Another bad day at the training ground: Coping with ambiguity in the coaching context. *Sport, Education and Society*, 10(1), 119–134.

Wrisberg, C. A., Loberg, L. A., Simpson, D., Withycombe, J. L., & Reed, A. (2010). An exploratory investigation of NCAA Division-I coaches' support of sport psychology consultants and willingness to seek mental training services. *Sport Psychologist*, 24(4), 489–503.

6
COACH–ATHLETE RELATIONSHIP CONFLICT

Introduction

This case presents readers with several issues which might require them to consider their personal and professional responsibilities to individuals in a lower-status role in a team. The case involves coach–player relationships, coaches' modeling behavior and decisions by a sport psychology practitioner who witnessed an emotionally charged event between coaches and a player.

Content implications

This case might be used for discussions concerning coach–player communication, conflict resolution, decision-making by the sport psychology professional, and the scope of sport psychology services that might be provided in a situation like this.

Purpose

The purpose of this case is for students to determine a course of action accounting for the ethical scope of the role and responsibilities a sport psychology practitioner has when they witness a difficult interpersonal situation and subsequently work with the individuals involved.

Student learning outcomes

At this end of this case study learning opportunity, students should be able to:

1. Identify the factors affecting the coach–athlete relationship
2. Recognize communication dynamics affecting the coach–athlete relationship

3. Demonstrate a critical understanding of the ways a sport psychology consultant might approach a situation where coaches and student-athletes experience interpersonal conflict
4. Discuss interventions which might improve the coach–athlete relationship
5. Demonstrate an understanding of the structure and process of a sport team and how they influence behavioral outcomes

Cast of characters in order of appearance

Jaime Varedo, Goal Keeping Coach, Men's Soccer.
Mark Champion, Men's Soccer.
Robin Marriot, Head Coach, Men's Soccer.
Javier Aguilar, Sport Psychology Consultant.

Athlete profile: Mark Champion, men's soccer

Mark Champion is a sophomore player on the men's soccer team. He is from the east coast of the United States and attends The U because it has a strong communications and business department. At the end of his playing career at The U Mark wants to work in politics. He is well spoken, articulate and knows his own mind. He is the middle brother of three, and his brothers are his best friends. They are very different from each other—one is a plumber, the other is a teacher—and their parents are both civil servants working for different government agencies. At home, Mark and his brothers were brought up to work hard, express themselves and challenge the thinking of the people around them. Conversations could get heated across the dining table but were always resolved. Mark's mother had been a city legal prosecutor before working from home and raising the boys. With all her sons away from home, she returned to work in the same office she left. She set the bar for discussions. Mark's father was in charge of a sanitation division responsible for dangerous cleanups around their city. He was used to working in direct ways with his teams in the field. His employees enjoyed working for him because he listened to them and made good decisions, and they felt respected. What you saw from Mark's parents is what you got from Mark too.

Mark is an attacking midfielder with a good range at passing, skill on the ball, and an eye for goal. His first season had seen him net 10 goals in 18 games and get 3 assists. Even as a freshman he showed leadership and communication skills, and always seemed at his best when the team was behind or in a fierce contest. He did not challenge the team's leadership and knew his role, but he was confident and knew when and when not to speak up; he let his play do his talking. But on one occasion he took exception to the way the goal keeping coach addressed him with curse words. The scene on the field caught the attention of the head coach, who sided with his assistant. Mark was admonished in front of his team for his behavior. He felt disrespected as a person not just as an athlete.

During his sophomore pre-season he had a slight groin muscle tear and was told he would be out for three weeks, which meant he would miss the start of the season. To be a member of the team, the head coach had him carry equipment, retrieve balls, run water bottles to the team, and make sure the pre-match meals were ready for his team mates too. Mark went along with this for the team without complaint until the goal keeping coach started to make disparaging comments about him within earshot. He confronted the coach on the field during practice when he heard one last comment which he could not let go. He asked the coach why he was doing this and the coach cursed at Mark as he had done the previous season. The two of them got into a heated exchange and the same pattern as the first year happened again, with the head coach taking sides and telling Mark off in front of the team. This time Mark responded strongly to both his coaches, and things got ugly.

The three of them stood glaring at each other like a western movie waiting for the draw. Training had stopped, and the players and the team's athletic trainer looked on. They could feel the tension between Mark and his coaches.

The case

JAIME: "What the hell is your problem kid? I'm the coach, when I tell you to shut up, you shut up, got it!"
MARK: "Some coach you are, you wouldn't cut it where I come from. All you do is stand around and say stupid stuff to us."
JAIME: "Who are you? You're nothing. You know I played pro and you know I know what I'm talking about. When I see a lazy person like you who's dragging around and showing a bad attitude I'm gonna say something."
MARK: "Bad attitude. Are you crazy?"
ROBIN: "Just shut up Mark! You don't talk back to your coach. Any coach. Do you understand? You don't talk until I tell you to talk."

Mark looked on. He knew from experience he was getting into a bad spot, so he changed how he approached this moment, but he was not going to back down.

MARK: "Coach, can you tell me why Jaime is cursing me out and making negative comments about me behind my back?"
ROBIN: "It doesn't matter what he says, you have no right to talk to your coach like that. Now apologize and let's get back to training."

Mark felt like he was in a different universe. None of his previous coaches cursed at him or run him down. He had three previous coaches—one of his dad's friends and a high school teacher who was almost too nice and the boys would have to ask him to be tougher on them. His club coach was a former professional player with a long career abroad who retired and coached because his daughter was in the same club.

He was a technical coach with a great sense of humor and got along well with Mark and his parents. Mark had no model for what he was experiencing at The U.

MARK: "Forget it Coach. No way. Jaime disrespected me and he's the one who should be apologizing. I've done nothing wrong."
ROBIN: "Shut your mouth Mark. Apologize and let's get on with it."
MARK: "No! I am not apologizing."
JAIME: [turning to Robin] "See this kid. What an attitude. You're lucky I don't kick your ass, you punk. When you get healthy I'm going ride you until you get better and give us the performance and attitude we deserve. If you don't, then maybe you shouldn't be here. There's always someone else to replace you."
MARK: [furiously and red with anger] "Are you threatening me? Is that what you're doing here? Wow! You need help, you suck."
ROBIN: "Mark! Shut it! Did I tell you to talk? No. So shut your yap and get off this field. See me in my office in 30 minutes. You totally screwed this session up for everyone. Get off now!"
JAIME: "You're never playing this season."The three had raised their voices, their faces were red and their focus was intense. It seemed like a moment of physical confrontation was going to happen. Mark recognized what was happening. He felt wronged. He stood his ground and he felt ganged up on. But he knew how heated this moment was. He turned to walk away and saw his team mates staring out like statues frozen in time.
ROBIN: "Get back at it boys. There's nothing to see."The players stood still as Mark walked past them into the athletics building where the coaches' offices were. Javier Aguilar heard the commotion through an open window he was observing the whole exchange through while he waited for a meeting.

Mark met Robin outside his office. He was still in his training clothes. He felt a lot calmer and reflective about what happened. He wanted to play this season and knew he had to deal with this situation even though he felt he was on the wrong side of things. Robin saw Mark, but did not speak when he arrived at his office. He opened the door and showed Mark to a seat across the round table. The two sat down opposite each other. Robin was still fuming when he began.

ROBIN: "Do you know why you are here?"
MARK: "I guess it's about what just happened."
ROBIN: "That's right. If you're going to play for me and you think you want to be a member of this team, you shut your mouth and you never answer a coach back. Do you understand?"
MARK: "Can you tell me why it is okay for Jaime to treat me like that?"
ROBIN: "Did you just hear me? You're doing it again. You don't challenge me or my coaches, ever!"

He banged his hand on the table so loudly passers by his office heard it.

MARK: [speaking calmly] "I've done nothing wrong. I've been a team player. I've done anything you asked me to do."
ROBIN: "That might all be true, but you never speak to a coach unless you agree with them. If we want your opinion we will ask you for it. Otherwise shut up, keep your head down and get on with things."
MARK: "Okay, so what do you want me to do?"
ROBIN: "At the next training session, I am going to call a team huddle at the beginning of training and you are going to apologize to Jaime for how you treated him and then me, and you are going to say in front of your team what you are going to do differently."
MARK: "You're making me do that? I'm the one who was being disrespected. I didn't start this, and how come you're taking sides? You're not even involved."

Robin felt a surge of anger rise up in him.

ROBIN: "SHUT YOUR FILTHY MOUTH! IF YOU WANT TO BE A PART OF THIS TEAM YOU WILL DO THIS OR YOU CAN GET THE HELL OFF THIS TEAM. YOUR CHOICE. GET OUT!"

Mark did not say anything. He pushed back quietly from the table, turned and walked out of the office. Javier Aguilar was walking out of the building and saw Mark come out of Robin's office. He saw the young man was uneasy.

JAVIER: "Hello"
MARK: "Hi."
JAVIER: "Are you okay?"
MARK: "No." Mark kept walking down the corridor, passing the team locker room and heading for the stairs to the administrative level. Javier watched him all the way down the corridor and begin to walk up the stairs when he went out of sight. Javier looked at his watch and saw he had a couple of minutes to spare. He knew Robin Marriot, and he imagined he and Mark had finished a meeting which had not got well. He turned towards Robin's office and then thought to himself he would leave it alone and not get involved. After all, he thought, if it's bad they will get in touch with me about it.

Mark went to Cissy Drew, The U's Assistant Athletic Director, and explained the situation to her. She told him call Javier Aguilar and get feedback from him about how to proceed. Cissy was not going to intervene, but she agreed to be present in a meeting with Mark if he wanted to take this up again with his coaches in private. Mark decided to call Javier.

MARK: "Hello is this Javier?"
JAVIER: "Yes, who is this?"
MARK: "It's Mark Champion, Miss Drew told me to call you today."

JAVIER: "Yes I know, she emailed me to let me know you might be reaching out to me."

MARK: "Did she tell you why I'm calling you?"

JAVIER: "She didn't have to."

MARK: "What do you mean?"

JAVIER: "I saw and heard what happened on the field, and you and me spoke when you came out of your coach's office."

MARK: "That was you? I didn't recognize you."

JAVIER: "Yes, it was me. So, tell me what you want us to talk about. I have 10 minutes before a scheduled client visits."

MARK: "Well, if you saw what happened that makes this quicker … I'm really mad about this. I don't feel like I've done anything wrong and I'm being treated badly and unfairly. Coach is totally overreacting. He threatened to kick me off the team, he's taken sides with Jaime and he won't even hear me speak … he yelled at me and banged his hand on the table. I mean I felt like he was going to punch me. He was like … totally out of control, do you know what I mean?"

JAVIER: "Sounds like this was in the office and things got out of hand. How did you respond to this?"

MARK: "I just got up and left, and I suppose that's when you saw me before I spoke to Miss Drew this morning."

JAVIER: "What do you want out of this situation?"

MARK: "I want to play. My injury is healing and I am nearly at 100 percent fitness. But the way they're treating me I feel is terrible and totally unfair, and I don't feel like anyone here is on my side."

JAVIER: "How much have you shared your thoughts with your team mates, friends or family?"

MARK: "I texted my parents that I want to talk to them tonight … I told them something went badly wrong today and Coach was out of control."

JAVIER: "Okay. So you have not spoken to anyone else?"

MARK: "No, but I will talk with my team mates, and if I get a chance I'll talk with my brothers first. I was brought up to talk things out before doing things."

JAVIER: "Okay, what do you want from me?"

MARK: "Ideas really … like how do you think I should handle this situation?"

JAVIER: "It depends what you want. If you want to play and are willing to go along with what your coaches want from you, or you want to play and stand up for yourself, or you want to stand up for yourself and see how things go, or you want to quit because you don't want anything to do with this team anymore, or there's something else you want. It all depends on what you want and what you can live with. In the end you must decide what is in your best interests."

MARK: "I know I want to play and I want to be treated fairly and with respect."

JAVIER: "Okay, so what do you think it's going to take to achieve that?"

MARK: "I don't know. I was hoping you would tell me."

JAVIER: "Well for sure, you should expect you are going to have to meet with your coaches to address this."
MARK: "Do you think I should go on my own?"
JAVIER: "No. You should have a mediator, and I recommend a team mate too, someone in the team's leadership you trust and respect."
MARK: "Would you be the mediator?"
JAVIER: "No. Miss Drew?"
MARK: "Why Miss Drew? What can she do?"
JAVIER: "She did not see or hear what took place today and she is your coaches' boss."
MARK: "Okay, why did you say I should take a team mate?"
JAVIER: "For two reasons—they saw what happened on the field and there are two coaches. You need someone there who saw it and to even the numbers up in the meeting. Otherwise it's a two-on-one situation, and we both know the coaches have the power."
MARK: "Coach Robin said I had to apologize to him and Jaime in public. Do you think I should apologize to them in public?"
JAVIER: "No. I think you should apologize in this meeting. Any right-minded person will see your coaches are trying to make you pay for the exchange but, based on what I saw and heard, this is not appropriate. If you can live with apologizing to your coaches and getting to play I advise you to do this; get what you want and learn as much as you can from this so that you don't experience this again."
MARK: "But they treated me unfairly and they threatened me."
JAVIER: "They might have done. But who has the power here to give you what you want?"
MARK: "This is a bad situation for me. I don't like this at all."

Discussion questions

1. What are the issues presented in this case?
2. What is the role of a sport psychology practitioner in this kind of situation?
3. What decisions might Javier Aguilar have made differently in this case?
4. How might you counsel Mark to cope in this situation?
5. What kinds of conflict resolution interventions might you recommend, and to whom?
6. If you were going to lead an intervention what might you do and who would be the recipients?

Author's notes

I find these kinds of situation challenging. I have witnessed coaches and players in on- and off-field conflict and it can be heated, hostile and unhelpful to all parties. The structure of teams is often vertical, and authority and power typically flows down from the head coach and is divested in coaching staff and players by the head coach. Understanding status, power, influence, authority, roles and responsibilities is necessary for sport psychology practitioner to navigate just like players, coaches and team support staff do. When I join a new team to consult, one of my first tasks is to determine the six variables outlined above to understand how the team is structured and operates to improve its performance, solve problems and communicate. I remind myself that all behavior is communication, so I pay attention and gather as much observational data as I need to analyze to make decisions about how I will operate as a part of the team organization.

When I have been involved in player–coach conflict resolution situations they have been unaware of my presence at the time of the conflict. I found myself carefully and quietly observing the incident, the reactions and responses of the people involved and those surrounding them who might have been affected too. I often wait and watch to see how the interactions develop over time. If harsh words have been exchanged this is different than a coach and player being involved in a physical confrontation of some kind. When this occurs the conflict has reached unacceptable levels and requires action. The timing of this action depends on the behavior.

If the exchange is words alone, I keep in mind that sport is an emotional context and emotional intensity is essential for athletes and coaches in competitive sport. If the exchange gets too heated and causes one or both parties to get upset, I prefer a cooling-off period to occur. I advocate for parties to take time to cool down to a point they can reflect and communicate their positions calmly and with composure. I prefer to encourage player and coach to communicate with each other and to focus on addressing the issues and expressing understanding and empathy for each other's viewpoint. At times I will recommend an apology be expressed. I focus on keeping the relationship respectful and positive; after all, in college sports the players and coaches often have similar desires, which are good performances and positive sport experiences. Focusing on common goals is a starting point for discussion. Having a third person present to mediate between the parties often helps reduce anxiety in the exchange. I often feel an experienced team manager or team administrator is a good choice for this role. When I have been in a mediating position I am careful to discuss ground rules and tone with the parties to set the stage for a productive conversation. I prefer meetings to be in neutral places in calming environments. Where the parties meet to address their issues I coach them on how to talk to each other, starting with "I feel" statements, and encourage them to communicate how they felt about what happened and what they hope might be accomplished by the conversation they are having, and to approach the meeting with a spirit of acceptance and understanding. I accept if there is no mediator role for someone else or me in this kind of situation, the player and coach will use their own skills to work through the process. On one hand this makes me feel positive because they are building resilience in the relationship as they are addressing their own issues and taking responsibility for their relationship. On the other hand the structural issues like hierarchy and the limits of the individual's personal communication skills can negatively influence the process and outcomes of this kind of meeting. When this happens I find I have to wait and see the results of the meeting before I take further action.

Further reading

Bekiari, A. (2014). Verbal aggressiveness and leadership style of sports instructors and their relationship with athletes' intrinsic motivation. *Creative Education*, 5(2), 114–121.

Mageau, G. A., & Vallerand, R. J. (2003). The coach–athlete relationship: A motivational model. *Journal of Sports Science*, 21(11), 883–904.

Mazer, J. P., Barnes, K., Grevious, A., & Boger, C. (2013). Coach verbal aggression: A case study examining effects on athlete motivation and perceptions of coach credibility. *International Journal of Sport Communication*, 6(2), 203–213.

Vealey, R. S. (2017). Conflict management and cultural reparation: Consulting "below zero" with a college basketball team. *Case Studies in Sport and Exercise Psychology*, 1(1), 83–93.

7
COMING OUT

Introduction

This case provides an opportunity for instructor's to facilitate a discussion with their students concerning issues facing student-athletes who might realize their sexual and/or gender identity orientation while at college. There are a range of experiences for individuals who self-identify as lesbian, gay, bisexual, transgender, queer, intersex or asexual (LGBTQIA). The developmental consideration of individuals recognizing themselves in a college context presents challenges and opportunities for sport psychology practitioners working with student-athletes. This case seeks to engage instructors and students in a meaningful conversation about how to approach and support a student-athlete in the early stages of recognizing their identity.

Content implications

The implications for this case include but are not limited to discussions and further reading on the experience of student-athletes realizing their gender and/or sexual orientation. Students might be encouraged to clarify their personal values and recognize their role in the process of working with a student-athlete like the one in this case. Students might also consider expanding discussions concerning developmental considerations for young adults at college not only experiencing new ways of learning and living but also transitioning between identities. Lastly, the training and role of the sport psychology practitioner to work with cases such as this is recommended for discussion too.

Purpose

The purpose of this case is to challenge emerging sport psychology practitioners to consider how they might work with a student-athlete who is realizing their sexual and/or gender orientation at college.

Student learning outcomes

At this end of this case study learning opportunity, students should be able to:

1. Identify the issues the athlete is experiencing
2. Explain how they might approach advising a student-athlete facing this situation
3. Express the difficulties in counseling student-athletes facing issues concerning sexual and/or gender identity
4. Discuss how a sport psychology practitioner might be effective in this scenario

Cast of characters in order of appearance

Sara Cooper, Women's Tennis.
Isabel Schmid, Women's Tennis.

Athlete profile: Sara Cooper, women's tennis

Sara Cooper grew up within a 2-hour drive of The U. She always wanted to attend The U because of its engineering department. She loved chemistry, math and computer science at high school. While she was a self-confessed science geek, she also loved to play tennis. Her tennis gave her the physical outlet her parents always thought she needed, and was a convenient sport because of their country club membership. Tennis was something most girls at the club tried. The club pro saw that Sara put in effort and tried hard, so he helped her become a very strong player at her private high school, and ultimately to be recruited by The U on an academic scholarship on account of her grades being so high.

Sara had the same high school classes as another girl called Becky, who enjoyed science even more than Sara did. When their teachers assigned them to the same project groups they would get excited because they knew each would push the other on. They became good friends, and even though Becky did not play sports she exercised and went to the gym regularly.

Through school-related activities Sara and Becky's parents got to know each other, and the families came to socialize and attend science fairs and activities the girls participated in. At the end of Sara's junior year, she and Becky stopped at an empty park while out for a walk around town. With the sun going down and nobody around, the two girls sat close under a tree and Becky kissed Sara on the cheek. Sara was surprised at first, but she kissed Becky back on the cheek. At that moment the two girls connected deeply. Their friendship was sealed and endured for the remainder of high school. They would find moments to be together in their senior year, but only kissed and hugged when they were sure they were absolutely alone. They felt no pressure to go further in their relationship, and kept their same patterns to avoid suspicion from friends and family. Both sets of parents would have been highly disturbed had they known the direction the girl's relationship had gone in.

The summer after they graduated high school, and before Becky would leave for another school a day's drive away, the girls spent as much time together as possible. Two weeks before Sara would start at the The U, she and Becky had their first sexual experience. Their families were away on vacation and left them behind to work summer jobs they got for themselves. Neither of them had much sexual experience with girls or boys before this encounter. They spent the two weeks at Sara's house, keeping their regular profile in front of neighbors who knew they were good friends. But whenever they could they took advantage of the time to be intimate. As the time wound down they resolved to communicate with each other when they could and looked forward to the winter break. They left as friends.

They started college well; they texted and Skyped each other two to three times a week, but by the middle of the semester, as exam time came for both girls, their communication slowed. Then Sara received a text from Becky which read: "So sorry. Met someone else. Can't explain. I still love you. Maybe talk at Xmas." Sara was heartbroken. She was a freshman finding her way at college, courses were hard, and the one close relationship she had in her life was gone.

The case

Sara and Isabel placed their kit bags and tennis rackets on the locker room benches and sat down alone in front of their personal lockers. The doors had their name, team number and an action pose on them. The two rows of five lockers faced each other and created a corridor leading the eye to motivational messages and goals the team listed for this phase of the season and posted around a large whiteboard with the message "DREAM BIG!" written on it in red marker. The room was painted white with outlined navy blue stars on the ceiling. Sara and Isabel arrived early as their classes finished at 12pm, which gave them two hours before training started to hang out. The two were freshman and shared one math class. They had not been overly friendly at the beginning of the semester but had grown to get along and trained well together. Sara studied engineering and Isabel studied human nutrition. They were completing their first semester and getting their general education requirements out of the way. But over time they began to confide in each other a little bit more, especially as they had midterm exams around the same time and shared difficulties trying to learn new material for them. They stared at each other for a bit.

ISABEL: "So what's up? ... You said you wanted to talk about something."
SARA: "Not much ... I just need someone to talk to and you're about the only person I could think of to talk to about what's on my mind."
ISABEL: "Me?"
SARA: "Yeah, I mean we're having the same kind of experience in school and you seem like someone I can talk to ... I mean I don't have many people I feel I can go to and just talk about stuff."
ISABEL: "Wow, I didn't know you saw me like that."

SARA: "Yeah, I know. I'm sorry. I'm not very good being personal with people. I'm better in larger groups and being around people, but it's different when I'm one-on-one or in small groups."
ISABEL: "I was like that too. Maybe things will change over time for you … so, what's up with you?"

Sara felt a pressure inside her build up. She felt alone and isolated now that she and Becky were not together. She felt nervous and embarrassed, and had a feeling this was the biggest moment in her life telling someone else about her private life, but she could not hold it in. She held a soft stare at Isabel and pressed her hands together so tightly her knuckles became white.

ISABEL: "What's up Sara? You look like something's really bringing you down."

Sara blurted out. "My girlfriend has left me," and she began to well up. She did not know how Isabel would respond, but at that moment she felt overwhelmed and frightened that she had spoken out loud something she had not said before to herself let alone anyone else. Isabel moved across the aisle to sit beside Sara and out her arm around her. There was a long pause.

ISABEL: "That happened to me last year before I got here."
SARA: "I had no idea you …"
ISABEL: "No, not many people do. I'm pretty good at acting straight and keeping things to myself, maybe a bit like you. Nobody else here knows about this bit of me. When I'm ready I'll tell people, but not right now."
SARA: "Does coach know?"
ISABEL: "Yeah."
SARA: "You told coach … how did that happen?"
ISABEL: "It was my dad. He made me tell her. He said if I was going off to school he wanted to make sure there were no secrets with the coach because he wanted me to be welcome and do well here."
SARA: "My parents don't know anything like that."
ISABEL: "That's a problem."
SARA: "I know. I feel they will be so upset or mad at me if they found out, but I don't know how to talk to talk about it with them. How did you do it?"
ISABEL: "Me … I had a high school art teacher I used to talk to."
SARA: "Were they like us?"
ISABEL: "I don't think so, they were married – not that that means much, but I never got that vibe from them. Anyway, they were easy to talk to, really positive and always on my side. You don't have someone like that?"
SARA: "I never told anyone, and as far as I know Becky didn't either."
ISABEL: "It helps to talk to someone. My dad was awesome. My mum was upset at first, but my dad sorted things out in the house. At school I kept things on the down low."

SARA: "Who did you date?"

ISABEL: "I met this girl from another high school at an ice cream place I used to go to. She was really cute. We got talking, and one thing led to another and we dated for a while, then she left for college before I did. She was a year older than me."

SARA: "Did you know you liked girls before her?"

ISABEL: "Not really. I kissed boys before, but when I was with her I felt different and I realized I preferred her to boys … If you are talking to me about this, does this mean coach doesn't know?"

SARA: "I can't tell her yet. My parents don't know. I had to tell someone and you seemed to be the best person to talk to."

ISABEL: "I think you should talk to someone else too."

SARA: "Why?"

ISABEL: "Coming out can be difficult. I mean it's really hard, it's not easy, you don't know how people around are going to handle it. When I came out to my parents I had the art teacher and a school counselor to help me through things. My close friends knew at the end of high school, but by then the worst of what it might have been like was over. You know how mean kids can be about being lesbian or gay. I couldn't face being bullied. That would have sucked."

SARA: "I don't know anyone to talk to. I'm not ready to talk to my parents, coach or anyone else here."

Sara sobbed at the thought of being alone with what she felt was a burden. Isabel gave Sara a hug.

ISABEL: "I heard from some of the seniors on our team that the sport psych guy called Javier was helpful and easy to talk to. At least you know he's there for you."

SARA: "A sport psychologist … but there's nothing wrong with me."

ISABEL: "I don't think anything has to be wrong with you to see a sport psychology person … I mean I think their thing is to help you focus and get on track towards your goals."

SARA: "But this isn't about tennis. It's about me missing Becky and feeling alone."

ISABEL: "It's not about tennis now, but it will be if you don't deal with it. That's one of the things my Dad told me. He played college sports; he was a wrestler, and he told me that his team mates always did worse at school and on the mat when things were not right in their personal lives. They could fake it for a while, but then things would break down. You don't want things to break down do you?"

SARA: "No. But I don't know how to handle this. Can you help me talk to the sport psych guy?"

ISABEL: "I can't talk to him for you, but I can reach out to him and ask if he has a slot for a friend going through a tough time."

SARA: "Will he tell Coach about me?"

ISABEL: "I don't think so. Not unless you tell him it's okay. My school counselor never told anyone about these things until I gave them permission. I think this will be the same."
SARA: "Can we contact him after today's practice?"
ISABEL: "Sure."

Sara felt relieved and grateful to Isabel for listening to her and being sensitive to her situation. She also learned a lot more about Isabel, and her respect for her was much greater than it was when the conversation started.

Discussion questions

1. What are the main issues presented in this case?
2. What do you think is at stake for Isabel if she attends counseling?
3. What contextual factors might influence Sara's sport and emotional experiences?
4. What challenges do student-athletes face when navigating their sexuality?
5. How would you advise Javier to approach Sara's case?
6. What kind of counseling approach do you feel is appropriate for Sara's situation?

Author's notes

There is a lot going on Sara's life right now. Firstly, I would want to establish a strong enough rapport with Sara to earn her trust and confidence to help her disclose the most important issues to her in sufficient depth to allow both of us to understand her current state. The next step would be to contract with her and agree to examine the issues she wants most to discuss. There are many issues present, including her perceptions of her sexuality and personal experiences, and her relationships with Becky, her parents, her coach and Isabel. Additionally there are prospective personal, social and academic issues that might be affected by her future choices concerning these issues. Working to prevent additional issues arising by mitigating the negative effects of the current stressors on Sara is my preferred route here.

I would approach this situation sensitively and at a pace Sara was ready for. I would be mindful not to focus too early on things I might be curious about. Sara's readiness and willingness to address her issues is the most important thing for me to acknowledge. How Sara determined her priorities would initially guide my decision-making. Once we were clear on the main issue, I would focus on problem solving to relieve any stress Sara might be facing. This phase might include eliciting and identifying coping strengths and skills; it might also demand creative and logical solutions given Sara's intellectual preferences.

From a theoretical standpoint I would take a rational emotive behavioral therapy (REBT) approach founded upon the core skills from person-centered counseling. I would take this blended approach because deep listening and appropriate reflection are needed to permit Sara's expression toward the depth of discussion necessary to explore challenges and identify possible solutions to Sara's situation.

If Sara decided to focus her energies on coping with her situation, I would explain the boundaries of my training to Sara and recommend a referral to a specialist counselor experienced in working with individuals in the LGBTQIA community. Based on Sara's decision I would want to re-establish the focus of our work together. If Sara decided to work with someone else I would complete the referral and compassionately terminate the working relationship.

Further reading

Fynes, J. M., & Fisher, L. A. (2016). Is authenticity and integrity possible for sexual minority athletes? Lesbian student-athlete experiences of US NCAA Division I sport. *Women in Sport and Physical Activity Journal*, 24(1), 60–69.

Greenspan, S. B., Griffith, C., & Murtagh, E. F. (2017). LGBTQ youths' school athletic experiences: A 40-year content analysis in nine flagship journals. *Journal of LGBT Issues in Counseling*, 11(3), 190–200.

Krane, V. (2016). Inclusion to exclusion: Sport for LGBT athletes. In R. J. Schinke, K. R. McGannon, & B. Smith (Eds.), *Routledge International Handbook of Sport Psychology* (pp. 238–247). New York, NY: Routledge.

Smith, C. V., Franklin, E., Borzumat-Gainey, C., & Degges-White, S. (2014). Counseling college students about sexuality and sexual activity. In S. Degges-White & C. Borzumato-Gainey (Eds.), *College student mental health counseling: A developmental approach* (pp. 133–153). New York, NY: Springer.

8

STAYING WITH OR LEAVING A TEAM

Introduction

Student-athletes come from all kinds of families and communities, and decide to attend colleges they hope will be a good fit for them based on where they come from and where they hope they are going. However, sometimes things do not work out as they hoped. This case introduces a common situation where a freshman feels they do not fit in with the college, team or sport culture they joined. Often the student-athlete is inexperienced in the transition to college and in navigating their new roles and responsibilities. They can often feel alone and isolated, and when this happens they begin to questions whether somewhere else might be better for them. This case deals with this dilemma.

Content implications

This case can be redirected in a number of ways: firstly, in the transition from high to school to college, and accommodation of the differences. A second option is to discuss how freshman athletes and coaches can build relationships, or how team members can develop friendships beyond the court or field. Lastly, an interesting discussion about how student-athletes make decisions and the role of the sport psychology consultant in the decision-making process might expand the vision and toolkit for emerging consultants.

Purpose

The purpose of this case study is to help students think through the circumstances they might face working with freshman student-athletes transitioning to college. In this case, a young man moves from a small high school environment and a community he knows well to a larger and seemingly more impersonal educational experience.

Student learning outcomes

At this end of this case study learning opportunity, students should be able to:

1. Identify the issues the athlete is experiencing
2. Explain the relationships between the issues presented in the case and how they might lead from simple to complex interventions concerning sport performance and life satisfaction
3. Select a counseling approach to respond to the coach's condition
4. Discuss the conflicting priorities the sport psychology practitioner might have
5. Discuss how a sport psychology practitioner might be effective in this scenario

Cast of characters in order of appearance

Mike Beck, Men's Basketball.
Javier Aguilar, Sport Psychology Consultant.

Athlete profile: Mike Beck, men's basketball

Mike is a 6 feet 6 inch, 185 lb freshman from Laberle, a small town of 1000 people in southern Minnesota. Mike was recruited from Laberle High School, which only had 150 students and was a historical "diamond in the rough" kind of school. About every two or three years as long as anyone could remember either a male or female basketball standout was recruited to play NCAA basketball at a prominent college. Mike was the most recent standout player, setting a new school record for offensive rebounds. While his team did not win championships, it was always a competitive team for opponents to play against. It was common for opposing coaches to tell their players, "If we can beat Laberle, we can beat anyone." The school and the town were basketball crazy. The high school gym was always with townsfolk, and the men's and women's teams and coaches enjoyed unwavering support no matter what the result. Stores in the town changed their hours to make sure everyone could get to the games. Only the gas stations and federal offices stayed open when the basketball teams played in conference playoffs. It seemed like when the boys were not winning their games the girls were winning theirs. The school and the town always had a team to cheer for.

Mike grew up as most kids did in Laberle. He felt he knew everyone in the town, and felt the warmth of a close community around him. His family had a haulage business. His mother ran the business and his father was the main driver of a fleet of three trucks. Their business served Minnesota's rural communities, and through his parents' business Mike felt connected with the people they dealt with. Mike felt there was not a place within 100 miles of Laberle he did not know.

When he was not at school or with his friends he would go with his dad to deliver shipments. Mike and his father became very close after many days traveling together.

When Mike was home he played outside with his friends without a care or fear of anything negative happening. Basketball was the sport of choice for practically every kid in the town. Mike's high school basketball coach was also the school's history teacher. He had played college basketball and returned to Laberle to marry his high school sweetheart. The coach believed the best way to learn to play was to play. His practice sessions were short, sharp and always fun. He kept the boys motivated with varied sessions and an uplifting environment, and often called them after practice or a game to highlight what they did well and how they could be better. Mike never did a fitness session or was punished by his coach with physical exercise consequences. He loved his coach for his attitude and fun way of getting the most out of him and the team. Even though Mike's high school team knew they were not always going to win, they always felt they were in with a chance, and that no matter what the result was their coach would support them and be there for them. It was Mike's coach and parents who helped him make his decision to attend The U.

The case

Mike sat in the waiting room at Javier Aguilar's office. After three sessions he was more comfortable with Javier and looked forward to their meetings. Although he disclosed quite a bit to Javier, he kept things back for only his dad and his friends from Laberle to know about. Working with Javier allowed him to get off campus. He liked having the opportunity to be in the local town and away from his coaches and some of his team mates. He felt much more at home being off campus and around people like those he knew before he decided to attend The U.

Javier walked down the corridor from his office to the waiting room. "Hi Mike, come on down. Good to see you." Javier stretched out his hand and Mike reached out to shake it. The two walked into Javier's office and sat in their normal positions: Mike opposite Javier, his chair angled toward him, with windows on his right showing outdoor greenery. He noticed music was playing in the background.

MIKE: "I didn't know you listened to music like that."

He pointed in the direction he thought the sound was coming from.

JAVIER: "Oh that, yes sometimes I like to listen to this kind of music, you know, to change things up."

Javier moved across to his desk to turn off the sound coming from his cell phone in an open desk drawer. He returned to his seat. Mike watched the counselor ease himself into his chair.

MIKE: "You seem tired to today Javier?"

JAVIER: "Yes, I am a little tired today."

MIKE: "Yeah, is it because you had tough cases coming in here taking it out on you?"

JAVIER: "Actually it's because I worked out harder than normal … I did a bit too much … I'm feeling it a bit."

MIKE: "What are you training for?"

JAVIER: "Well, I want to get stronger and I might take a hiking vacation later this year. I just want to feel a bit better."

MIKE: "Okay then … you sound motivated."

JAVIER: "I am … so tell me Mike, what would be most helpful for us to talk about here today?"

MIKE: "You get right to it don't you … well I had this thought this week. At first I thought it was weird that the team manager would tell me to talk to you. I wasn't sure what to expect, and to tell you the truth I'm not really sure what I'm getting out of this other than time off campus and time away from the team, but it feels okay to be here and I do feel understood … I suppose what I want to discuss is how I will know whether I want to stay here or leave."

JAVIER: "So, you're still a bit unsure about what is going on here—it feels a bit weird but you have something on your mind to discuss. Do you mean you want to leave our working relationship or leave the school, or something else?"

Mike shifted in his seat. He had only talked to his dad about this topic so far, and he was not sure he could totally trust Javier.

MIKE: "How will I know I can trust you not to tell anyone at The U about our conversations?"

JAVIER: "Good question. What have others at The U told you?"

MIKE: "They told me you could be trusted, that you were easy to work with and open-minded."

Javier nodded quietly as Mike spoke.

JAVIER: "You will decide for yourself Mike if I am trustworthy or not. Share as little as much as you like with me. It is your choice; you have authority over your information."

MIKE: "Do you promise not to say anything to my coach or anyone connected to the team?"

JAVIER: "Providing you don't intend to hurt yourself or someone else. Yes, I will not talk to your coach or anyone connected with the team. Do you want to tell me something about what is on your mind right now?"

Mike looked to his right and stared out of the window at the green leaves. The basketball season was winding down, and early warm temperatures encouraged leaves on trees to flourish earlier than expected and the evergreens outside stood proudly in the hopeful spring sun bathing the scene Mike looked out on. It made him feel relaxed. Javier got up and, respecting the moment, stretched quietly and sat down again.

MIKE: "I feel like I don't belong here. I don't really enjoy the basketball here and I think my coach doesn't know what he's doing."
JAVIER: "Okay, that's quite a bit Mike. Which part do you want to tackle first?"
MIKE: "Basketball."
JAVIER: "Okay, what is it about basketball you don't like these days."
MIKE: "Well, when I got here I thought basketball would be fun, fast and something I would always look forward to … but I don't. Our style is boring, every workout is exhausting and, you know, it makes no sense. We play two times per week and we get no time to rest, and Coach just wants to run us again and again. I never feel like I am 100 percent when I play because I am always tired … everything is regimented. There's no free play. I don't get it, we can beat every team but we play like we're chained. If we do one thing that doesn't fit his plan he just rips into us."
JAVIER: "Okay, so you're upset at the way Coach runs practices and sets up the team. You don't think the team is playing up to its potential."
MIKE: "Yeah, but it's more than that. Coach and his assistants just tell you what you're doing wrong; they don't really show you how you to improve. They just tell you … it's like when we watch game film. We all watch the game film together and Coach tells us what we've done wrong but not how we could have done it differently. He calls you out all the time in front of your team mates. All I hear is what I haven't done. I'm a freshman, how do you think that makes me feel? … I mean he recruited me because I can do some things well, but I never hear him talk about what I do well."
JAVIER: "You sound frustrated and upset with this situation Mike. Is this why you feel like you don't belong here?"

Mike looked out of the window again. This time he was feeling determined. He shared some of the things on his mind, and Javier seemed to listen without judging. He kept looking out of the window.

MIKE: "It's more than that. There's no fun and my team mates are as a negative as my coach. Nobody says anything—they talk behind Coach's back but say nothing to his face. They don't seem to have fun either. Nothing about this team is like my high school team or my high school coach."
JAVIER: "You're feeling like this is very different than what you're used to and it doesn't feel right for you."
MIKE: "Yeah, why do you keep repeating what I'm saying, it's getting annoying."

Javier raised his eyebrows, paused and breathed deeply. He sensed Mike was irritated he was talking to him while he still looked out of the window.

JAVIER: "Mike, you have not invited me to discuss anything with you. You are driving here. You are expressing your thoughts. I am listening. Do you want me to do more than that right now?"

MIKE: "Sorry. That was a bit mean. I'm frustrated."

JAVIER: "I feel you're frustrated too. Tell me a bit about this feeling of isolation you're experiencing. Does it have something to do with your coach and your team?"

MIKE: "Kind of. I miss my family and my friends. I knew everyone in my town, and here it's different. I only really know people connected with my team. We do everything on campus—we don't go anywhere other than away games and to the same restaurants to eat as a team on campus. Most of my team mates are from larger cities and their parents are not self-employed. I feel like I don't have much in common with them. I don't really have any friends here."

JAVIER: "It sounds like you're feeling lonely, maybe a bit homesick?"

MIKE: "Yeah."

JAVIER: "How have these feelings affected you outside of basketball?"

Mike chuckled and picked at his navy blue t-shirt with the school logo on the front and a silhouette of a basketball player dribbling the ball.

MIKE: "There's this professor I have in the finance department. He's a real old guy, you know, maybe about 50 years old. He makes me laugh, he tells stories and the way he teaches reminds me of my dad."

JAVIER: "Oh, how's that?"

MIKE: "Well when he gives us problems to do in class it's like he's with you but he's not."

JAVIER: "What do you mean?"

MIKE: "When I was younger I'd go all over Minnesota with my dad. I always knew he was in charge, but he never got down on me and he would ask me what I thought about things and how I might solve a problem if I was in his position. Sometimes he would even do something I suggested ... Anyway, this professor's like that; he treats everyone fairly—even the students who are not very smart. He's always upbeat, and he seems to love what he does. He's cool."

JAVIER: "This sounds like a good professor. What's his name?"

MIKE: "Professor French. Have you heard of him?"

JAVIER: "No, but I'm wondering if there's anyone else who you connect with on campus."

MIKE: "I like the strength coach Thompo. He seems like he's a good guy, but you know he's a trainer and he works for Coach."

JAVIER: "So you don't have friends on campus after seven months?"

MIKE: "No, not really."

Mike and Javier looked at each other for a moment, Javier thinking where to go next in the conversation and Mike considering telling Javier what he told his dad the night before. Mike initiated.

MIKE: "I called my dad and told him I'm thinking about transferring schools."
JAVIER: "Go on."

Javier immediately began to feel uncomfortable. Two years ago a freshman player transferred after the men's basketball team invested significant resources into recruiting him. That time the player's interaction with the coach was the chief issue. The head coach and Javier had several conversations, and the latter felt the ire of the coach for not telling him the player was intending to leave. Javier momentarily zoned out of the conversation with Mike and replayed one of the conversations with the head coach that resulted in a heated exchange. It took two months to repair the relationship between them. Javier felt a sense of dread come over him as he refocused on Mike's presence.

JAVIER: "Transferring schools, that's a big decision."
MIKE: "Yeah, I feel like I don't belong here. The coach is nuts, my team mates aren't really team mates. There's nothing here for me, so I'm wondering why I should stay here."
JAVIER: "Have you talked to your head coach?"
MIKE: "No way. He would go mad."
JAVIER: "Have you talked to anyone else about this?"
MIKE: "No."
JAVIER: "Okay Mike, do you realize that making this decision so close to the date when recruits choose which college to go to could leave your team in a bad spot."
MIKE: "Yeah, but what have they done for me? I don't feel like they respected me or looked after me. I mean I got here and they were like, 'talk to your academic adviser to get your classes sorted out and the team manager to secure your housing.' It's not like they've been great to me."
JAVIER: "So you want revenge. You want them to pay for what you feel they didn't do for you. How much did you speak up to your coaches about your needs?"

Mike paused and stared at Javier. Nobody had ever asked him this question before, and he was not sure what to say. He started to work back in his mind and visualize as many moments as he could to find a time when he had spoken to someone on campus, in the team, the athletic department support staff or the coaching staff about how he was feeling and what he needed.

MIKE: "I haven't spoken to anyone."

As Mike spoke he felt a sense of disappointment come over him. The other night the call with his dad had been all one way. His dad listened and was supportive but did not question him, instead saying they could talk more about it at the weekend, which was two days away. Mike knew his dad would probably ask him the same question Javier did. If his dad knew Mike had not talked to anyone he would tell him to start doing so immediately, and not just to the counselor.

Discussion questions

1. How do you feel Javier handled the interaction between himself and Mike?
2. What difficulties does Javier face given the information he has following the session with Mike?
3. What risks does Javier face in his role with the team now he knows Mike's intentions?
4. What counseling approach might you have taken in this case?
5. How might you deal with ethical dilemmas presented in this case?

Author's note

This case is quite typical of the characteristics of athletes I have worked with who come from small communities and were outstanding high school players. These players were often well known and championed in their community, and were encouraged to leave to attend college in a larger city because of the opportunities (athletic, educational and career) afforded to them. However they often experience difficulties transitioning from where they grew up—and the familiarity and certainty this experience gave them—to a new set of circumstances and individuals who are mostly unknown to them.

In this case Mike's previous life still dominates his current situation. His difficulties center on the discrepancy between his life in Laberle and what he experiences now. Key relationships are missing, including his high school coach, family, friends, team mates and surrounding community. Mike is on his own for the first time truly making his own decisions and having to adapt rapidly to changing circumstances. His readiness for college life and coping with uncomfortable relationships and situations demonstrates opportunities for him to grow and develop. Additionally, having not communicated with anyone at The U about his idea to transfer from the college speaks to the possibility of perceived threat, fear and concern about the outcomes of this conversation; but it also signals that things have gotten further than they needed to for all concerned.

For me, this case centers on three aspects of critical importance to athletic performance which concern interpersonal relationships: 1) communication, particularly conflict resolution: 2) affiliation and belonging in mutually rewarding relationships; and 3) problem solving and coping skills. These are difficult skills and approaches even for seasoned and experienced athletes to adopt and apply with confidence. Expecting a 19-year-old to have mastery in these areas is a bit unrealistic. Most likely Mike will need to be coached along with understanding he is doing this for the first time and might be a bit unsure of how to handle himself during interpersonal dealings with others.

In this instance my preferred course of action would be to float the idea of a facilitated conversation with an individual connected with the team who Mike had the most faith in to discuss his issues with knowing that the head coach, team manager and athletic support staff might have to be engaged too. Although Mike is the client, I would be mindful of retaining the working relationship with the head coach of the basketball team and the team, particularly as this kind of situation happened before. Working through the process with Mike, my first goal would be to address his concerns at The U because another transition might not be helpful, and the fact Mike is considering leaving does not mean he wants to. Instead, maybe he does not know how to communicate exactly what he needs or wants to happen and just wants to get out of the situation, and this is his way of communicating this. My second goal would be to work with Mike to develop skills and approaches to address the issues that came up; and my third goal would be to connect with the basketball head coach and his staff to develop and implement a behavioral plan aimed at improving Mike's basketball, college and personal experience over time.

However in this situation I would need to be aware of several matters out of my control that might negatively impact the process. Firstly, the head coach has to commit to working on this in some fashion, as does Mike. Mike must make his own decision about how he wants to progress. He cannot be forced, and although I have an agenda it does not mean we share that. If our goals are different difficulties will arise between us. Secondly, Mike's interpersonal skills development will happen over time, and he will have to see it as important for him to commit to working on these skills. Lastly, it is possible the academic experience might trump the basketball experience. If Mike's academic goals are strong enough for him to see himself staying at The U, I might consider reaching out to Professor French to engage him in the consulting process too. He could be an asset if he mentored Mike and supported him academically and interpersonally. This case could require quite a bit of effort on the sport psychology consultant's part. Before progressing I would want to know exactly what Mike's goals and aspirations are at The U before deciding how much energy I should direct to a client who is likely to leave the college.

Further reading

Association of Applied Sport Psychology. (2017). Ethics Code: AASP Ethical Principles and Standards. Retrieved from www.appliedsportpsych.org/about/ethics/ethics-code/

Fletcher, D., & Maher, J. (2013). Toward a competency-based understanding of the training and development of applied sport psychologists. *Sport, Exercise, and Performance Psychology*, 2(4), 265–280.

Papanikolaou, Z., Nikolaidis, D., Patsiaouras, A., & Alexopoulos, P. (2003). The freshman experience: High stress-low grades. *Athletic Insight: The Online Journal of Sport Psychology*, 5(4).

Spieler, M., Czech, D., Joyner, A., Munkasy, B., Gentner, N., & Long, J. (2007). Predicting athletic success: Factors contributing to the success of NCAA Division I AA collegiate football players. *Athletic Insight*, 9(2), 22–33.

9
HAND INJURY

Introduction

This case introduces several elements quite common in NCAA sports, including a foreign coach and athlete and an Olympic sport dominated at the national level by west coast college teams. Additionally, students are asked to consider multiple angles concerning the causes of a hand injury and the role of coach, athlete and trainer in recovery from the injury.

Content implications

This case deliberately mixes several elements commonly found in college sports when an athlete gets injured: for example, coach–athlete conflict; intrapersonal conflict; the role of the sport medicine professional; out-of-season recovery; and the influence of family on the mental state of the student athlete.

Purpose

The purpose here is to identify the key facts and apply appropriate theoretical models and evidence-based solutions to a typical case of an athlete experiencing a injury which occurred outside their sport.

Student learning outcomes

At this end of this case study learning opportunity, students should be able to:

1. Demonstrate appropriate theoretical application to a given set of circumstances
2. Understand the range of influences and complexity in a sport injury context

3. Consider how time, transitions and physical distance might impact outcomes
4. Recognize the role of a sport psychology practitioner in the context of a sport medicine rehabilitation team

Cast of characters in order of appearance

Jenny Johnston, Athletic Trainer.
Sime Radic, Men's Water Polo.
Viktor Varga, Head Coach, Men's Water Polo.
Javier Aguilar, Sport Psychology Consultant.

Athlete profile: Sime Radic, water polo

Sime Radic was expecting to be a starting senior on the men's water polo team in the upcoming season. He was one of two full scholarship athletes recruited from Croatia for the team and was the team's defensive leader. He was a powerful force in the water, and recognized as another top foreign recruit for the team. Sime's normal training routine was to combine training for water polo with his love of boxing. Although he was considered gentle and mild-mannered outside of competition, during a water polo match he was seen as exceptionally aggressive, almost hostile, toward any opponent except when the opponent was equally as vicious and aggressive. In this case he seemed to settle down and just play. To the trained eye it looked like Sime had respect for someone as aggressive as him and wanted to play hard and skillfully at his best level and not just dominate his opponent with force and aggression.

Sime's water polo coach, Viktor Varga, promoted Sime's attitude in competition and preferred his gentle nature outside of competition too. He supported Sime's boxing and encouraged him to train with local boxers in town to grow his social network. After a slow start building relationships in Joe's Boxing Gym (mostly due to his spoken English skills), Sime made firm friends at Joe's and trained with several boxers at the same or heavier weights, eventually competing in the local Golden Gloves competition.

Just before this year's Golden Gloves competition Sime received news that his younger brother had been diagnosed with a serious medical condition and that the prognosis for recovery was unclear. Sime was naturally devastated by the news. His brother was his best friend and the most important person in his life next to his parents. He was also the main connection to the team mates and friends Sime had left behind in Croatia.

Sime was well liked by his university team mates, but his main support system was at Joe's Gym. His friends there were more to his liking, and they reminded him of friends he grew up with in his home country. Sime did not feel as comfortable talking to his water polo team mates as he did his sparring partners. He felt their friendship was based on his use to the team not how he was as a person, whereas his friends at Joe's saw him more as one of them and good fun to be around. He felt like he belonged, and he enjoyed that feeling very much.

At the Golden Gloves competition, Sime approached his boxing with fury, letting loose what seemed to onlookers like a flurry of punches of retribution. It was during the first round of a semi-final bout that Sime landed a vicious and powerful right hook to his opponent's body and felt a searing pain from his hand. He knew immediately something was not right. Even though the pain was intense, he finished the match by jabbing and resting his right hand. He lost the bout on points and his best friend from Joe's—a local called Esteban who worked on a construction site—took him to the hospital to get X-rays. The pictures revealed a typical boxer's fracture to the fourth metacarpal.

The case

It was the last Monday in April when Sime would meet with his coach, Viktor Varga, four days after his injury occurred. He would be expected to report for pre-season training on the first Monday in August. But before meeting Viktor, Sime would meet with Jenny Johnston for a treatment plan.

JENNY: "Come in Sime, take a seat over here." (Jenny pointed to a bench where athletes normally received treatment.) "I heard about your hand. How are you doing?"

SIME: "Okay ... what am I going to do about this ... I mean I just hit the guy and boom! This happened. It's my throwing hand too. I can't grab anything and they told me at the hospital it will take 8–12 weeks to heal. Come on! How can a tiny thing in my hand take that long take to fix itself?"

JENNY: "I see you're frustrated, anyone in your position would be. I heard you lost your temper during the bout ... I heard you were even more aggressive than you usually are in the water ... I've seen you 'go' at guys Sime, but I heard you really went after the guys you boxed against. What happened to you?"

SIME: "My brother Sasha is sick." (Sime looked up with tear-filled eyes.) "It's my brother. I don't know if he will make it."

His hulking 6 feet, 6 inch frame and 240 pounds of sinewy muscle tensed as he drew a deep breath and exhaled, trying to prevent his tears from spilling over.

JENNY: "I'm sorry Sime."

Jenny got up and, facing Sime, put her hand on his left shoulder. The big Croatian leaned in and clutched Jenny, and cried quietly on her shoulder. He was a long way from home.

Viktor Varga swiveled around in his chair from the computer screen when he saw Sime's reflection in the window of his office overlooking the water polo pool.

VIKTOR: "Sit down Sime. How are you doing? Jenny told me you have a treatment plan." Sime sat down opposite Viktor by the door with enough clearance for the door to close. His injured hand was splinted and resting on his lap. Happily for Sime the fracture was simple. Significant angulation had not occurred and surgery was not necessary.

SIME: "Hi coach. Yes Jenny gave me a plan for when I get back to Croatia to follow. She told me I needed to video call her weekly to check my progress and answer my questions."

VIKTOR: "She's good isn't she."

Viktor smiled. Then he paused and his face became calm; no lines or wrinkles could be seen by Sime.

VIKTOR: "You put me in a tough spot Sime. I supported your boxing so you could make friends and stay sharp for us. Not to get injured. Not to put the team in jeopardy, and not to put me in a position where I might have to reduce your scholarship because you might not be ready to play until mid-season if your hand does not heal well. Do you see what you've done Sime?"

Sime was not expecting this. He thought his coach would show some care towards him.

SIME: "Coach, I was not thinking. I lost it … I …"

VIKTOR: "I know about your brother Sime. I get it and I am very sorry. But this was not a good move on your part."

Viktor leaned back in his chair with frustration and a sigh of ambitions being lowered.

VIKTOR: "I had plans Sime. I was going to try to finalize our recruiting with you as the defensive anchor. Now I might need to find a replacement for your role on the team."

SIME: "Coach, I can't afford to study in America without the scholarship you give me."

VIKTOR: "I know Sime. But what am I supposed to do here?"

Viktor paused again and looked straight into Sime's eyes.

VIKTOR: "Listen! Be ready by August 1. Come back here ready. Do what you have to do. Do what Jenny tells you to do. Be ready. We want you here Sime. We made an investment in you. Now, you pay us back!"

SIME: "I get it coach, I didn't mean to get injured. I just lost it. It's not easy for me. I keep thinking about my brother. I mean he's my best friend too. He's a great guy."

Sime crumpled and welled up again. Viktor felt himself getting upset too. His own family was divided. His wife and kids were in the United States but his parents lived in Hungary. He missed them terribly too.

VIKTOR: "Sime, I am not good with these kinds of things … Look, don't worry about your scholarship. I'll figure it out. I am frustrated at the situation not you … how are you doing at school?"

SIME: "Not well. I'm getting poor grades. I'm capable but I can do better. It's just ever since this happened with my brother I can't concentrate like I should."

VIKTOR: "Okay, have you spoken to Javier?"

SIME: "The psych guy?"

VIKTOR: "Yes."

SIME: "No."

VIKTOR: "How much have you thought about seeing him?"

SIME: "It's not a thing for me Coach. We never saw a sport psychology person in Croatia."

VIKTOR: "Me neither. We never did that in Hungary. But I know him, he's a good guy, he's easy to talk to … it's more like talking to a friend who listens."

SIME: "You mean he does not want to analyze me and tell me what my problems are and what I should do to fix them. I'm not a bad person."

VIKTOR: "No he's not like that."

SIME: "What can he do for me?"

VIKTOR: "He might be able to help you not worry as much, concentrate and help you get through the summer."

SIME: "Does he do Skype or FaceTime?"

VIKTOR: "I don't know. He's pretty much up for most things. Why don't you ask him?"

SIME: "Can you call him for me? I don't know what to say."

VIKTOR: "I don't mind calling him. But you need to speak to him when I call him and tell him that you want to meet up."

SIME: "How long do I need to meet with him for?"

VIKTOR: "It depends, the first meeting might be 30–40 minutes … you'll meet on campus, and then you and Javier will work things out from there. He's a straightforward guy. You won't have any problems."

SIME: "Okay."

VIKTOR: "I'll call him right now." Viktor picked up his cell phone and called Javier. Sime heard only heard Viktor's side of the conversation: "Hi Javier, yes it's Viktor, do you have a minute … you do … okay … Javier I have a player who needs a bit of help. Can you talk to him for a minute … you have two minutes, okay here he is." Viktor passed his phone to Sime.

SIME: "Hello. My name is Sime … hello Javier … Coach thought you might be able to help me … my challenge? … My brother is sick and I am very worried … about 6 weeks … yes I am returning home to Croatia … I injured my throwing hand boxing … I'm not doing great in my studies … can I meet on Thursday at 9:00am? … Let me check. Yes I can meet … yes I'll meet at Coach's office. How long will it take? … 30 minutes … okay … thank you. Good bye."

Sime turned off his phone, put it away and handed Viktor's phone back to him.

VIKTOR: "That went well didn't it ... do what I said earlier and listen to Jenny. Get things sorted out. Make the most of things with Javier this week. I want you to update me every Friday from this week until you return here. Give me even more confidence in you Sime."

SIME: "I will coach. You can trust me. I won't let you down."

VIKTOR: "I hope so Sime. I told you how I feel, now you have to follow through. Go and see Javier. Listen to Jenny. I know when you get back to Croatia things will be tough, but I expect you to work your ass off. Stay positive and believe your brother will recover."

SIME: "Sure Coach."

Discussion questions

1. What are the antecedents of injury related to Sime's state of being?
2. What kind(s) of anxiety might Sime have demonstrated?
3. How relevant is the cognitive appraisal model to Sime's case.
4. What are the sociodemographic, psychological and social/contextual factors that might influence the sport injury rehabilitation process for Sime?
5. How might a sport medicine rehabilitation team operate in this case?
6. How might Javier operate in this case?
7. What strategies might Javier apply in this case?
8. How might Sime's return to Croatia influence the outcomes of this case?

Author's notes

There is a lot going on in Sime's case. For me, the first thing is to understand his current experience and work to appreciate the full scope of the context he sees himself in. I would be careful not to evoke feelings of premature grief for Sime's brother. Instead I feel a stronger choice is to fully understand the sport, life and injury stressors affecting Sime from the point of view of his narrative—that is, Sime telling stories of his own experience. I would want to understand his appraisal of his situation and the degree to which he felt personally responsible and empowered to take action and help himself while he was in the United States. Given the time frame I feel behavior change is unlikely to happen quickly, so support for Sime's coping capabilities would be my focus here.

The next step I would take is to work closely with Jenny Johnston. She seems to have the strongest and most structured relationship with Sime. I see my role here as to provide support to Jenny as she works with Sime through the summer and not to get in the way of their working relationship. I would recommend she use goal setting, sport rehabilitation and performance profiling to help Sime maintain focus and work toward a successful return. At this point I would recruit Viktor Varga to engage with this process too. Based on the evidence of this case, medical, technical and informational support and relationship security are the approaches I would advocate for. The discord between Viktor and Sime during their meeting might create doubt in Sime's mind later in the summer, particularly if his brother's recovery does not go as well as expected. I would encourage Viktor to respond positively to Sime and occasionally send him a motivational or compassionate message depending on circumstances.

I would expect to conduct an initial consult with Sime and then arrange to join Jenny Johnston and recruit Viktor Vargas for a short sport rehabilitation team meeting with Sime before he leaves campus for the summer. The purpose of this meeting would be to ensure everyone understands the plan for the summer in terms of expectations, roles and responsibilities, and to show support for Sime and the process. Lastly, as mentioned above, I would work with Jenny as needed through the summer and, if the need arose for increased contribution on my part, I would step in as required.

Further reading

Andersen, M. B., & Williams, J. M. (1999). Athletic injury, psychosocial factors and perceptual changes during stress. *Journal of Sports Sciences*, 17(9), 735–741.

Ray, R., & Wiese-Bjornstal, D. M. (1999). *Counseling in Sports Medicine*. Champaign: IL. Human Kinetics,

Wadey, R., Clark, S., Podlog, L., & McCullough, D. (2013). Coaches' perceptions of athletes' stress-related growth following sport injury. *Psychology of Sport and Exercise*, 14(2), 125–135.

Williams, J. M., & Andersen, M. B. (1998). Psychosocial antecedents of sport injury: Review and critique of the stress and injury model. *Journal of Applied Sport Psychology*, 10(1), 5–25.

10
COACH DEVELOPMENT

Introduction

This case focuses on coach awareness, coach education and coach development. Instructors are encouraged to bring their own experience to bear on this case, and to remind students of the implications for coaches working with the same athletes over a four-year college sport cycle.

Content implications

Students will be able to consider the implications of working with a coach who operates like they were coached, and who holds firm beliefs about their role in the coach–athlete relationship based on their own experience. A range of coach education and development discussions might develop from this case, including coaching philosophy, the coach's role in developing their athletes, communication and leadership styles, practice design, and creating a motivational sport climate. Students are encouraged to consider how coaches develop their coaching philosophies and motivational approaches to athletes.

Purpose

The purpose of this case is to consider the role of a sport psychology consultant in coach education and development in a day-to-day college setting.

Student learning outcomes

At this end of this case study learning opportunity, students should be able to:

1. Identify the issues underlying coach behavior
2. Select coach behavior interventions

3. Determine coach development priorities
4. Discuss how a sport psychology practitioner might be effective in this kind of scenario

Cast of characters in order of appearance

Robin Marriot, Head Coach, Men's Soccer.
Tina Morrison, Head Coach, Women's Tennis.
Celia "Cissy" Drew, Assistant Athletic Director and Women's Sport Administrator.

Coach profile: Tina Morrison, women's tennis head coach

Tina Morrison was the second head coach of women's tennis at Unity University. She was in her eighth season at The U and was enjoying it more than ever. Tina had been a member of a successful NCAA Division II team who won two national championships in her sophomore and junior year at a public university in the California State University system. She had been a standout high school singles player and a highly rated doubles player. She was less strong as a singles player, but was recruited by the team's coach to fill out her college team roster.

Tina was a walk-on, and an above average student. As a freshman, if it was a choice between playing tennis and going to class she would choose tennis. She grew up with the game, and the tennis court was her favorite place to be in life. All her friends at college were tennis players or coaches. Tennis was fun to her.

Tina's college coach was Sabrina Hudson. Her tone was strong and demanding. She was very aggressive in her communication, and she seemed to favor some of her athletes over others. She put her top players under least pressure and her lower-ranked players under the most pressure. Her thinking was that her top players were already under pressure but that the lower players needed more motivation and fear to play better. Hudson allowed Tina to settle in, and then midway through her first semester as a freshman she confronted her in a training session and told her in no uncertain terms that if she did not shape up she would be out and another recruit brought in who could do what Hudson wanted.

This experience left a deep image in Tina's mind of how to coach. For the next four years Tina worked harder than ever to play on the team and please the coach. She made sure she was always on the coach's right side, including volunteering do extra duties for the team and being seen to do extra in practice. Tina felt if she could please the coach she would keep her place. At the time tennis was all she wanted to do.

At the end of her junior year and the second national championship Hudson left for a NCAA Division I school in Florida and a new coach came in. The second coach contrasted with Hudson in several ways, including her desire for the players to find meaning in their own tennis, to identify ways to develop their own game, to focus on the process—and to call her by her first name. Tina's senior year was somewhat successful but did not hit the heights of the previous year. In Tina's mind the way the new coach operated was too agreeable, and she vowed not to be like this coach if she ever coached. However, Tina was influenced differently when her coach asked her to stay on as a graduate assistant while she finished her master's degree in education studies. Tina recognized in her junior year more schooling would be a good idea, and decided a teaching certification in math and health would suit her.

After being a graduate assistant and seeing how difficult coaching could be Tina realized she had been harsh with her head coach, but she still felt she could tighten up on some things. But she did learn that you did not always have to be hard on players to get the most out of them. It was her second coach who suggested that she try coaching because she felt Tina could develop players and had a winning mindset. She recommended Tina to the Athletic Director of a small NCAA Division I school where the coach was soon to retire and they needed a young replacement to enliven things up and teach classes too. Tina fitted in well and turned the program around in three years. They did not get further than conference championships, but their winning record was consistent and the players connected with Tina. She brought out the best in several Mexican-born players, which endeared her to the majority Hispanic and Latin institution.

Tina was recruited to her current position by Cissy Drew, the Senior Women's Administrator at The U. It was a big step up for Tina in terms of role and responsibilities. She was 28 when she joined The U eight years earlier. She was mentored by the women's soccer coach for a year and then cut loose. At first things went well, but the students at The U were more balanced between school and athletics than at her last college or her own college for her playing career. The students came from different social, economic and cultural backgrounds than she was used to, and they were more willing to speak up and present their own ideas. The differences would make her uncomfortable and agitated. At times she would call out her players; in particular, European players were the ones Tina felt caused her the most grief. They always had an opinion; she felt it was always different from hers and they should play for her first and the team second.

She decided she would work to make The U in the image of her college team and she would be like her college coach was: tough and competitive, because in her mind that was the way to The U would win.

The case

Robin Marriot passed Tina a book he had read on sport psychology and motivation called *Mental for Sport*, written by a renowned sport psychology practitioner.

TINA: "I didn't know you were much of a reader Robin."
ROBIN: "Yeah, when I started coaching I realized pretty quickly not everything I did with the players worked and it bothered me. Sometimes I would ask

myself why the players don't just do what I tell them to do, and then one day, like you, I had a falling out with one of my players. I totally blew up. I was frustrated and I just let them have it. I mean, I just went off on this kid, you know what I can't even remember for what."

TINA: "What happened then?"

ROBIN: "Well, I went home and talked to my wife about it, and she told me that I did not act that way with our children. If anything my youngest daughter would walk over me, and she felt I was wrapped around my eldest daughter's finger pretty well too. When she said it, I was like 'she's right, what's going on here?' So then I went online and found a soccer coaches' online group through my professional association and I started to talk with other coaches who experienced similar things. From one of those conversations I heard about this book and purchased it online. It's two years old now, but you're welcome to have it."

TINA: "Okay, but what happened? What did reading this book do for you?"

ROBIN: "Well I picked up some tips. The first thing I learned was players need autonomy, and if I get on them and they perceive I am controlling them or trying to push them when they are not ready, all I am going to get is them doing it just because I want them to, not because they believe it is the strongest thing for them to do for their performance."

TINA: "But what about them just following your directions. I mean you're the coach, they're the player. At some point they do need to get on your page, not just the other way around."

ROBIN: "You mean you feel I should be the coach and they should do what I tell them to do?"

TINA: "Kind of. I mean that's why we are hired to focus on our athletes and get the performance. Most college athletes I know don't know how to improve what they do, that's why they need a coach to help them."

ROBIN: "Okay, let's say you're right and I do that for my players. Do you realize my players have been playing for about ten years before they come to college, and sometimes they have had a new coach every season because youth teams often change coaches to freshen things up? They have seen lots of different coaches and they have a sense of what they like and don't like. That's one of the things I learned from the book. My job is to impart knowledge, but the way I coach is often more important than what I coach. If they don't want to listen to me and I lose them, no matter how hard I try they will tune me out and that is not good for them or me."

TINA: "Well okay, but in tennis it is different. Tennis is special. You have a coach and they know what you need. You work with them sometimes for your whole time in a club and you depend on them for, you know, everything."

ROBIN: "What does 'everything' mean?"

TINA: "It means tennis coaches identify what the player is doing well and not doing well; we tell them how to improve, we set up the drills and they do it. We invest in them; our repayment is their performance."

Robin paused and his brow furrowed. He chose his next words carefully.

ROBIN: "Do you really think this the best way to reach your athletes Tina?"

TINA: "What else did she [Cissy] tell you?"

ROBIN: "Nothing. You know Cissy, she's one of the good ones. She is not going to say anything—she just makes 'it' happen. She knew you and I talk sometimes, and she thought I might be able to share some coaching pointers with you."

TINA: "Okay … well it's like history all over again. I have a couple of players who are not coachable. They think they know more than me and they think they do not have to do what I tell them to do."

ROBIN: "What are they doing that makes you think that?"

TINA: "They say things like 'This does not work for me' or 'This is not improving me' … things like that, and recently one of them blew up on me for no reason."

ROBIN: "Okay, when are the players like this?"

TINA: "During practice."

ROBIN: "When they say their thing what is your response to them?"

Tina paused; she felt Robin was getting too close to uncovering things she did not want to talk about.

TINA: "I just tell them to get back to work and get on with it."

ROBIN: "Okay, I know you played a high standard of tennis. How did you feel when your coach said that to you?"

TINA: "Well it's different. I always felt my spot was under pressure …"

ROBIN: "Yes, but how did you feel about it?"

TINA: "I didn't like it."

ROBIN: "And you think your players do?"

Tina sighed.

TINA: "But I am the coach!"

ROBIN: "Yes you are, but is this the only way to go? Do you only know this way of coaching? I mean, if I acted like this with my players I would lose most of them. Have you lost your players yet?"

Tina got up from the round table in Robin's office overlooking the soccer field. She walked to the window and looked on as the sun bathed the playing fields in golden light.

TINA: "It's beautiful outside."

ROBIN: "What's wrong Tina?"

TINA: "It's not that anything is wrong. I just can't handle it when the players answer me back, especially my top players. It's like they are undermining me in front of everyone ... I mean why can't they just get on with it?"
ROBIN: "How long have you been coaching Tina?"
TINA: "Eleven years now. Feels like a lot longer with some players."
ROBIN: "Does this have anything to do with what happened with that player you had a few years ago? You know, the one you had a big fight with—the one from England?"
TINA: "Yeah, that's why Cissy thought we should talk. I know you heard about it, you had just started here then. This is not as bad as that, but I know Cissy's worried about it ... the thing is the player I fell out with is really good; she could be the best player we have ever had. I just can't reach her. She won't let me coach her. She fights me. It sucks. I just want to help her be even better. I want her to be the team captain, but I can't tell her that after what happened."
ROBIN: "So you like this player?"
TINA: "Yeah, she's great."

Tina shook her head and returned to her chair opposite Robin, who had remained seated the whole time.

ROBIN: "Can I give you some pro tips?"
TINA: "Sure, lay 'em on me."
ROBIN: "With my best players I bring them in and ask them what they feel we might work on. I don't always do what they want, but I listen, and you know what?—sometimes they have great ideas and sometimes we do them. They give me their trust and respect because I treat them this way. With one player in particular whose dad is a great coach and I know the kid is very well coached I'll ask him for drills he thinks might work too. This works with this player because he is a team-first guy, and even when he is on the bench he gives 100 percent whether he players no minutes or the whole game. He's the kind of player you love to have."

Tina sat and processed all that she heard from Robin. This kind of coaching was nothing like her two college coaches, especially Hudson, and not like she had ever done before.

ROBIN: "I can see you're thinking about things Tina. What's on your mind?"
TINA: "Don't you feel weaker for not having all the answers as a coach?"
ROBIN: "No. I only know what I know. I have 24 players. I can't know them all, and they and my staff collectively have strengths I don't."
TINA: "It does not concern you what they think of you as their coach?"
ROBIN: "Sure it does, but I want them to know how much I care about them first before I care about how many x's and o's I teach them."
TINA: "Do you do things differently often in training?"

ROBIN: "Pretty much every day. I have a couple of rules: 15 minutes max on any one exercise, and no two training sessions are exactly the same. I always modify something. It keeps things fresh for me and for them too."

TINA: "How do you do that? I mean how do you keep it fresh, you train a lot and year around?"

ROBIN: "Me and my assistants read a lot, we go to seminars, watch a lot of soccer, we take courses … our sport is always changing and somebody is trying something new and we want to be where the leaders are. Remember, we have taken some big losses in championship games recently and I can't keep losing big games otherwise a decision will be made about my employment. What do you do to keep fresh?"

TINA: "Keep fresh? Well, that's a good question. I don't have an assistant and I don't have a team manager. It's just me. I have to do everything myself."

ROBIN: "How do you change things up for you and your team? Surely you must do something?"

TINA: "I haven't really. I've been doing the same old things for some time now. They seem to work."

ROBIN: "Can you really say that Tina? We both know your team has hit its peak and you need something new to get your team over the hump, whether it's talent or different coaching. We're both under a bit of pressure."

TINA: "Okay, if you were me, what would you be doing differently?"

ROBIN: "If I were you I would be making a plan to change things up in how I worked with the team. I'd get this top player on my side without forcing it, and I would talk to Cissy about working with one of our sport psychology professionals."

Tina jumped on the last suggestion.

TINA: "That's what the team needs, a sport psychology person to talk to them."

ROBIN: "No Tina. Not for them, for you."

TINA: "Oh! Me? Why me? I am not the problem here. I am the one with the problem of handling these players. I have no assistant and no team manager. I am on my own. Nobody sees the work I do behind the scenes and I get no thanks for what I do. I feel like there's always someone looking over my shoulder."

Tina was indignant and her face red with anger. Robin thought carefully about his next words; he did not want to upset Tina even more than she was.

ROBIN: "How about we call it a day and we pick this up again when you're ready, maybe sometime in the next week? Text me when you are ready, okay?"

Tina left Robin's office. Once she was out of sight he got his cell phone out and called Cissy.

CISSY: "Hello this is Cissy, who is this?"
ROBIN: "It's Robin. I just finished with Tina."
CISSY: "Hi Robin, how did it go? Did she get upset?"
ROBIN: "Well, we started off okay but I think Tina left upset. We said we'd talk again."
CISSY: "Okay, so what do you think we should do?"
ROBIN: "I think Tina needs to work with one of our sport psychology people. Maybe Javier?"
CISSY: "Okay, send me an email and outline the conversation. Can we work with Tina?"
ROBIN: "Yeah we can. She wants to coach well. I feel she just needs more tools to do her job well."
CISSY: "I'll follow up with our sport psychology consultant, talk to him and let him know where things are with Tina. I'll make an appointment for her too. I think it's the first time they might have met."
ROBIN: "It's a start. Hopefully things will improve for Tina and her team."

Discussion questions

1. What is going on in this case?
2. What are the central issues in this case?
3. What might the role of the sport psychology consultant be working with the tennis coach in this case?
4. What might the scope of practice for a sport psychology consultant be considering the range of issues challenging all the individuals in this case?
5. How do you feel Robin and Cissy conducted themselves in this case?
6. What course of action would you recommend a sport psychology consultant take in this case?
7. How might you deal with Tina when you meet with her for the first time?
8. What other things are going on in this case that might be important to address?

Author's notes

This is a tricky case because there are a number of elements to work with, including coach–player relationships, organizational matters, conflict management, interpersonal relationships, coach education and development, and perhaps a touch of coach burnout too. Additionally we have a coach-to-coach interaction which reveals significant information supplementing what we already know about Tina's personal history. In this instance I feel the steps I would take include the following. First, I would work to address the issues facing Tina and what created the situation in the first place. Next, I would work with Tina to address her desire for change and her personal and professional needs. In this phase I might even elicit Tina's vision and value for her coaching too, but I would be mindful that there is not endless time allocated to this work, and it is likely some form of coach behavior change is being sought by the client (the Athletic Department) for the recipient is expected. With this in mind I would focus on the small, significant behavior change that would get more of what the coach wanted in terms of her team's performance and less interpersonal hostility.

In these kinds of situations I prefer to use experiential exercises with clients because I want to raise personal awareness and encourage the client to voice their position and the position of the athlete or whoever they are working with so that they can hear the different ideas for themselves. In this case I might use activities like role playing, empty chair and whiteboard work showing the issues. I find they get issues out quite quickly and engage the client in the work more directly and collaboratively.

At the same time as working with the coach I would seek to engage the tennis team too. I would want to have a solution focused conversation while hearing the players out. The top players would need a side conversation to work through their position and point of view. Then a third step would be to get the team and the coach together for a mediated conversation. In the back of my mind, working with Robin and Cissy would be necessary too because of the hierarchical relationships and the need to provide them with updates. I know that some consultants prefer to keep information to themselves, but I prefer careful transparency. For me this means informing and updating individuals without giving too much detail, and leaving the primary individuals to communicate their own stories.

In the longer term, I might approach Cissy about support for Tina. I feel like Tina's tension is partly induced by the range of tasks she feels she is having to complete because she does not have an assistant. The tension she expressed with Robin about not having organizational team support indicates she might be feeling burned out and overextended, which in turn makes her vulnerable to outbursts she might not normally have. Lastly, I would work to understand the range of coach education opportunities available to Tina and share them with her and see if progress might be made in this area to freshen her coaching up too.

While Tina might be a bit rough on her players, there seems to be sincerity in some aspects of her coaching and she wants the players to be successful. She is experienced and her coaching has developed over the years. I feel she can be an asset to The U.

Further reading

Gould, D., Damarjian, N., & Medbery, R. (1999). An examination of mental skills training in junior tennis coaches. *Sport Psychologist*, 13(2), 127–143.

Kelley, B. C., Eklund, R. C., & Ritter-Taylor, M. (1999). Stress and burnout among collegiate tennis coaches. *Journal of Sport and Exercise Psychology*, 21(2), 113–130.

Poczwardowski, A., Sherman, C. P., & Ravizza, K. (2004). Professional philosophy in the sport psychology service delivery: Building on theory and practice. *Sport Psychologist*, 18(4), 445–463.

Santos, S., Mesquita, I., Graça, A., & Rosado, A. (2010). Coaches' perceptions of competence and acknowledgement of training needs related to professional competences. *Journal of Sports Science & Medicine*, 9(1), 62–70.

11

TRANSITION OUT OF COLLEGE SPORT

Introduction

This case introduces students to the complexities of student-athlete transitions from the college sport and academic context to a different phase, and most likely a change in lifestyle, following their initial undergraduate experience. There are several elements in this case which are usual and customary for prospective graduates, including considerations for future sport participation, career development, and specific pathways to ongoing personal and professional development and growth. Uncertainty is a common experience for many students in their senior college year unsure of what the future holds. This case relates all these factors in a single scenario for students to examine.

Content implications

This case may foster discussions about sport retirement, life skills support and programming, coping with anxiety, interpersonal communication, problem solving, goal setting and stress management. There are multiple sources of pressure which challenge student-athletes to determine an approach to support them in a timely and relevant manner, with defined time constraints acting on any intervention undertaken.

Purpose

The purpose of this case is for students to determine the role and scope of services a sport psychology practitioner might have in supporting a student-athlete transitioning from their undergraduate sport and academic experience to a different lifestyle and context.

Student learning outcomes

At this end of this case study learning opportunity, students should be able to:

1. Identify and explain the issues presented in this case
2. Discuss the challenges facing student-athletes as they transition out of college sport
3. Explain the impact of career transitions on student-athlete identity
4. Express the developmental nature of a student-athlete sport career
5. Discuss the role and limits of a sport psychology consultant as part of a transitional team

Cast of characters in order of appearance

Shawndra Banks, Women's Basketball.
Carolyn Banks, Shawndra's Mother.
Quang Tham, Career Adviser.
Javier Aguilar, Sport Psychology Consultant.

Athlete Profile: Shawndra Banks, women's basketball

Shawndra was a communications and marketing major, and recently returned to The U after a brief break between games for Christmas Eve and Christmas Day at home with her family. She was entering the second semester of her senior year at The U and her final season as small forward (SF) with the women's basketball team. While she was at home her parents had asked her about graduation and her career prospects.

Shawndra had been recruited by Becky Washington, The U's women's assistant coach, who became the head coach in Shawndra's sophomore year after she replaced the previous head coach. Shawndra had a good relationship with Becky and regarded her as a mentor. One of the reasons Shawndra was recruited was that basketball was such a high priority and her goal of playing abroad was very strong. She was academically moderate in high school, but she always did very well in public speaking, presentations and demonstrating how things worked. She was well liked in her school, getting along with most people, all of her teachers and having friends in different social groups. Close to the time Shawndra was being recruited by Coach Washington, her high school academic and career adviser recognized her strong interpersonal skills and recommended she study a major in communications and marketing. Luckily The U had a program that focused on communications and public relations, which several other student-athletes registered for too.

Shawndra's basketball and academic studies progressed well. She was a positive player for her team on and off the court. Her coaches enjoyed working with her and found her positive and low maintenance. She never caused them any problems, and went about her training and play with a positive attitude. She was a consistent player, always getting good enough results but not getting the public recognition her consistent play deserved. While her basketball experience had been mostly positive, her academic career had stalled a bit.

At the end of her junior year, two faculty members left her major. One retired unexpectedly because of health reasons and another took a position at another institution. The second one was responsible for coordinating internships, shadowing and networking students to their professional pathways. This role went unfilled into the second semester of Shawndra's junior year, which meant her summer work experience was quite poor. She ended up shadowing an intern in The U's marketing department. She got along with the intern but did not learn much, get to try new things or extend her professional network very far. She was frustrated and disappointed at the end of this experience. It was not what she wanted. She looked forward to her last season of college basketball and putting these things behind her.

Over the years, Shawndra's parents had taken a pragmatic view of her college career. They hoped her dream of playing professionally in Europe and traveling abroad would come true, but they also hoped that her studies would lead to an entry-level job close to home. They tried to be understanding and supportive but they were concerned. At Christmas, Shawndra had no immediate career or basketball prospects after graduation, and was unclear about what she would do. Shawndra's mom, Carolyn, would be at the New Year's Day home game against Barton College and arranged to have dinner together after the game. She intended to talk to Shawndra about her concerns for her future and offer some ideas for her daughter to consider.

The case

The team won their match against Barton, spirits were high, and Shawndra looked forward to meeting her mother at her favorite diner, Manny's on Main, which her mother also liked Manny's.

Carolyn smiled broadly as her daughter entered the diner and got up to give her a hug. The two squeezed each other until they both laughed, and then sat down to look at the menu. Shawndra was very hungry and ordered her favorite meal, which was breakfast at dinner time. Carolyn ordered her favorite house salad too. After settling in the conversation began.

CAROLYN: "It's lovely to see you Shawndra … you and team played great tonight."
SHAWNDRA: "Thanks Mom. We really had it going tonight. My team mates, well you saw them, everyone was 'on' tonight."
CAROLYN: "You did well too, another double-double with points and rebounds … how many is that this season?"
SHAWNDRA: "It's my second … I was close to a third last week but didn't make it. I'm playing well but not always getting what I want."
CAROLYN: "I know dear. How do you think things are going for you this season?"

SHAWNDRA: "Well, they're okay. I'm doing a little bit better than last season. Coach is happy with me, and my team mates are too. I'm starting every game and I'm contributing. I just don't seem to be getting the recognition I need to reach my goals."
CAROLYN: "You mean you still want to go abroad?"
SHAWNDRA: "Yeah Mom. I still want to do it. I always wanted to travel. I'd love to play in Spain or Italy. I'm not going to get into the WNBA league, but I think I can make a European team."
CAROLYN: "But you have no agent, your coach hasn't talked to you about it, and it seems a long way off honey."
SHAWNDRA: "I know, but that's now. I have to change this. Can we just eat and not talk about this for a while?"

Carolyn understood her daughter well and knew that talking more right now would upset her. The two most important relationships in Carolyn life were with Shawndra and her husband, Martin. They were a tight-family. Martin was a former Marine officer specializing in logistics. He and Carolyn met after he had left the military and was working as a manager at a large logistics company. Carolyn had been a first grade teacher until Shawndra was born. They brought her up to think for herself, take responsibility, and have a positive attitude. They wanted her to live the life she wanted to live, but these days were concerned because for the first time the future for Shawndra was uncertain.

SHAWNDRA: "I know you and Dad are worried, but I still want to do this. I always wanted to travel. Dad did ... why can't I?"
CAROLYN: "Your dad and I know you want go to Europe, but things are different now. You're not a kid and you're finishing college in a few months. We're concerned you'll be a difficult spot when you graduate and we want to help, but we don't know how. You've always played basketball and you've been a good student, but we don't see your prospects and we don't see how you're going to be successful. You don't tell us about any career-related things and we're a bit lost too."
SHAWNDRA: "I know things don't look good right now. But I still have time."
CAROLYN: "Time for what honey? What do you have time to do?"
SHAWNDRA: "I scheduled a meeting with our team's career adviser and I'm going to talk to my coach about Europe."
CAROLYN: "You mean you haven't done this before?"
SHAWNDRA: "No."
CAROLYN: "Why not? Honey, you waited all this time to do this? Me and your dad thought you had done this way before now."

Shawndra began to well up as she felt her mother's disappointment.

SHAWNDRA: "I don't know why I didn't do it. I just hoped things would work out, but they haven't gone the way I hoped they would."

CAROLYN: "Honey, we taught you to have a plan and go do it. I'm just surprised you had no plan and, like your dad says, 'Hope is not a strategy.' What were you hoping for—an agent would come for you and a job would fall in your lap?"

SHAWNDRA: "Don't be mad at me. It's not helping right now. I'm not one of your students either. I'm not a bad person … I didn't do this to upset you and Dad."

CAROLYN: "I know you didn't. We're worried about you that's all, and we're worried we don't know what to do. You're our baby and we want what's best for you."

SHAWNDRA: "I know you do, but you're upsetting me."

CAROLYN: "When are you seeing the career counselor?"

SHAWNDRA: "Tuesday."

CAROLYN: "Okay, in three days. Will you call us and tell us how things go?"

SHAWNDRA: "Sure. Can we just eat now and not talk about this anymore?"

On Tuesday Shawndra was early for her meeting with the team's career counselor, Quang Tham, in the student-athlete academic center in front of a lifesize media picture of Shawndra's team. Quang stood up from behind the study desk he had selected to spread out the papers he always brought for initial meetings with student-athletes. He reached out to shake Shawndra's hand.

QUANG: "Hello Shawndra. I recognize you from the photograph I saw on the team webpage. I am happy to work with you."

SHAWNDRA: "Thank you. Nice to meet you."

QUANG: "Please sit down over here."

Quang guided Shawndra to a seat opposite him overlooking the papers laid out on the table.

QUANG: "You're the second student-athlete I have worked with this year. Normally my colleague Norma works with the athletes. I am excited to be helping you."

Shawndra was surprised, she had expected Norma to be working with her.

SHAWNDRA: "Okay, so what do we do?"

QUANG: "Well, I brought several career interest inventories for you to complete so that we can determine what careers you might like and perhaps be motivated by. I know we have little time before you go to practice, so you can take them with you to complete later."

SHAWNDRA: "Okay, but what are we going to do here right now … how are you going to help me? Do you know what my major is?"

QUANG: "I read that you are a communications major. Perhaps something in the media would appeal to you?"

SHAWNDRA: "So, this is just a meeting for me to fill out these forms and return them? I need real help. I graduate in five months and I need a plan. I need a bit of direction and I want help!"

Quang stared at her. He seemed unprepared for Shawndra's requests. Non-student-athletes were a bit more passive and allowed things to unfold on his timeline.

QUANG: "Okay, look, let's meet again in two weeks when you have done the forms. I am sorry I am not able to help you right now, but I can when you return the inventories."

Shawndra sighed and agreed to Quang's plan and went off to practice. When she got there, her mind was filled with her mother's questions, ideas swirling around her head about her graduation situation, and feelings of frustration and anger. She was not herself.

Practice got underway and the team went through its usual training routines. Shawndra got into the flow of practice and then her coach decided to introduce a progressive match situation which pitted team mates in one-on-one, two-on-two, three-on-three, and then five-on-five situations. Play was at maximum intensity and players were competing very hard with each other. A shot was taken and hit the rim of the basketball hoop. Shawndra contested with a team mate and was accidentally knocked in the face. Her team mate had no intent and was focused on the ball. Shawndra lost her cool; she started yelling, pushing aggressively, and trying to grab at her team mate. The other players intervened and the coach got between Shawndra and her target. Nobody had ever seen Shawndra behave like this before. Everyone was startled and there was a moment of silence. Shawndra froze, then after several seconds realized what she had done. She grabbed her hair and started to tear up; she tried to apologize at the same time. It was all too much, and one of her team mates took Shawndra to the locker room to calm down. The coach returned to practice with shooting drills for the team to cool the situation down. After practice the coach talked to Shawndra about her conduct. She was shocked at what she witnessed and instructed Shawndra to work with the team sport psychology consultant. From her point of view this was a one-off from Shawndra, but she wanted her behavior handled and settled as the New Year was approaching and she wanted the team to have a strong run of victories going into conference championships. She also directed her to apologize to her team mates. Shawndra did as her coach asked but was racked with guilt and shame at her outburst. She did not tell her parents about the incident. She was to meet with the sport psychology consultant in the next few days, well before her next career counseling session with Quang Tham.

Javier Aquilar sat waiting with his coffee at his usual table in the coffee lounge of The U's main library. He happened to be on campus that day and had time to meet with Shawndra. They had spoken before in team meetings Javier facilitated over the years but not worked together one-on-one. Javier had no feelings either way about the basketball player, but he knew from the coach's email telling him about the incident that the coach was concerned about the player. They asked Javier to help get the player "right" for the weeks ahead into the championship part of the season. For Shawndra's part she knew very little about Javier besides his working with the team and helping a couple of her team mates through their injury recovery. She had not worked with a sport psychology consultant before and did not know what to expect. By the time she met Javier she was more balanced in herself and feeling like this was something extra to satisfy her coach.

Shawndra came from the side and sat down without Javier seeing her. His eyes were on his iPad. He looked up with surprise.

JAVIER: "Hello Shawndra."
SHAWNDRA: "Hello."
JAVIER: "Can I get you a coffee?"
SHAWNDRA: "No thanks. I have my water bottle" (which she placed prominently on the coffee table as she sat down).
JAVIER: "How's things?"
SHAWNDRA: "Okay, I suppose. Coach contacted you about what happened?"
JAVIER: "She did."
SHAWNDRA: "Well, I think we're supposed to talk about what happened."
JAVIER: "Are we? ... I was thinking we might talk about something you would find helpful to talk about first."

This was not the approach Shawndra was expecting; she was not sure how to respond and sat quietly.

JAVIER: "Tell me Shawndra, what would be most helpful for you for us to talk about first?"

A silence settled in the space between them as the basketball player stared at her water bottle and thought for what seemed like minutes but was only seconds.

SHAWNDRA: "Graduation ... graduation is on my mind."
JAVIER: "Okay, say more about what's going on. We don't know each other, for me to understand your experience you need to tell me how things are for you right now."
SHAWNDRA: "How do I know you won't talk to Coach about this?"
JAVIER: "I will talk to your coach. We have an agreement. Besides, at the end of our conversation I will summarize what we talked about, give some key points back to you and ask if you if I can use those key points in my conversations with your coach."
SHAWNDRA: "So you will talk to Coach?"

JAVIER: "Yes. I always talk to the coach. I give no details, only the big picture. I have to—it's part of my job and I need to do it to show them you and me talked and I have an idea of what is going on. But if you tell me very little or tell me things in a way that is comfortable for you but leaves me in the dark, there's nothing I can do about that. You have the power; it's up to you how you go about this. So, how do you want to go about this?"

Shawndra sipped from her water bottle.

SHAWNDRA: "I have no prospects after graduation. I thought I would have an agent, or have a career path by now and I don't. One of my team mates has an agent, she's Serbian. She seems to have things figured out. My major is a joke. I have no internship experience to rely on and the career adviser I just met was a joke too … they didn't even really know me; and on top of this my parents are upset with me and getting on me. I know they love me but they don't seem to understand."

JAVIER: "You mean you want to play professionally and have a career back-up if that does not happen?"

SHAWNDRA: "How did you figure that out? We've never talked before."

JAVIER: "Well you started off talking about the agent and then the career. It was a bit of a guess on my part."

SHAWNDRA: "Good guess."

JAVIER: "Can I tell you something?"

SHAWNDRA: "Sure."

JAVIER: "I think you're graduating in a few months and it's normal for student-athletes in your position to come to this realization. It is scary and unsettling. Not only are you thinking of the next thing, but you also have to be considerate of the current thing you are doing. But too much thinking about the next thing gets in the way of the thing you are doing now."

SHAWNDRA: "Okay."

JAVIER: "Are you scared Shawndra?"

SHAWNDRA: "A little bit. I don't know what to do. I feel totally stuck, like I'm boxed in. It's like making a defensive rebound and not having an 'out' pass to one of the guards with Coach yelling at me to move the ball quickly."

JAVIER: "Ah okay. You need options is what you're saying."

SHAWNDRA: "Kind of, but it's more than that. My parents are upset and worried … we're really close and I feel this is between us. My parents are very responsible and this is difficult for them, especially my mum."

JAVIER: "What makes it difficult for them?"

SHAWNDRA: "They think I don't have a plan … I don't. I have a dream."

JAVIER: "A dream, what is it?"

SHAWNDRA: "I want to play in Europe and I want to travel. Ever since I was really young I looked at a map and pointed to places I wanted to go. My dad encouraged me too. He said I could do anything I put my mind to."

JAVIER: "Who else knows about your dream?"
SHAWNDRA: "Only my parents."
JAVIER: "Who else do you think should know about this?"
SHAWNDRA: "My coach."
JAVIER: "How come you haven't told her already?"
SHAWNDRA: "I figured she would talk to me about it if she thought I could do it."
JAVIER: "Can I give you feedback about your approach here?"
SHAWNDRA: "Sure."
JAVIER: "You have to be focused on your future not your coach. You have to make this happen for yourself. Your coach is focused on the team now. That's where her mind is. Do you blame her? No! You expect it. Okay, so you said a Serbian team mate has an agent. How much have you talked to her about this? How much research have you done to make this happen for yourself?"

Shawndra was unprepared to hear Javier's comments. She felt startled, and pushed back from the coffee table.

SHAWNDRA: "Are you blaming me for not doing enough?"
JAVIER: "No, I didn't mean that. What I mean is this … and you have to rely on my experience a bit here. I have worked with a number of athletes at this stage of their career like you. They have taken control of their own future and put themselves first in their thinking. Many of have been team players, but they know their careers are short and their dreams are important to them. The ones that are successful have a good playing record, a good head on their shoulders and know how to get help to progress to their goals. That is all I meant."
SHAWNDRA: "Okay, but what about my career if I am unsuccessful in achieving my dream?"
JAVIER: "I don't know much about career matters. I know that this is a time of transition and you need the best resources around you possible. I know sport and mental health well. I can't really advise you on which career would be best for you. I can help you identify some strengths, help you problem solve and come to a decision, but the technical issues are beyond me. It would be like a center trying to play point guard."

Discussion questions

1. What are the main issues present in this case?
2. How would you prioritize the issues facing Shawndra?
3. What challenges does Shawndra face during this phase of her student-athlete career?
4. What role might anxiety have in Shawndra's case?
5. What might the range of problem solving options be in this case?
6. How might you approach counseling Shawndra during this time?

Author's note

I often work with student-athletes in their final year of athletic eligibility who want to play their sport after college. Sometimes they want to continue in the United States and sometimes, like Shawndra, they want to play in Europe. I found several things in common with these athletes:

- They are highly motivated but inexperienced in the process of getting to the next level of performance.
- The individuals in their network are well meaning but often inexperienced in these things too, which makes it difficult for the student-athlete to rely on them for instrumental help—that is, help which advances the student-athlete to their goal in practical and pragmatic terms.
- Team coaches have to be engaged in the process. Many are connected with agents and professional scouting networks; therefore the quality of the relationship between student-athlete and them is essential for successful transition.
- Some student-athletes focus early in their academic careers on a professional and career skill set that will help them after their college lives have finished. On the other hand there are a number of student-athletes who start concentrating on this in their final year, and especially their final semester when their sport is over and they will leave shortly thereafter. At these times anxiety, a sense of loss, even grief might be experienced.
- Often student-athletes have given some thought to their transition, but in my experience it has been hit and miss solely because they concentrated on what they were doing at college, which meant things slowly crept up on them.
- And, finally, the quality of their career expectations often depends on family, coach, faculty, academic/career adviser, peer group, and faculty influences and experiences. Few student-athletes are successful alone in their transition from college.

Transitions are tricky moments in the life of a student-athlete. In general they are tricky for many individuals in many walks of life. I approach the conversation thinking about three phases: 1) the approach to the transition; 2) the process of going through the transition; and 3) emerging from the recent transition into the new state of being. Considering this three-step process helps me consider the desire, abilities, reasons, needs and commitment necessary for the student-athlete to be successful. I see my role in the student-athlete transition as supplemental to a collective approach too.

Lastly, one of the professional challenges I faced over the years is not seeing the outcome of the work done. Often a student-athlete graduates and does not communicate whether the work we did has been successful or not. This can sometimes feel a bit empty, but it is a common experience for many helping professionals. It has been hard to measure the effectiveness of the work under these circumstances.

Further reading

Murphy, G. M., Petitpas, A. J., & Brewer, B. W. (1996). Identity foreclosure, athletic identity, and career maturity in intercollegiate athletes. *Sport Psychologist*, 10(3), 239–246.

Park, S., Lavallee, D., & Tod, D. (2013). Athletes' career transition out of sport: A systematic review. *International Review of Sport and Exercise Psychology*, 6(1), 22–53.

Tyrance, S. C., Harris, H. L., & Post, P. (2013). Predicting positive career planning attitudes among NCAA Division I college student-athletes. *Journal of Clinical Sport Psychology*, 7(1), 22–40.

Wylleman, P., & Lavallee, D. (2004). A developmental perspective on transitions faced by athletes. In M. R. Weiss (Ed.), *Developmental sport and exercise psychology: A lifespan perspective* (pp. 503–523). Morgantown, WV: Fitness Information Technology.

12
UNDERPERFORMANCE

Introduction

It is common in NCAA competition for student-athletes to transfer between schools in search of new opportunities in their sport and academic studies. Transferring between institutions and teams often means transition from one way of operating to other ways of doing things, often leading to different forms of personal stress affecting the student-athlete. This case has a range of issues that might influence sport psychology students. The title is deliberately vague to induce the reader to discern what they perceive to be the critical aspects of the case.

Because this case originates with an individual transferring between institutions and teams, it presents sport psychology students with issues seldom discussed in the sport psychology literature, be it peer-reviewed research or text book—namely, the issues surrounding a transfer between teams. Typically, the concept of transitions is dealt with in issues like retirement from sport or graduating from college to the world of work, but it seldom contends with in-sport transitions. It is possible that neophyte sport psychology practitioners might not address the challenges presented by a transition and instead focus on the technical aspects of performance without addressing the underlying causes of underperformance.

Content implications

The case deliberately infers nuances for consideration by sport psychology students, including but not limited to, coach–player interactions, coach–coach interactions, athlete support, transitions between teams, life balance between academic studies and sport performance demands, concentration during competition, situational decision-making during competition, stress management, interpersonal relationships, goal setting, and visualization. The literature on underperformance evokes terms like choking, stress, fatigue, burnout, and overtraining. However, this case does not concern these issues. If these aspects are brought up it might indicate the details of the case are not well understood. Instead, this case is based on the cognitive and emotional responses the student-athlete experiences in the situation.

Remember, it is possible students will find links between the content, characters and the solutions you and I did not consider, which is one reason for using the teaching case method.

Student learning outcomes

At this end of this case study learning opportunity, students should be able to:

1. Identify the issues causing lapses in concentration
2. Select psychosocial interventions for enhancing concentration
3. Consider strategies for psychosocial program implementation to enhance performance
4. Discuss how the effectiveness of a mental skills training program might be evaluated

Cast of characters in order of appearance

Mike Landing, Head Coach, Men's Basketball.
Jake Johnson, Assistant Coach, Men's Basketball.
Yannis Papadopoulos, Men's Basketball Coach.
Celia "Cissy" Drew, Assistant Athletic Director and Women's Sport Administrator.
Vivian Moreno, Sport Psychology Consultant.

Athlete profile: Yannis Papadopoulos, men's basketball

Yannis Papadopoulos is a 22-year-old junior transfer student on The U's men's basketball team. He is a 6 foot 4 inch point guard. He is originally from Thessaloniki, Greece, and played on high-level Greek youth and men's teams. He was an Olympic hopeful with a strong range of passing techniques coupled with effective decision making, speed, and a high free throw percentage. His favorite shot was a mid-range jump shot.

He was originally recruited by a college in a neighboring state before he transferred to The U. He started on this team as a sophomore and won conference honors, being named to the All-Conference Team at the end of the previous season. He was very happy with his team mates and his coach. Things were going well academically and the transition from the Greek education system to the higher education in the United States had been smooth.

Yannis is not on a scholarship; he receives no money from The U. His mother is a school teacher and his father is a senior engineer for a Greek shipping company. They have stable incomes, investments, and savings to send Yannis to America to play basketball and complete a degree. Their hope was he would become an engineer too and return to Greece to work in the same company as his father. His parents are very rational people.

Soon after returning for his second season Yannis's coach informed him he would be leaving his position for personal reasons at the end of the season. Yannis was very disappointed. He liked the coach and the way he dealt with him. He also liked his team mates and felt settled in school. As the season went on, whatever his coach was going through affected his mood and the team's performance. Yannis did not play as much or as well as his first year. About a month before the end of the season his coach spoke to him about transferring to another school. The coach apologized for how the season had gone and they communicated they were unsure Yannis would get the experience he wanted if he stayed for his junior year. The coach mentioned he knew the coach at The U and he would be interested in receiving Yannis as a transfer. But moving to The U was a step up in playing level and in academic demands compared to where he was now.

Yannis talked the move over with his team mates and his parents. The U's coach contacted him and told him he was impressed with Yannis's play and attitude, and he respected the judgment of his current coach. He also told him he would not guarantee playing time or an easy time academically. Knowing this, Yannis asked to transfer to The U. He met all the eligibility criteria set out by the NCAA for Division I athletes transferring between academic institutions. He arrived a week before summer training began to move into his new accommodation, register for classes, and meet his new team mates and academic support advisers.

The case

Mike Landing and his assistant, Jake Johnson, looked on from the sideline as their team cooled down after an intense training session before their fifth game of the season. The team came off a productive pre-season, integrating two freshman forwards and a new point guard—Yannis Papadopoulos, who had transferred from another college—and their current record was 2–2.

JAKE: "Coach, I just think we should sit Yannis for the next game. He's making too many mistakes and costing us turnovers. He still looks uncomfortable with our playing schemes."

MIKE: "I still want to try him. I have faith in the kid."

JAKE: "We have benched other players for less. I just think right now he's our second option."

MIKE: "I hear you Jake, but I want to try him. I'm going to start him and monitor how he does in the first 5–6 minutes. If it looks like he is struggling I will bring him out. This is a short trip to Mumford College for this non-conference game. We should win … it's a good time for him to grow his confidence."

Jake folded his arms and rocked back and forth on his heels. The team circled up.

MIKE: "All right boys, good session! I'll talk to you in the team meeting tomorrow morning before the game. Yannis, let's talk."
MIKE: "Yannis you're going to start the game tomorrow."
YANNIS: "Okay"
MIKE: "Are you good with this, can you handle starting?"
YANNIS: "I can handle it. I thought after the last game you would sit me because of the turnovers and free throws."
MIKE: "I'm giving you a chance. You're a good player but you need to show more quality in your decision-making otherwise you give me no choice but to bench you, and you know it might be hard to get minutes once you're benched."
YANNIS: "I get it. Is there anything else I should know about what I need to do tomorrow?"
MIKE: "Just don't give me a reason to bench you."

Later that day in the campus cafeteria Jake Johnson and Cissy Drew were having lunch.

JAKE: "What's the word on the team Cissy?"

Jake was responsible for knowing how the team was performing academically and how the mood of the team was in general terms. Cissy was the senior women's administrator, but she was also the person the players would most likely talk to about most things going on in the team or in their lives. She and Jake would have lunch once a week to talk about the team.

CISSY: "Pretty good, but this new kid Yannis is struggling a bit."
JAKE: "What do you mean?"
CISSY: "Well, I'm hearing from a couple of the guys that he's struggling to see the game the same way as they do ... they like him and they feel he's a good addition to the team but he seems to lose concentration a bit ... his passes are just a bit too long, making them look bad, or those bounce passes he tries get cut out or you know ... sometimes he does not see the help coming ... it feels like he is forcing the play and the offense is not working properly."
JAKE: "Wow! They do tell you a lot. That's all been on my mind too. I talked to Mike about Yannis this morning. I like the kid but he's making too many errors."
CISSY: "I heard he was finding it tougher to adjust here than he thought it would be. The academics are more demanding, the rural location is different than he thought, and the way we play is also different than he's used to. He's become friends with Dewayne, and he told me Yannis is all up in his head about his grades and school work. Apparently, he studies really hard and he gets really moody if he feels like he's slacking in class. Dewayne has to tell him to take a break and chill out a bit."

JAKE: "Do you think we should step in be more proactive with Yannis? I know Mike likes him."
CISSY: "You're the coach ..."
JAKE: "Okay, I'll talk to Yannis after tomorrow's game."

The U's men's basketball team won the fifth game by two points. Yannis was replaced after 7 minutes. He passed the ball straight out of bounds twice and the timing of his passes was off. The previous season's point guard managed the game well and closed the game out. As the team walked down the tunnel Cissy noticed Yannis seemed sad and disappointed. She took him by the arm and led him into a quiet area away from the dressing room.

CISSY: "Yannis, you doing okay?"
YANNIS: "Not really."
CISSY: "You're disappointed about how you played?"
YANNIS: "Yeah ... but ... well ... I just feel like things are much harder than I expected ... it's hard keeping my mind straight."
CISSY: "Do you want to talk about things?"
YANNIS: "With you?"
CISSY: "No, Jake told me he was going to check in with you after the game."
YANNIS: "Jake? I don't think he likes me that much. He seems frustrated since I came here. Is there a person who does sport psychology here? ... There was a sport psychology person at my last college and we had a psychology adviser to my teams in Greece."
CISSY: "I don't know much about psychology but I know we can work with Vivian Moreno, our sport psychology consultant."
YANNIS: "Do I still need to meet with Jake?"
CISSY: "I think you should."
YANNIS: "Okay, but when can I talk to the sport psychology person?"
CISSY: "I'll text you in the morning ... most likely you'll be able to meet after your recovery session around 5pm."

Jake called Yannis across the court before the recovery session began.

JAKE: "Hey Yannis, I just wanted to check in with you and see how you're doing."
YANNIS: "I'm fine. No problems."
JAKE: "Okay, well it's been a few weeks since you came here and I hoped we could talk about how things are for you."
YANNIS: "They are fine."
JAKE: "So you're fine?"
YANNIS: "Yeah, I'm good."
JAKE: "Okay, just wanted to check in."

Yannis turned and jogged down the tunnel to join his team mates in the sport medicine center. Jake looked on as the point guard entered the locker room, sighed, and put his hands on his hips. Cissy was on hand to witness the interaction between the coach and the player.

CISSY: "I saw you talk to Yannis … if you can call it that. How did it go?"
JAKE: "The kid hardly said anything. It's like it didn't matter to him that I reached out to him."
CISSY: "Well you're right … He thinks you don't like him for some reason, so you catching him like this probably felt weird to him."
JAKE: "Okay … so what do you think I should do now?"
CISSY: "Nothing."
JAKE: "Nothing! But I'm his coach."
CISSY: "Yes but you are making it difficult for him right now. Give him a break."

Jake raised his eyebrows, put his hands in his pockets, and puffed out his cheeks.

CISSY: "I contacted Dr Moreno and she's going to meet Yannis this afternoon."
JAKE: "Dr Moreno? Whoa, I did not see that one coming."
CISSY: "Yannis asked for it."
JAKE: "He did. I didn't know he needed that kind of help. We don't really talk about that stuff. We try to recruit the kids you know … who have 'it'."
CISSY: "Well, according to Yannis it's normal for him to work with a sport psychology consultant. It seems like that's what they do where he's from. I mean look at this way. It got him to the USA and he caught Mike's eye and he ended up here, so this boy has some quality, and maybe we just need to help him figure this situation out."

Jake stood dumbfounded. Cissy pointed her index finger at Jake and pressed it into his chest.

CISSY: "You said you wanted to help him."

And with that she walked past him toward the exit.

Dr Moreno was in the 15th year of her psychology career. She was paid a retainer, had consulted at The U for three years, and was a trusted adviser to administrators, coaches and athletes. She was highly valued for her professionalism. She had a clinical psychology practice in town, and about one-third of her work was with athletes from The U and the other two-thirds with individuals usually experiencing anxiety and depression. She sat at her favorite table in Cherry's Campus Café with a latte. Her table allowed her to see the long view of people who might arrive from campus turning left around the corner and walking towards Cherry's. She preferred to meet athletes off campus, and in this case Cissy Drew had told her Yannis was Greek and she imagined a coffee shop might put him at ease. Yannis approached from the direction Dr Moreno expected. She knew what he looked like from his photo on the team roster, but she had not done any research to learn more about him; she wanted to discover Yannis for herself and then decide what she would do. Besides, she did not know if she and the point guard would be a good fit. As Yannis approached the door Dr Moreno waved at him to catch his eye.

VIVIAN: "Hello Yannis, I'm Vivian. Can I get you a coffee?"
YANNIS: "No, it's okay, I'll get my own."

Yannis purchased a coffee and sat with Vivian.

VIVIAN: "Thanks for being on time to meet me."
YANNIS: "I know I am Greek but we can be on time." [He smiled.]
VIVIAN: "Of course ... Cissy told me you wanted to talk to a sport psychology consultant."
YANNIS: "Yes. I used to work with a sport psychology consultant with my last two teams. It was normal, but it seems not so normal here. I did not even know you were available to us."
VIVIAN: "That can happen. I am usually called by the team's coach when they feel they need me. But this is different—you asked for me, and so, here I am."
YANNIS: "Good."
VIVIAN: "Tell me what made you ask to talk to someone."
YANNIS: "Well, I don't really feel like I can talk to anyone on the team and I get the feeling the assistant head coach, Jake, does not like me, and the one kid Dewayne is a good kid but a bit loose for me ... it's hard because I don't know anyone well and it seems like everyone knows each other really well."
VIVIAN: "So you're feeling a bit isolated and alone right now without too many people to confide in."
YANNIS: "Yeah. On top of this, I keep making errors during games. Well, what I mean is I am making the same errors but I don't know why. It's like I am blocked ... like, I think I see what's going on in the game and then I don't. This has happened before but not like this."

Yannis sipped his coffee.

VIVIAN: "So you've been through this before but this time it's different. What's different?"
YANNIS: "I'm not sure. Things mostly happen on a fast break after we've rebounded their shot on our basket. The coach wants me to push the play and get them in transition. He wants us to play really fast to create three versus two or two versus ones and off steals too, but I am still learning the team and how each guy plays. I'm off by centimeters in my passing. When the game's slower

I can play ... but the pace of play ... I'm fine in training but in games I can't seem to see the right things at the right time ..."

VIVIAN: "It sounds like you know what's going on but you're not sure exactly what's causing your errors. Maybe it's learning the players around you, maybe it's the situation ... maybe you're not sure."

They both drank their coffee.

VIVIAN: "It's my understanding you transferred to The U in the summer ... What made you move here?"

YANNIS: "My last coach was having personal problems and told me he was leaving. He set me up with Coach Landing and I moved here."

VIVIAN: "Okay, and how has the move here been for you?"

YANNIS: "To tell you the truth, not what I expected. The academics are harder. I thought I would do okay, but in the first two weeks of school I saw the difference. I liked my last school but, coming from Greece, I did not know the difference in schools here in the USA would be so great ... it's really a massive difference."

VIVIAN: "You take your academics seriously?"

YANNIS: "For sure. I want to be an engineer like my father, but I have to get the grades you know."

VIVIAN: "How much time are you giving to school?"

YANNIS: "As much as I can do. I mean these days it's more important to me than basketball because that's why I am here."

VIVIAN: "Does your coach know this?"

YANNIS: "No."

VIVIAN: "Do you think Coach Landing should know about this? He committed to you by recruiting you when he didn't have to."

YANNIS: "It's not like I am trying to screw the team. I try to give as much energy as I can to the game. I'm serious about my game, but right now I am struggling to balance things."

VIVIAN: "Okay, so balance is an issue for you. Tell me how much mental skills training you do these days? About how much visualization do you use?"

YANNIS: "I used to do it quite a lot in Greece but here not so much."

VIVIAN: "How well did it work for you?"

YANNIS: "Good. We used goal setting and visualization all the time. It was part of training with my men's team. But here it seems like no coaches use it, so I don't use it. I don't see any of the players using it either, so I think it's not important."

VIVIAN: "So you think it's not valued here and you don't need to use it. Do you really think that?"

YANNIS: "No, not really."

VIVIAN: "You're a bit confused about what to do here, but you know some other things might work you too."

Yannis nodded and they both sipped their coffee.

Discussion questions

1. What are the main issues affecting Yannis's performance?
2. What kinds of mental skills training might Yannis use to enhance his performance?
3. How might the team coaches and the sport psychology practitioner collaborate in this case for the benefit of Yannis and the team?
4. What might the role of the sport psychology practitioner be in this case?

Author's notes

This is the kind of case where I am likely to use a functional technical perspective. I am likely to use a cognitive appraisal model to understand the situation an athlete experiences from their own point of view. I find in real time using this kind of straightforward model is a strong first step to recognizing how personal and situational factors influence thoughts, emotions and behaviors. I prefer to use this kind of approach in a case like this because I feel it has the necessary elements to assess the issues. I can explain my approach easily to athletes and coaches using phrases that are jargon free, and it gives me a guide to inquire through.

Transitions like those outlined here can be planned and prepared for. An individual is leaving a mostly known situation; they pass through a process of arrival and begin again in a somewhat unknown situation. There are three phases in a transition, and it seems like this process was not necessarily managed effectively. Based on the facts of this case the Assistant Athletic Director seems to have some awareness of the difficulties Yannis might be facing because of the transition, which is not surprising because they are viewing the situation from the side. I might consult them during my process of working with Yannis.

Yannis seems to be experiencing difficulties adapting to the academic demands, and it appears possible his desire to achieve academically is greater than his motivation to commit to the basketball program in ways the head coach and his team needs him to. This is not to say he is not motivated to play basketball, but he has made the choice to engage with his academic studies more seriously than his sport because he might have underestimated the difficulty or overestimated his ability to cope with the academic challenges he was going to face. Solutions I might consider in this case would be to work with Yannis to profile his academic strengths and weaknesses and match him with enhanced academic support and tutoring through the university's student support services. In this case my role might be to help Yannis engage with the available resources to relieve pressure or stress he might experience concerning his studies.

This is a challenging situation because of the communication gaps between Yannis and his coaches. His coaches have information and awareness they might not have shared; likewise Yannis. Additionally, he is not playing well and is aware of his underperformance at key situations, unlike his coaches, who do not express an understanding of the specific nature of his errors. But they both see him not playing well. Yannis and his coaches have more in common than they are aware of. This seems like a classic situation of two or more elements of a team having information the other could benefit from to deepen understanding and enhance interpersonal relationships and reduce prickly and difficult interactions. Several solutions I might consider here include facilitating a meeting between Yannis and his coaches to have each express themselves openly from the starting point that both parties want Yannis to be successful. I favor processing the transition to The U first and helping everyone understand the process and its outcomes so far, then moving to discuss and learn about the important stressors the athlete faces, which in this case is the academic challenges. Finally, I would address the decision-making and concentration elements at key moments in the game with Yannis and foster a problem-solving session between Yannis and his coaches. Most importantly, I want: to address this issues using the strengths of the player and the coaches; to align and employ academic resources to support Yannis and create the conditions where the coaches can use their strengths to mitigate their own issues concerning Yannis's performance; and to work with him to get the best performance from him given the challenges of the transition.

Yannis has previous experience with sport psychology practices and achieved success using mental skills training. I would encourage him to fall back on his previous practices and begin to train them again in 10–15-minute goal setting and visualization on-court exercises. These activities would be aligned with the plays the team needs executed based on the task cues Yannis should perform in his role on the team.

In a situation like this there has to be tangible outcomes coming from the sport psychology consulting process: for example, decreased academic stress, grade point average maintenance (at least), and enhanced basketball performance based on the metrics the team uses. Additionally, informal attitude measures gained from Yannis and the coaching staff would be useful to evaluate the change over time from the interventions and meetings that took place. Sometimes external distractions have significant effects on student-athlete performance. By interviewing the athlete and knowing the underlying causes of cognitive disturbance and emotional responses it becomes clearer why Yannis acted the way he did and what measures might be taken to help him and his coaches reach an understanding for all to progress and achieve their goals.

Further reading

Baker, J., Côté, J., & Hawes, R. (2000). The relationship between coaching behaviours and sport anxiety in athletes. *Journal of Science and Medicine in Sport*, 3(2), 110–119.

Moran, A. P. (2016). *The psychology of concentration in sport performers: A cognitive analysis*. New York, NY: Psychology Press.

Wulf, G. (2013). Attentional focus and motor learning: A review of 15 years. *International Review of Sport and Exercise Psychology*, 6(1), 77–104.

13
COACH PERSONAL DEVELOPMENT

Introduction

This case introduces students to a common occurrence in NCAA sports, which is when a coach seems burned out: they are underperforming; their job might be at stake; and in general terms things are not going well for them. The coach in this case is an immigrant to the United States and is skeptical about sport psychology or counseling approaches. He holds the belief that counseling is something done *to* someone, not *with* them. He also holds the belief that counseling is problem focused, not solution oriented.

Content implications

This case might extend itself to discussions about coach burnout and alternative counseling approaches such as solution-focused and narrative therapies. You might even consider discussing self-management and lifestyle behavior change approaches in the context of sport, or consider conversations about leadership styles too.

Purpose

The purpose of this case is to consider the role of the sport psychology consultant working with a coach for the latter's personal development. It is possible in a college sport environment in specific sports which have a Eurocentric culture that foreign cultures will be found. Therefore, the challenges facing individuals in their sport, personal, and cultural lives have to be accounted for. This case aims to prompt discussion about these matters.

Student learning outcomes

At this end of this case study learning opportunity, students should be able to:

1. Identify the issues affecting the coach's performance
2. Select a counseling approach to respond to the coach's condition
3. Discuss variations in counseling approaches to coaches presenting issues
4. Discuss how a sport psychology practitioner might be effective in this kind of scenario

Cast of characters in order of appearance

Javier Aguilar, Sport Psychology Consultant.
Viktor Varga, Men's Water Polo Coach.

Coach profile: Viktor Varga, water polo

Viktor Varga has been the head water polo coach at The U for ten years. He was born in Hungary and completed his degree in physical education at a leading university in his home city of Budapest. He met his American-born wife (Cindy, from Minnesota) when she was on a yearlong study abroad program. When Cindy returned to America they kept their long-distance relationship going while Viktor played professional water polo for one of the oldest and most successful teams in the national league. At the same time Cindy qualified as a registered nurse, and while they would see each other during Cindy's holidays, things were tough for them. Viktor represented Hungary at water polo many times, but due to a shoulder injury his career ended after three seasons of top-flight competition, which also caused him to miss out on the 2000 Olympic Games. Cindy and Viktor got engaged in Budapest and married in Minneapolis in 2003.

Viktor was a quick study in his new home. He learned English quickly. He had contacts with American water polo coaches due his role on the Hungarian national team. His water polo network was based in California and he would attend and work at clinics there whenever he could. He was hired as water polo head coach at a private high school, where he coached boys and girls and taught physical education. In many ways it was his dream job because he and Cindy were settled, he was earning more money than he had ever earned before, and life was good. He settled in well with his colleagues at the high school and was well liked and respected. He brought a level of professionalism and fun the school was glad to have, and he had a demeanor his players enjoyed. They found he could be disciplined without being overbearing, although they also knew he was a bit rough and not always understanding of their American upbringing. But they also respected that he trained every day too. They knew his shoulder had been badly damaged, but through what glimpses they had of his ability they instantly saw his quality. In particular, Viktor was popular with the boys because he was athletic and would play around in the water. After all, he had grown up in a country emerging from the Cold War where rough and tumble for boys was normal and children were expected to sort themselves out in social situations including physically.

After four years of coaching the high school teams Viktor had become a favorite in the athletic department. He adapted to coaching girls too, and accepted advice and assistance from some of the mothers of his female players. Due to their reaching out to Viktor and including Cindy in the conversations Viktor was able to adapt himself to the girls' needs and coach them more effectively. Each year he got better and better in his coaching. He talked regularly with "the Mothers" (as he called them) and the team captains, and together they enjoyed enjoyable and successful seasons. Things were going well for Viktor when he saw an advertisement for a new position, with a new program doing what he was doing but at college level and with higher pay. Viktor had not forgotten what it felt like to be at a high level. He loved his life with Cindy and the opportunities he had, but nothing had replaced the feeling he got in the water or on the pool deck during the intensity of a match. He applied to the The U with the support of his high school principal, and beat out several candidates in a round of interviews to become the The U's first women's and men's water polo head coach. He presented a vision of what the program might look like, which led him to be responsible for building the program. Cindy and one of the Mothers helped him prepare and investigate the opportunity as thoroughly as he could.

It took five years for Viktor to build The U's program so that the teams were competitive. His learning curve—concerning recruitment; quality of players; coaching student-athletes; working with faculty members, administrators and sponsors; and always focusing on the big match against Barrow twice per year—was steep. In his eighth year Viktor finally won a men's NCAA national title, but the team leaders graduated and there was a gap in class which meant years nine and ten would be filled with freshmen and sophomores. Results were moderate and the emotional highs of the championship year were replaced by bad moods and disappointment. The women's team improved steadily and made the semi-finals for the national championships twice in the last four years, but performed flatly in the most recent season. Life had got very demanding. He and Cindy found family and work–life balance hard to achieve. Their kids, Lucas and Laura, were doing well in school but they had cut back on their own time together. Viktor gave up on his training too. He had gained weight, slept badly, did not enjoy his coaching every day, and, although he loved America, his family in Budapest had not seen him and his family for several years and his parents' health was not good. Viktor was 39 years of age and facing a midlife crisis.

The case

Viktor met Javier at his office in the small town of Lake Beyond the Hills. He did not want to meet Javier on campus. He preferred to see him on his way home after practice so he could use the drive home to wind down after what was his first ever meeting with a sport psychology counselor, and a person he did not know very well. He parked on the street about a 2-minute walk from the office in case anyone saw him going in or he had time to walk past or delay his approach. Javier was a licensed professional counselor and a certified sport psychology consultant; his regular practice was with anyone who presented with a mental health issue. Sports tended to be about 10–20 percent of his weekly clinical work and about 10 percent were workshops on campus. He worked on a retainer basis with The U, dealing with any team.

Viktor entered the reception area and checked to see if he knew anyone. He spoke to the front desk assistant, confirmed his appointment, and was told to take a seat. He decided if he saw someone he knew he would leave, but he sat down and waited. Just as he was getting comfortable, Javier walked from his right down a well-lit corridor colored with bright yellow and green hues.

JAVIER: "Hello Viktor, thank you for coming."

Javier smiled broadly and shook Viktor's hand. To Viktor it was as if Javier imagined they were friends. Javier was dressed casually in a black short-sleeve shirt, khaki pants, and brown loafers. He had thick black hair with silver streaks in it, and he wore a small stud in his left ear. Viktor was surprised by his appearance and wondered if he had already made a mistake coming here. Javier led him down the welcoming corridor to an office with several comfortable chairs and no couch. The room had large, broad windows looking out onto a garden; it had a clean whiteboard surrounded by pictures of children, people without names, coaches, and student-athletes Viktor knew.

JAVIER: "Viktor come in, sit down, choose a seat where you might be comfortable. We have an hour so make sure you choose the one you feel is right for you."

Javier sat down in an orange comfy chair at a 45-degree angle. Viktor chose to sit with his back to the corner and the window to his right so he could see out of it, see the door, and find his way out if he wanted to leave.

JAVIER: "Comfy?"
VIKTOR: "Yes, I am okay."
JAVIER: "Thank you for coming today. I appreciate you being on time and I recognize it might have been hard for you to be here today."

Viktor was taken aback by Javier's disarming response.

VIKTOR: "Thank you … No offense to you Javier, but this not what I had in mind when I went to the administration and they recommended I talk to you … I mean I don't understand what's going with me and how seeing a shrink is going to help me."
JAVIER: "I appreciate you do not feel like this might be for you and you have some doubts about how us being here might helpful to you right now."
VIKTOR: "Yeah."

JAVIER: "Viktor, what would be most helpful for us to talk about first?"
VIKTOR: "Tell me what we're going to do and how this is going to help me."
JAVIER: "I will do that. First though, can you tell me how much experience you have with sport psychology or counseling?"
VIKTOR: "Experience? None. In my home country we don't use therapy as a crutch like people do here. Only when people are not right in themselves and perhaps criminal do psychiatrists get involved. I never used one and I am embarrassed for being here. I hear our student-athletes see you. I tell them to come here because that's what happens here, people always talk about their experiences. But for me it is different and I don't understand what you can do for me that I can't do for myself."

Having said this Viktor felt a bit guilty for what he shared with Javier; after all, he had only met Javier a few minutes ago and now he was telling him how he felt about things. Javier nodded all the while he listened; he had heard this from sport coaches and athletes since he started working with The U.

JAVIER: "Hm, you're frustrated, you're here and you don't know what I can do for you. In fact the very thought of you being here makes you feel less for having done so."
VIKTOR: "Yeah. Can you tell me what we are going to do?"
JAVIER: "It depends. What would be most helpful for you to talk about Viktor? I am interested to know what you want for yourself while you are here, and to work together to see how we can collaborate on achieving the goals you have for yourself."

Viktor felt flipped around. He had attended this meeting expecting intensity and some form of interrogation, but what he got was not what he expected. He felt Javier was just being with him, just quietly sitting in the same space observing home. This made him uncomfortable.

VIKTOR: "Why aren't you asking me questions or trying to solve my problems?"
JAVIER: "That's not how this works. My role is to listen and help you see the solutions for yourself and help you decide what you want to do when you are ready to do it."
VIKTOR: "I can do that for myself."
JAVIER: "Sure you can do this, so tell me how are things working out for you these days if you are dealing with this yourself?"

Viktor felt himself tighten. Javier's tone was gentle but his question packed an emotional wallop. The truth was Viktor was not doing well; he was not himself and he did not know what to do in his life right now. He felt lost.

VIKTOR: "I am getting by, I am fine doing day to day things … I have my family, my work … things are good." Javier let the words linger and sat silently looking out of the window for a moment; then, as if compelled by an unseen force, Viktor leaned back in his chair, his neck arching backwards, expanding his chest. He hauled himself forward to stretch his hands above his ahead, took a deep breath, and sat down again.

JAVIER: "Comfy?"

Javier had watched this performance with curiosity but without surprise. In his experience it was normal for his clients to move around.

VIKTOR: "Yes, comfy."
JAVIER: "So how are things for you Viktor?"
VIKTOR: "Not so good."

He felt weight shifting and falling.

JAVIER: "Go on"
VIKTOR: "Well … I don't know what happened, one day I woke up and it was not 2003 anymore—it's now. I have a job, family, kids. I am fat, my teams don't win. I don't train. I don't see my family back home. I don't see my wife like I want to. I am getting older. I am not the man I used to be. I am getting soft and I am here now … what's good about any of that?"

Viktor bit his lip when he finished speaking as if he had committed a terrible crime.

VIKTOR: "I didn't mean it. I love my wife and kids. I love my life … I just … I just don't know what happened and I am here in this place with you. No offense."
JAVIER: "None taken."

They both sat quietly for what seemed like minutes to Viktor but in reality was about 30 seconds. This time Javier got up and moved to the whiteboard on the wall opposite the windows and clearly in Viktor's vision. Javier took a black marker and drew a line from one side of the board horizontally to the other side. At the top of the board he wrote the words 'My Life Story'.

JAVIER: "Viktor for me to help you I need to understand you. I cannot get into your head. I cannot tell you what to do, but if you are willing to tell me your story I believe I can help you identify some things that might give you relief. You're in pain right now and you seem a bit confused. Help me to know you and let's see how we can progress."
VIKTOR: "My life story? Nobody has ever asked me this before. How long do we have?"
JAVIER: "Well let's try to finish in 30 minutes, or do you have a two-volume story?" Viktor grinned. Javier drew lines and wrote words relating exactly as

Viktor spoke them. The board was full of notes, drawings, quotes, and a timeline showing Viktor his life as he said it was up to that moment. When the 30 minutes was up Javier and Viktor looked at the board in silence together. There were 10 minutes left in the session.

JAVIER: "So this is your story right now. When you look at it, what do you see?"

VIKTOR: "I see I have had a lot of transitions. I never really stopped to think about my life like this. I've really lived. I mean all the changes I have lived through, it's crazy. All the immigration stuff, kids, marriage, water polo … so much. I don't get how I'm here though. I suppose I'm tired of all the changes. It's crazy when I see what I have done and how far I have come. It makes me proud, but I also see problems."

JAVIER: "Viktor, what are the one or two things that you want to focus on, the problems you want solutions to?"

VIKTOR: "Well, I did not realize how much not training was affecting me. I swam since I was a baby. The pool, coaching and teaching, is in my blood—it's who I am. It affects everything and everyone in my life."

JAVIER: "You want to begin training?"

VIKTOR: "Yes but how? See for yourself, it is impossible. I'll never be able to manage it under these circumstances. I am trapped."

JAVIER: "Okay, which other issue up there on the board is really on your mind right now?"

VIKTOR: "I want to feel like I want my kids to see me healthy, fit, and strong like I used to be. You have no idea what it's like for me to be in this body now. I am puffy and soft. It's not good. I get on my athletes if they are not in shape. Look at me!"

Viktor pinched his body and grasped a thick wedge of belly skin.

JAVIER: "So you want to be in better shape, you want to be a role model for your kids, and you don't want to be a hypocrite?"

VIKTOR: "Exactly! Now, what can you do for me to help me with this?"

Viktor looked at the clock

VIKTOR: "Great! Now I have 3 minutes."

JAVIER: "Viktor, you identified important things tonight. If you have your cell phone, take a picture of this material. You can chew on it and we can discuss it first thing next week."

VIKTOR: "How do you know I am coming back?"

JAVIER: "Are you coming back next week?"

VIKTOR: "Yes, I'll be back, but you still have not assessed me, told me what is wrong and how you are going to fix me. But I learned some things. I don't know everything what I learned right now, but I think about it when I drive home—it will come to me."

They rose from their chairs and shook hands. As Viktor opened the door to leave, Javier continued.

JAVIER: "Don't worry. You're the last client here. Nobody's in the waiting room. You can leave by the front door."

Viktor did not mind Javier at all.

The week passed and Viktor reflected on his encounter with Javier. He talked about it with Cindy and she felt he made progress. As a nurse she was used to the idea of counseling and had known patients in her cardiac rehab clinic get good results from group counseling sessions during their rehabilitation programs.

The following week Viktor and Javier repeated the same greeting ritual as the first meeting. The photo of the whiteboard's content from the previous session was showing on Javier's tablet. He handed it to Viktor to look at.

JAVIER: "I'm glad you returned here. How was your week?"

Viktor examined the image of the timeline of his life on the tablet, expanding it on the touch screen to get a more detailed view.

VIKTOR: "Your handwriting needs to be bigger."
JAVIER: "True. So how have things been for you this week?"
VIKTOR: "Not bad, same old, same old …"
JAVIER: "Agh, so not as bad as last week?"
VIKTOR: "About the same … I talked to Cindy about things and she said I took a first step. She is always positive and supportive with me. Ever since we met she has been positive. It's one of the things I liked about her from the beginning. She is always looking for the bright things in life … it makes it tougher for her when I feel like this."
JAVIER: "You mean you feel guilty for feeling the way you do and you want it to have less effect on Cindy?"
VIKTOR: "Yes. The more I try not to think about things the more difficult the day is for me. I hate it. I feel like I am going crazy because I feel this stress."
JAVIER: "Go on."
VIKTOR: "Well this week my women's team had a game. They played and some of them gave a great effort and the others kinda did what they normally do. You know, they're consistent but not great players. We don't have too many of those kinds of players. We played well and we won, but not in the style I like. I wanted to explain how important it was to win with style, win perfectly if we can. But I could tell they don't care about that. They're happy just to get results. Sometimes it is very important to play with great style."
JAVIER: "You sound like you're happy with the result but not how it was achieved, and you want your players to care about style as much as you do."

VIKTOR: "Yeah, and it drives me crazy. When I was younger winning and style went together. These days I guess just winning is enough for people … sometimes I just want to tell them how things can be, how good they can be and how they can achieve great things if they work harder, listen more, and play perfectly … but I don't think they can handle the truth about what it takes."

Javier paused and looked at Viktor; the water polo coach looked very intense. His eyebrows were furrowed, his face tense, and his jaw set. The tablet had been set down on the small coffee table next to his chair tightly placed between it and the wall of windows.

JAVIER: "Viktor, are you talking to yourself out loud?"
VIKTOR: "What do you mean?"
JAVIER: "I am wondering if the standards you held for yourself for so long you fear slipping away and you are missing the experiences of the past. I am imagining you are feeling like those great days you had as a player and maybe as a coach are behind you, and you are concerned they are not coming back … is it possible that not training and your team not playing like you did are signs of losing something for you?"

Viktor drew back into his chair. He gazed out of the window and sighed. Javier had hit on something and Viktor felt it. He could not put words to it but he sensed himself getting upset. He took a breath.

VIKTOR: "Water polo, Cindy, my kids, and my family are my life. Not always in this order of course. I miss my family, my parents are getting older and cannot physically travel here, or afford to even if they could. I keep thinking about how things were. I hate the way I look … I mean look at me. I am fat. I used to be trim and feel strong every day, always on my game."
JAVIER: "It sounds like you are grieving for the life you had Viktor, and wondering who you are now and concerned for the way life is for you now."
VIKTOR: "Yes. Things suck right now."

Discussion questions

1. What do you think is going on in this case?
2. What do you think are the main issues presented in this case?
3. How might you determine what to focus on with Viktor?
4. How do you assess Javier's approach to counseling Viktor?
5. What challenges does this case present the sport psychology practitioner?
6. What counseling approaches might you use if you were presented with this case?

Author's notes

Working with Viktor would be a real challenge because he is a genuine person who cares deeply about the people around him and his coaching. His mind is clear about what is important in his life, and there is a sense he knows his values and purpose to himself—his family and his teams. However it seems like he is facing a life transition and experiencing anxiety, depression, grief, and physical change in different ways.

From a life perspective the prospect of his parents getting sicker and possibly dying is weighing on his mind. Focusing on his wife and children is essential for him, and his physical self is important to his self-image and optimal feeling. He also wants more from his water polo team. He is focused on the past quite a bit too, and the sense of loss feels real to him.

My impression is that this is a mindset and lifestyle intervention in the making. The challenge I see here is knowing what to focus on first with Viktor and keeping him attentive to the process. He is skeptical of counseling, so pushing or pulling too much could tip him over and send him away. A gentle approach is required; in this way I prefer to adopt a values clarification process first to elicit from Viktor the vision he has for his life going forward. I would likely adopt an adaptive counseling approach of awareness raising, education, homework, and reflection utilizing motivational interviewing, cognitive behavioral therapy (CBT), and solution-focused therapy. One area I might go for quite early on is working with Viktor to identify ways he might be more physically active. My sense is that his physical identity is linked to his mood, self-esteem, and perception of his life.

By utilizing a broad set of approaches to engage Viktor and help him process his experience and make progress, I feel more comfortable focusing exclusively on his needs. I would not engage any team members or sport administration until I gained Viktor's trust and he expressed readiness for this to happen (it might not even happen, but the option to do so should remain). I might seek to engage Cindy in the process at some point too. Her influence is positive and strong, and I see that Viktor values her input greatly. Cindy is an asset in helping Viktor's development.

Working with Viktor might involve an extended period, possibly up to a year, to see him through two seasons of play and help him adjust towards his 40th birthday too.

Further reading

Fletcher, D., & Scott, M. (2010). Psychological stress in sports coaches: A review of concepts, research, and practice. *Journal of Sports Sciences*, 28(2), 127–137.

Sharp, L. A., & Hodge, K. (2013). Effective sport psychology consulting relationships: Two coach case studies. *Sport Psychologist*, 27(4), 313–324.

Sharp, L. A., Hodge, K., & Danish, S. (2015). Ultimately it comes down to the relationship: Experienced consultants' views of effective sport psychology consulting. *Sport Psychologist*, 29(4), 358–370.

Stebbings, J., Taylor, I. M., & Spray, C. M. (2011). Antecedents of perceived coach autonomy supportive and controlling behaviors: Coach psychological need satisfaction and well-being. *Journal of Sport and Exercise Psychology*, 33(2), 255–272.

14
EATING DISORDER

Introduction

This case concerns the eating disorder bulimia nervosa. However, the disorder is purposely not named so that the instructor can prompt and probe their students to identify the symptoms and signs of this particular condition. This allows the instructor to introduce other conditions like anorexia nervosa and muscle dysmorphia into the discussion as comparisons to the condition described here. The case is written so that students have a third-person view of an unfolding situation facing three characters. Two characters (David and Thompo) are members of the Performance and Sport Medicine Team (PSMT) at Unity University; the third (Jenny) is a student-athlete one of the PSMT suspects may be experiencing bulimia nervosa.

Students are often presented with characters and cases concerning eating disorders which are clear and unambiguous. This case presents the complexity of the conversations, ideas, and thoughts leading the characters to operate the way they do around this issue. Cases usually employ characters with well-established behaviors, but this case takes a different approach. The emphasis here is on early intervention, and while criticisms might be levelled at David and Thompo for their words and actions, David shows care and leadership in this respect.

The final part of this case leads David to the Athletic Department's sport psychology consultant. This is done deliberately so that students can approach the case on two levels. First, it is common for sport psychology consultants to be approached by other trained and licensed professionals in sport performance and sport medicine for feedback and guidance. Students should be exposed to peer-to-peer communication and consider the qualities and expectations concerning these types of interactions. Second, the sport psychology consultant has a role to play in this case, particularly if they are a licensed or accredited mental health professional in some form. It is possible Jenny and her team mates might be referred to the sport psychology consultant, or to another provider.

Students should be encouraged to consider how they might operate given the training path they are currently on. For example, students preparing to become licensed mental health professionals might approach the case differently than students working to attain a sport performance-focused credential. The case finishes with David seeking out the sport psychology consultant and is left deliberately open-ended so that you can facilitate your class discussion in the direction you want it to go.

Content implications

The case takes the point of view that the student-athletes engaged in the behaviors shown are quite new to acting in the ways described. Issues that are embedded in this case include, but are not limited to, scope of practice, professional conduct, body image, labeling, stereotyping, biases (gender, race, sport, and ethnicity), sport demands, coaching behavior, team dynamics, weight expectations, professional preparation, and training of sport and performance professionals. It is possible students will find links between the content, characters, and the solutions you and I did not consider, which is one reason for using the teaching case method.

Purpose

The purpose of this case is to encourage students to consider how to approach athletes and sport medicine professionals about eating disorders and the issues they present so that they can determine the role and scope of practice for a sport psychology practitioner who is an unlicensed mental health professional.

Student learning outcomes

At this end of this case study learning opportunity, students should be able to:

1. Correctly identify the different symptoms of eating disorders
2. Recognize the influences on the decision-making of a student-athlete to engage in eating disordered behavior
3. Demonstrate a critical understanding of the ways to approach an individual showing eating disordered behavior
4. Demonstrate an understanding of the role and responsibilities of a sport psychology consultant faced with an eating disorder-related case

Cast of characters in order of appearance

David Dean, Athletic Trainer, Swimming and Diving.
Mike "Thompo" Thompson, Assistant Head Coach, Strength and Conditioning.
Jenny Yang, Women's Diving.

Athlete profile: Jenny Yang, women's diving

Jenny Yang is a sophomore on the Unity University diving team. She is originally from Shanghai, China, and moved to the United States when she was three years old because her mother married an American business executive. Before she started diving she was an enthusiastic ballet dancer and gymnast. Since she was very young she had been attracted to aesthetic movement and music. She loved how her body felt when she moved through the air. She found the sport of diving by accident as a freshman at high school in Illinois. She had heard from her friends the sport was fun and she should try out. They told her the coach was easy to get along with. Jenny found the coach very positive and supportive to all the high school team members and rarely put pressure on the divers. The coach focused on improvement, learning, and enjoying the sport. Jenny thrived in her high school team and her academic performance improved too. In her junior year, Jenny performed very well at several events, and a number of colleges in the Midwest courted her for their diving teams.

By her senior year, Jenny decided to join Unity University because it offered three things she really liked: she wanted to study music and art in the art history department; she wanted to continue playing the violin and there were opportunities to play in The U's orchestra; and the diving team seemed to operate like her high school team did. She was not going to receive an athletic scholarship, and her parents were going to pay for her tuition for the first two years of school. Jenny and her parents agreed she would take a small part-time job or volunteer in her junior year to get some experience of the work world. Her career ambition was to become a curator at one of the 'big' museums in the US or China. After all, she spoke English and Mandarin fluently.

The case

It was Monday morning and David Dean was sitting in his favorite chair in the training room. He looked up from the most recent report from the NCAA about the prevalence of eating disorders in student athletes. He felt a bit overwhelmed at its findings, which claimed that 25 percent of female student athletes experience eating disordered conditions. Female athletes in aesthetic sports like gymnastics, synchronized swimming, and diving—where technical and artistic qualities are the basis for judged performance—are more likely to experience these conditions than other athletes such as lacrosse or tennis players. David was feeling frustrated by this knowledge because one of his teams was women's diving and he had suspected for a month or two that things were going on with the athletes' eating patterns but he could not put his finger on it. He noticed several of the girls seemed to be hiding food and being very careful not to eat in front of anyone else apart from one or two of their closest team mates. In particular he noticed that Clara, Jenny, and Sara seemed to be in on this behavior together, but not at every snack or meal time. He also noticed that these divers in particular went to the bathroom at irregular times; there seemed to be no pattern to this, whether they competed at home or away.

He read on and learned that restrictive eating, excessive concerns about body weight, shape and appearance, and laxative abuse were signs of eating disordered behavior. David felt a little confused; this was his second year working with the women's diving team and he felt he was still getting to know the athletes. There were ten team members—3 seniors, 2 juniors, 4 sophomores, and 1 freshman. The team had two full-ride scholarship athletes, one freshman and one senior. David faced difficulties in his first year, more so with the incoming freshman than the juniors and seniors who had seen him around the training room. He leaned on his knees with the pages of the report drooping in front of him. He was gazing at the top of the last page he read, thinking about the team, when Mike Thompson arrived.

THOMPO: "Morning' Dave. Man, you looked zoned out. What's up with you this morning? It's the start of a big week, we've got men's soccer and women's volleyball ... and your girls are diving this week in a conference match up. Why be so miserable? ... This is why we're here. It's another day at The U!"

David liked Thompo but he found him too chipper sometimes.

DAVID: "How much do you know about eating disorders Thompo?"
THOMPO: "Not too much. I mean I focus on the athletes making weight and being healthy. Why, what's up?"
DAVID: "I'm not sure, but I think there might be some women's diving athletes who are having difficulties with their eating?"
THOMPO: "What do you mean difficulties with their eating?"
DAVID: "I mean I've seen some things with the team that have me concerned?"
THOMPO: "Dave, have you talked to any of the girls?"
DAVID: "I'm not sure how to ask them. I mean it's tricky. The female athletes I work with have seemed sensitive to conversations about food, weight, and all that ..."
THOMPO: "Listen ... if I was you Dave, I would talk to one of the girls you feel is having these food difficulties and ask them some questions ... of course be careful but if you don't talk to them you won't know will you?"

David thought ahead to the training session this afternoon; the conference match up was in four days. He wondered who might be the best athlete to talk to. Since she came to The U last year he noticed Jenny Yang seemed to be well adjusted; she had a lively personality, she was smart and really enjoyed being part of the diving team. They had several conversations over the 16 months she had been part of the team. He helped her recover from a repetitive wrist injury, allowing her to compete in the 3-meter platform event, which was her favorite. David decided he would "check in" with Jenny to set up a longer meeting later, when he planned to ask Jenny a few questions to check his assumptions about her behavior.

David duly spoke to Jenny before training and explained he wanted to talk to her as a routine check-in during the season. They agreed to talk in the training room after the training session.

JENNY: "Hello David, what's up?"

Jenny smiled and sat down in David's favorite seat. David sat on the bench opposite where the athletes normally sit when he talks to them.

DAVID: "Hi Jenny, thanks for coming in ... So, how's life for you this semester?"

Other athletes and trainers were entering and exiting the training room. David saw one of Jenny's team mates go into Thompo's area.

JENNY: "It's good."
DAVID: "Just good?"
JENNY: "Yeah, you know, same old, same old."
DAVID: "So what's new with you?"
JENNY: "Not much."

David was feeling awkward and Jenny was wondering why she was there.

JENNY: "So, what's up David, what did you want to talk about?"

David was relieved Jenny asked the question.

DAVID: "Well Jenny it's a bit delicate ..."
JENNY: "Go on"
DAVID: "Well, I've been noticing some things going on with you, Clara, and Sara and I wondered if we could talk about them?"

Jenny stiffened and shifted in the seat. She grabbed for her water bottle in her kit bag and clutched it tightly to her body.

JENNY: "What do you mean things you've seen?"
DAVID: "I mean I've noticed some things you have been doing with your eating and the crazy bathroom schedule you keep around training and competition."
JENNY: "Wait, what? What are you talking about?"

Jenny sat back and stared at David.

DAVID: "I've seen you hiding you're eating, and it seems like there might be something going on."

Jenny was startled by David's direct questioning.

JENNY: "You brought me here to talk about this? How is that fair David? How is this right?"

Just as Jenny spoke, her team mate came out of the strength and conditioning room and headed toward the training room. David sensed from Jenny's angry and upset response he was losing control of the situation. He already felt uncomfortable with this situation.

DAVID: "Jenny, I'm not accusing you of anything. I'm just worried something is going on with you, Clara, and Sara. It's my job to monitor the health of the team and report what I know to my boss and the head coach."

Jenny sat straight up, still clutching her water bottle. Tears rolled down her cheeks.

JENNY: "I don't really want to talk to you about this. It's private."
DAVID: "Can you tell me anything that is going on?"

Just as David spoke, Jenny's team mate walked into the training room without saying anything, just glancing at David's serious looking face as she walked into the back room to pick snacks off the table by the back wall. As she bent over to grab her snacks she looked over her shoulder and met Jenny's gaze. She got her food and walked out, nodding at Jenny on her way through the door.

DAVID: "I'm sorry Jenny. This is not the best place for this kind of conversation."
JENNY: "Close the door."
DAVID: "Sure."

David turned, stretched out his right arm, and pushed the swing door closed.

JENNY: "I've never been like this before."
DAVID: "What do you mean?"
JENNY: "It started about five months ago in the summer."
DAVID: "What started?"
JENNY: "When we did our end-of-year exit interviews with Coach Paula, she told all of us individually that to be more competitive we had to manage our body weight more and not to look 'soft.' It was kind of tricky. I mean, look at me ... I'm already skinny ... at high school sometimes my friends would call me 'Bones' because sometimes I would be so thin. I knew they were joking, but it still kinda hurt."
DAVID: "Go on ..."
JENNY: "Clara, Sara, and I texted each other. We really like being on the team. It's how we met each other, and Sara especially loves being on the team. She

would do anything to be more competitive. So we decided to … you know … do some things to control our weight. At first it was just dieting; we texted each other and started a private Facebook page posting our eating habits and encouraging each other to keep our eating in check. It was really hard to get my weight down … they found it hard too. By the time we got back to summer training we were all around the same weight give or take an ounce or two. Then Coach told us monthly weigh-ins were going to be started this semester as an incentive. So every final Friday of the month we weigh in."

DAVID: "So you're feeling a lot of pressure to manage your weight for the diving team?"

JENNY: "Yeah … but things have got tough in the last few weeks. Sara is really going for it. She's trying to get down to a body fat count of 12 percent before the weigh-in. I'll never make that but I am supporting her."

DAVID: "How's that?"

JENNY: "I mean I'm around and I do some of the things she does, but I don't want my hands to suffer because of my violin playing."

David listened attentively. He was aware he had started a conversation he could not finish.

DAVID: "Jenny can you give me a minute? I need to go to the bathroom."

David pushed through the swing door, turned left, and walked to the bathroom. As he was going in Thompo was coming out. David motioned Thompo back into the bathroom.

DAVID: "Can I talk to you Thompo?"

THOMPO: "Sure."

DAVID: "Listen, I spoke to one of the divers about this thing that's on my mind. It feels bigger than I can handle."

Thompo nodded and snorted gently.

THOMPO: "Is it in their head? Those girls, they've always got something going on. Try the shrink."

DAVID: "You mean the sport psychology consultant?"

THOMPO: "Yeah, if that's what they're called these days."

DAVID: "Where would I find the shrink's details? I don't think I've ever met them?"

THOMPO: "Not surprising you've not met them, they typically only get called for urgent things with the aquatics program."

DAVID: "Do you think I should call them now, just before the competition this week?"

THOMPO: "It's your call Dave; you started this, it's up to you."

With that, Thompo walked on. David dried his hands and returned to the training room. As he pushed the door he glanced down and saw Jenny's thumbs moving quickly on the phone. He sat down on the bench and noticed Jenny had drunk about a third of her water in the time they'd been apart.

DAVID: "Thanks for telling me your story Jenny. I'm inexperienced with this kind of thing. I'm not really sure I know what I'm doing here … I'm concerned for you and the others. What do you think we should do now?"
JENNY: "I don't think we should do anything. Sara's already upset I told you what's going on. We don't want any trouble especially, with Coach Paula."

Discussion questions

1. What is going on in this case?
2. Which eating disorder is central to this case?
3. What is the role of the sport psychology consultant in this case?
4. What is the scope of practice for a sport psychology consultant when facing a case concerning eating disordered behavior?
5. How do you feel David and Thompo conducted themselves in this case?
6. What course of action would you recommend David take in this case?
7. How might you deal with Jenny when you meet with her?
8. What else is going on in this case that might be important for David, Thompo or anyone else connected to the case to address?

Author's notes

Knowing the difficulties and challenges eating disorder behaviors present for the individual experiencing them and the possible affects these can have on bystanders, I would approach this by completing a thorough interview with David to understand the full scope of the issue from his perspective. Depending on the outcome, I would prefer to talk to Jenny myself with David present. I would choose this way forward because they had a preexisting relationship, and Jenny and I might not have a strong enough relationship for us to get to the issue in a comfortable way for Jenny. I would want to approach this situation gently, carefully, and with compassion to focus on understanding the issues from Jenny's point of view.

Also depending on the outcome of the interview, I would seek out and talk with Sara and Clara using the same approached as with Jenny. As a non-licensed mental health provider, I would simultaneously contact a trusted mental health counselor skilled in working with eating disorder cases. This would help me make a referral for the student-athlete at the time if they were willing to take it as a next step solution for them. The considerations I would have about the referral would include the licensing of the provider, their location, and their affiliation with the institution. Each of these variables can act as a barrier to attendance and adherence by a client; but they can also attract a client depending on the peace of mind, convenience, and optimism the individual approaches the referral with.

I would prepare to talk with the women's diving coach about their understanding of the situation and their perceived role in it. My goal would be to raise their awareness of how they can support the athletes in the future. If the behavior seems persistent and damaging I would refer one of more of the athletes. Jenny's information about Sara would be particularly important in this instance, and I would have to be particularly sensitive to Sara's experience and how I approached her about her behavior.

In a case like this, I would expect to have ethics and boundaries challenged, and I would have to keep in mind who my client is. The issue is presented by David, but I see the student-athlete as the client because they are the direct recipient of my efforts. But there are indirect clients too. At the same time, I will need to have respectful and useful relationships with both the head coach of women's diving and with Thompo. This particular case reminds me that coaches and sport medicine professionals might need detailed and specific education to raise awareness of the variety of eating disorders they can unknowingly promote in athletes, causing negative effects on their health, wellbeing, and performance.

Cases like this require a lot of communication in different ways to many individuals. I would expect to communicate the same facts to each person in a different way with a different expected outcome from the conversations. In my view, my first responsibility is to the student-athlete; therefore, my communication has to be aimed at enhancing their condition and then working to take steps to prevent this kind of situation happening again with the team, coach, sport medicine team and the necessary representatives from the athletic administration.

Further reading

Turocy, P. S., DePalma, B. F., Horswill, C. A., Laquale, K. M., Martin, T. J., Perry, A. C., & Utter, A. C. (2011). National athletic trainers' association position statement: safe weight loss and maintenance practices in sport and exercise. *Journal of Athletic Training*, 46(3), 322–336.

Greenleaf, C., Petrie, T. A., Carter, J., & Reel, J. J. (2009). Female collegiate athletes: prevalence of eating disorders and disordered eating behaviors. *Journal of American College Health*, 57(5), 489–496.

Ismailova, D., & Gazdowska, Z. (2016). Eating disorders in sport: Review of prevalence, risk factors, and studies of eating disorders in highly competing athletes. *Journal of Education, Health and Sport*, 6(6), 351–358.

Voelker, D. K., Petrie, T. A., Neumann, C. S., & Anderson, C. M. (2016). Psychosocial factors as longitudinal predictors of bulimic symptomatology among female collegiate athletes. *Psychology of Sport and Exercise*, 26, 123–129.

15
BINGE DRINKING

Introduction

This is a richly complex case involving a student-athlete who is self-sufficient and experienced in life looking out for themselves and taking responsibility for their behaviors; but they are at odds with their coach and show a calculating and aware approach to their addictive behaviors.

Content implications

This case provides the platform for discussions concerning: functional alcohol and gambling behavior, interpersonal relationships, mandated counseling, health behavior change, motivational interviewing, and the role and scope of a sport psychology professional.

Purpose

The purpose here is for students to consider the complexities of a case from a range of viewpoints, roles, and conditions in order to determine how they might operate in difficult interpersonal and behavioral conditions and remain effective.

Student learning outcomes

At the end of this case students should be able to:

1. Discuss effective ways to work with individuals presenting lifestyle issues affecting athletic performance
2. Consider different approaches to working with a complex case

3. Recognize the scope of practice for a sport psychology practitioner
4. Discuss how to approach a client mandated to attend counseling
5. Recognize the effects of counseling behaviors on treatment processes
6. Relate their approach to working with issues concerning alcohol use

Cast of characters in order of appearance

Robin Marriot, Head Coach, Men's Soccer.
Drake Payton, Men's Soccer.
Michelle Ball, Graduate Intern, Counseling Center.

Athlete profile: Drake Payton, men's soccer

Drake Payton is a fifth-year senior having been redshirted because of injury in his freshman year. He took a gap year between high school and college to travel around the United States, and he is the oldest member of the men's soccer team. After his senior year in high school he went to a soccer camp in the Midwest well known for college coach scouting, and it was here Robin Marriot, The U's head coach of men's soccer, saw him play. Drake played in center midfield, and was his usual highly combative self. Drake saw himself as a ball winner and distributor with an eye for long-range efforts on goal. Throughout the camp he was one of the most consistent players in his position, making good decisions and few errors, chipping in with a goal here and there. He was feisty and commanded respect for his athleticism, composure, and commitment in play. Robin did not see Drake much off the field, apart from a couple of conversations about possibly going to The U to play. Drake agreed on the spot after the first conversation, which surprised Robin. Drake agreed with his new head coach that he would take a year off and then join the team. While not ideal for The U, Robin Marriot agreed to this because of the promise Drake's play showed, and his potential as an asset to the team.

Drake's decision to take a year off came after a high school experience punctuated by his parents' bitter divorce which left him Drake his father and his sister with their mother. Drake then witnessed his dad go through several relationships with other women soon after the marriage break-up. His dad drank heavily once or twice a week, and although not physically abusive, was often extremely critical of his son. Drake often chose to stay at school to do his homework and his regular training (and extra if he could), or he would just drive around. He felt quite isolated in his hometown. He got on with his teachers and team mates but never felt confident enough to share what was going on at home. He talked to his sister whenever he could. His mother was also drinking heavily, and more regularly than his father. She lost her job after the divorce but landed another but much lower-paid job, which meant selling the family home and moving herself and her daughter to a smaller home in an unfamiliar part of town where they had no friends.

Over time, Drake developed significant self-reliance. He felt he had to look after himself, so he worked through high school, including double shifts during the summer vacations to pay for a beat-up car. His goal was to escape his life. He invested time in his relationships with academic counselors, and his teachers would often remark that he was a 17-year-old with a 37-year-old's mindset. What he could not get at home he would get elsewhere.

Drake loved his soccer and he was a good student in high school. He wanted a break from both for a while and, although playing at college was somewhat of a goal, he went to the summer camp because of a teacher's recommendation. The same teacher was his coach who gave him confidence and support—which had more benefit to Drake than the teacher knew.

Drake's plan was to drive around the United States and play men's open league soccer and get by with jobs he could pick up. He thought it would be fun to play in North Carolina for one season and then drive across the country to play in California. He imagined he could explore and experience life, keep fit, and maintain his college eligibility. In the year between high school and college Drake grew up even more. He developed a lifestyle of responsibility and recklessness wherever he was. On one hand, in his jobs and soccer he was on top of things—he made friends and his co-workers and bosses liked him. On the other hand, away from these responsibilities, he had a series of short-term relationships and alcohol binges—but never when he thought it would affect work or soccer. However, when he drank, he went all out—and mostly in the company of strangers.

Over the year Drake experienced a series of high points. He was rewarded with good work and team relationships. He had developed great confidence in dating women, and believed he could cope with his drinking so that it would not affect his life. Things were good until he joined The U's soccer team and fell badly and dislocated his shoulder at the end of pre-season before the first exhibition game. His introduction to life at The U would be from the bench.

The case

Robin Marriot met Drake Payton alone at his office on the first day of pre-season training.

ROBIN: "You know why you're here, right?"
DRAKE: "Yeah."
ROBIN: "I'm sick of your bullshit Drake! If you want to play this year, get your shit sorted out. If I'd known when I saw you at that summer camp that you'd caused me headaches every year there's no way I would have recruited you. It's just been one mess after another with you. You just don't get it, do you? You just don't get it … you have talent, but boy do you have attitude. You think this shit is gonna fly anymore? No way!"

Drake looked his coach up and down. He had heard this kind of thing when he was growing up but now, at 24 years of age, he knew how to let it roll off his back.

DRAKE: "Look Coach, what do you need me to do?"
ROBIN: "To do? Get your shit together. I can't believe you got a second driving under the influence [DUI] charge. I bailed your ass out of the first one in your sophomore year and I thought we were done. But this time, you just had to go further didn't you? You just needed to push things out there. Remind me just what you got for this go around with the law."
DRAKE: "I got a $390 fine plus about $150 costs, 18 months' probation, suspended 1-month jail—and another mouthful from the judge."
ROBIN: "You just don't seem to give a shit do you?"
DRAKE: "Coach, I'm here, I want to play. What do you want me to do?"
ROBIN: "Do you even care how much effort I've put into you since you've been here? It's been one screw-up after another. I don't understand you at all. You do well in school, you do well in sport, and you totally screw up your personal life. What the hell is wrong with you? I mean, what have I done to deserve your irresponsible behavior?"
DRAKE: "You see Coach, that's your problem. You think this is about you when it's about me. You think I wronged you or I'm out to get you. You're in your own world Coach. That's your problem. When I'm here, I'm with the team. You know that, I know that, but you're too closed minded to see what's around you."
ROBIN: "My problem, what's my problem? You're the one with the problem son."
DRAKE: "I don't have any problems Coach."

The coach laughed out loud and shook his head.

ROBIN: "Listen Drake, I know what you have not told me."
DRAKE: "Oh yeah, what's that?"
ROBIN: "That you've got to attend mandatory alcohol treatment programming and have a breathalyzer installed in your car until your alcohol intake drops to 0.02."
DRAKE: "You did your homework Coach. That's all true."
ROBIN: "You don't seem to care about this at all."
DRAKE: "Coach, it's not that. It's just that you're just a coach, nothing more, and let's be real about this. The only thing you ever care about is the effect on the team. You're a soccer guy, you never related to me and you never will. You never showed a real interest in me, so why should I give a care about you?"
ROBIN: "Well maybe I'll give you something to care about now. If you want to play, on top of the program the court ordered you to do, I want you to go the counseling center this week and next week, and every week of the season to

work on yourself. I might not know you, but it doesn't mean I don't want something better for you."

DRAKE: "Okay Coach, I'll go if it means playing."

ROBIN: "You're damn right you will. I already made the appointment. You're going to go tomorrow morning at 9am after practice, then at the same time every week for 12 weeks. I know your class schedule too, so just show up and do as you're told."

DRAKE: "Twelve weeks! Okay Coach."

Drake snorted in disbelief.

ROBIN: "How are you going to pay your court fees?"

DRAKE: "From my winnings?"

ROBIN: "Your winnings? What does that mean?"

DRAKE: "I played a few hands of poker over the summer and won more than I lost. I got it covered."

ROBIN: "Geez! There's no end to you is there?"

DRAKE: "Nope."

ROBIN: "Get out Drake!"

DRAKE: "Surely will Coach."

Drake left Robin's office. The coach felt empty and exasperated; he could not remember being that angry at any player before. He thought he had done the right thing: tough love was what Drake needed, just like he got as a boy from his father, and just like he gave his own kids when he felt they needed it.

Drake showed up at The U's counseling center 10 minutes early. He had not drunk since the night of his DUI two months ago. He was scheduled to see a new graduate sport psychology intern for the first time. As he sat in the waiting room he wondered if the person he was going to work with had any idea about how they were going to approach him. This was not his first time in the counseling center. His coach had made him go after the first DUI. He met an intern then and flirted with her in every meeting they had over six weeks. At the end of the sessions he got what he wanted, which was a date. It did not go further, but he reached his goal. Perhaps he would be lucky again this time he thought.

Michelle Ball walked into the waiting room and called out for Drake Payton. They looked at each other. Michelle was dressed formally and looked organized and professional; Drake was in his tracksuit from practice, but wore deodorant in case the counselor was attractive as he wanted to make a good impression.

MICHELLE: "Come on through Drake."

Michelle shook his hand and led him to her office. She showed Drake to his seat and closed the door. She sat down opposite and took a pad of paper and a pen and set them on her lap.

MICHELLE: "Thanks for arriving on time Drake, especially from practice."
DRAKE: "No problem."
MICHELLE: "It's my understanding you know I'm an intern here under the supervision of Javier Aguilar, who works with some of the teams here at The U. I'm going to record our time together so that we can review my work and discuss things for next time. I'm going to start recording, okay?"
DRAKE: "Sure."
MICHELLE: "Do you know why you're here?"
DRAKE: "Yeah. Do you?"
MICHELLE: "Yes, your soccer coach called on Friday and told me and my supervisor about what happened with you and that you got a second DUI with several conditions."
DRAKE: "Yeah, but let's talk a bit about you. You know me. Let me get to know you a bit."
MICHELLE: "Sure. I'm a doctoral student from another college. I'm here for the academic year completing my internship. I used to be a physical education teacher but I wanted a bit more than what I was doing, so I enrolled in school and now I'm studying to become a licensed professional counselor focusing on health and sport."
DRAKE: "Nice. You married?"
MICHELLE: "Yes."
DRAKE: "How long?"
MICHELLE: "Since college. Why, is that an issue for you?"
DRAKE: "No. Just curious."
MICHELLE: "Okay, so you know a little about me, tell me a little bit about your situation Drake. How did you come to be here today?"
DRAKE: "Well, no offense Michelle, but I didn't want to be here. I was told to be here."
MICHELLE: "I understand this is not your favorite thing to do right now Drake, but tell me a bit more."
DRAKE: "That's right. I mean this DUI thing is bullshit. I was at 0.08, right at the level. That female cop had it in for me. I think she wanted a date or something. So, no offense but this whole thing with my coach and you is overkill. I've already been found guilty."
MICHELLE: "You do understand what you did was against the law right?"
DRAKE: "Yeah."
MICHELLE: "So how come you did it twice?"
DRAKE: "Are you setting me up here to make me angry?"
MICHELLE: "No, I just want to be clear that you know the law."
DRAKE: "Yes. Of course I know the law. It's my second time. I suppose you know from my coach that this happened before."
MICHELLE: "Yes. How have things changed since the first time for you?"
DRAKE: "You mean in school, soccer ... what?"
MICHELLE: "I mean in your life."

DRAKE: "Oh ... well I got a bar job that pays great tips when I'm not playing soccer and it allows me to get out and play some poker after hours. In the summer I make good money when I work the weekends and I go to the casino and play a few hands. This summer I did really well. My best winning yet."
MICHELLE: "How often do you drink when you play cards?"
DRAKE: "I never drink when I play cards. I focus. You can't play well if your mind's gone."
MICHELLE: "So it's like soccer and school for you. When you have a job to do you focus and it takes priority."
DRAKE: "Yeah, you could say that."
MICHELLE: "How are things different when you drink?"

Drake paused and rubbed his face and looked away from Michelle. He was not prepared for the questions he was being asked.

DRAKE: "What do you mean different?"
MICHELLE: "Well, I'm wondering if there's something different going on with you because you seem capable and confident in areas of your life where there's some kind of performance to give, and I'm wondering if there's something about life outside of this that's uncomfortable for you."
DRAKE: "I wouldn't say uncomfortable really."
MICHELLE: "Okay, what would you say?"
DRAKE: "I would say it's none of your business why I drink, and it's got nothing to do with me being here at The U or being in this room with you."
MICHELLE: "You're upset. What was it about what I asked you that made you feel angry?"
DRAKE: "I don't want to talk about it."
MICHELLE: "Okay, but I don't know what 'it' is."

Drake could feel his body tensing. He wanted to escape the room. This exchange was not going as he wanted and he felt like he was being cornered.

DRAKE: "I don't want to talk about it."
MICHELLE: "Okay Drake. Perhaps another time. Can you give me an idea of how your drinking happens? Don't tell me what causes it; just give me a picture of how you go about it."

Drake felt much more comfortable with this line of questioning because of his court experiences.

DRAKE: "I drink alone. Somewhere between eight and nine drinks. I like beer but I prefer shots of straight bourbon; sometimes I'll chase them down with a beer ... on average I'd say about once or twice a month, or more depending on my responsibilities."

MICHELLE: "Thank you for sharing that with me."
DRAKE: "No problem."

Drake felt at ease relating the facts. This was the easy part for him.

MICHELLE: "Do you mind if I give you some feedback Drake?"
DRAKE: "Feedback, like what, telling me I have a drink problem?"
MICHELLE: "No, I mean, can I share some understanding of your situation and then you tell me if I'm on the wrong track."
DRAKE: "Doesn't sound too bad. Go ahead."
MICHELLE: "It sounds like you binge drink, but I don't get the sense you're rebelling against someone or you're curious about alcohol. You are an experienced drinker and I see that you're confident, and peer pressure doesn't seem to influence you either. You get along with people and you're not a loner, but I wonder how much your drinking is to cope with something else, and the something else is the 'it' you don't want to talk about with me."

Michelle's reflection shook Drake to his core. She was the first person for some time who seemed to understand what might be going on with him. He felt scared and nervous that he might let slip what was on his mind and his personal demons that led him to drink. He did not want to give in to Michelle's invitation to confirm or deny her thoughts, so he sat looking at her with as little emotional expression as possible—showing he was alive and present but sharing nothing to give the intern the satisfaction she might be onto something important.

Discussion questions

1. What are the issues presented in this case?
2. What is the role of a licensed mental health practitioner in a complex case like this?
3. What is the scope of practice of an unlicensed sport psychology practitioner in a case like this?
4. How might the source of referral influence the therapeutic relationship?
5. How might you work with Drake over the course of the soccer season?

Author's notes

I would approach Drake carefully and somewhat cautiously. I would need to check in with myself and my beliefs and attitudes concerning drinking and drinking and driving. This is because I would want to avoid potential traps like judging, shaming, or blaming Drake. These behaviors would get in the way of the communication between me the Drake, and potentially cause unhelpful friction at the beginning of the relationship. I would want to understand why he is being mandated to visit the counseling center because the source of referral can impact the nature of the initial interaction. In this instance the coach might intend something positive by requiring attendance at the meeting, but it could be experienced as a negative punitive consequence by Drake. Settling down hostility between Drake and Robin might be a goal of mine early on so that tension was reduced in the sport environment. I see my initial role as a person seeking to understand Drake and his position first, and then concerning myself with how best to progress with his case.

Determining if the issues presented by Drake are within my scope of practice, I would parse these into those I could tackle; but separating the ones I could not tackle would lead me to my second consideration. If an issue was presented that was outside of my scope and had more importance than I felt I could manage a referral to a licensed mental health professional would be in order. In this case, binge drinking and the decision-making leading to Drake's DUI led him to be counseled, but there are a number of underlying issues in his back story and his recent life contributing to making these issues outside my scope of practice. My focus would be on taking a full statement and learning as much as possible with the goal of referring Drake to a licensed mental health professional who has specialist training in alcohol-related behaviors. I do not think that Drake's case is completely related to sport psychology. The case concerns non sport-related issues outside of performance, but they infringe on the sport performance because of the timing. Nonetheless, for Drake's wellbeing as a person the issues presented should be attended to simultaneously.

I would rely heavily on reflective listening and hypothesis testing when I interviewed Drake. I would use open questions to elicit the differences in behavior, time, location, and activity to get a sense of how things changed for him. I would also want to draw connections for both of us between events to illustrate out loud in the discussion the links for us to explore. Of course, this all depends on the rapport and alliance built in the session to the extent Drake was willing to share information. If he was not willing to share information, I would still try to learn and understand and maintain the goal of referring Drake to an appropriate professional practitioner for him to work with. I would also communicate this decision to Drake's coach and stay within the bounds of proper confidentiality.

Further reading

Donohue, B., Pitts, M., Gavrilova, Y., Ayarza, A., & Cintron, K. I. (2013). A culturally sensitive approach to treating substance abuse in athletes using evidence-supported methods. *Journal of Clinical Sport Psychology*, 7(2), 98–119.

Mastroleo, N., Scaglione, N., Mallett, K., & Turrisi, R. (2013). Can personality account for differences in drinking between college athletes and non-athletes? Explaining the role of sensation seeking, risk-taking, and impulsivity. *Journal of Drug Education*, 43(1), 81–95.

Pitts, M., Chow, G., & Yang, Y. (2017). Athletes' perceptions of their head coach's alcohol management strategies and athlete alcohol use. *Addiction Research & Theory*, 1–9.

Weaver, C., Martens, M., Cadigan, J., Takamatsu, S., Treloar, H., & Pedersen, E. (2013). Sport-related achievement motivation and alcohol outcomes: An athlete-specific risk factor among intercollegiate athletes. *Addictive Behaviors*, 38(12), 2930–2936.

16

ON-COURT AGGRESSION

Introduction

This case introduces students to a coach demanding a capable player show mental toughness in ways the coach can identify when they see it during competition. Students are invited to examine the case from three perspectives—those of coach, athlete and sport psychology consultant. Attention might be given to the consequences for the player and/or reprisals if they fail to show the competitive toughness the coach is seeking from them.

Content implications

Students might consider discussing this case through the lens of mental toughness; but they might also elect to examine the situation from the perspective of instrumental aggression, concentration, arousal regulation and mental skills training. They might also address the role of the sport psychology consultant and how they approach sport psychology to educate athletes and help them acquire the mental skills necessary to perform in competition.

Purpose

The purpose of this case is for students to consider the application of mental toughness training to enhance competitive performance.

Student learning outcomes

At this end of this case study learning opportunity, students should be able to:

1. Identify and explain the issues presented in this case
2. Discuss how aggression might be developed

3. Explain the impact of mental toughness on performance
4. Express the developmental possibilities for learned instrumental aggression
5. Consider how to integrate mental toughness training into sport psychology consultation
6. Discuss the role and limits of a sport psychology consultant in this case

Cast of characters in order of appearance

Dominique Xavier, Women's Basketball.
Becky Washington, Head Coach, Women's Basketball.
Javier Aguilar, Sport Psychology Consultant.

Athlete profile: Dominique Xavier, women's basketball

Dominique Xavier was entering her sophomore year at The U. She was recruited from a rural high school in Wisconsin after a strong high school career. She came from a small private school of 150 students where she knew everyone and grew up and played alongside the same girls year on year. Her parents were self-employed; her father was an accountant and her mother ran her own day care center for pre-kindergarten children. Dominique and her two sisters were brought up to be self-reliant, personally responsible and accountable. Getting along with others, working hard, having good manners, doing well at school, and being goal focused were promoted in her home life.

Dominique studied psychology and business. One of her sisters was studying biology as a route to medical school, and the other was studying business and political science as a pathway to becoming a lawyer. Her sisters were not athletic; instead they preferred theater and photography. Nobody in Dominique's family was particularly interested in sport. Her family was hugely supportive of each other, but sport and outside interests were seen as a distant second to career and professional development.

Dominique enjoyed basketball at her school mainly because her coaches were Mr and Mrs Johnson, who were the teachers in social studies and math. They were light-hearted and fun coaches to play for, and their organizational and communication skills carried over from their classrooms. They got along well together, with the team, and with the families of the players. They emphasized doing your best, playing well in a team, being respectful to your opponents and doing well in school. Mrs Johnson gave Dominique extra help with her math class too.

Dominique played basketball at high school because it was fun. The more fun she had with the team the better she played. She felt no pressure to be perfect or be better than anyone else. She and the team were coached to be technically good, in good physical condition and to achieve the team goals they all agreed to; but the focus was always that studies came first. The latter was so important that Mr Johnson would check how their studies were going, and if a player needed more time he would allow them to complete their homework before practice. This approach made Dominique's parents very happy and supportive of her playing basketball because they felt their family values were matched by Mr and Mrs Johnson. It was not until Dominique got to The U that she realized her high school basketball experience was completely different. She had been recruited without a scholarship offer and informed about the demands of student-athletes and the idea of being a student first and an athlete second. While on one hand this seemed true, on the other hand she felt an uptick in pressure from coaches and team mates to be more competitive and individually focused to be the best she could be and beat her opposite number. The focus and fun in her basketball environment was different. She found balancing studies and basketball difficult in her freshman year. Her parents reminded her to put her academic studies first and suggested she give basketball one more year and decide at the end of her sophomore year if she wanted to continue to play. As a non-scholarship athlete she was playing because she wanted to, not because she was financially beholden to The U or the coach who recruited her.

The case

Becky Washington blew her whistle to end practice after her players had completed a grueling one-on-one match-up against each other. She was unhappy with her team's level of aggression during rebounding in the preceding game. The team had won comfortably but she thought she recognized weaknesses in this area of their performance. She speculated to her assistant coaches whether the players would be strong enough against tougher opponents; in particular she had questions about Dominique's toughness and consistent levels of aggression over a whole game, and not just when she was "tuned in."

The last hour of practice had been all 12 players playing 5-minute games with 5-minute breaks between games. Six games played at once; the winner of each match moved up to the next basket and the loser moved down. No coaching took place, but the results of every game were recorded as part of performance profiles to rank and rate each player. Becky wanted to see how her team would compete with each to be on the top court, who could keep winning, and who would keep losing. Just as in a game, Dominique won a game and lost a game. The team did this kind of practice about every 2–3 weeks.

As the players walked off court, Becky approached Dominique.

BECKY: "Let's talk a while Dominique."
DOMINIQUE: "Sure Coach. What's up?"

Dominique knew what was coming.

BECKY: "The other night, you seemed 'off', like you couldn't compete for every ball."

DOMINIQUE: "Really?"
BECKY: "You know the last two practices like this, you've been the same. You win, you lose … you're always in the middle, it's like you can and you can't play tough in the same game. You train like you play. It's 50-50 … I don't get it because you're a good athlete; you have bright moments but you don't seem to be able to put it altogether."
DOMINIQUE: "What do you mean 50-50 … not tough enough?"
BECKY: "I mean you're inconsistent and I get the sense you're not aggressive. I don't know how much you want to win a game."
DOMINIQUE: "Win a game? I want to win every game I play. I do my best, I support my team mates, I'm easy to coach, I try to do everything you tell me to do."
BECKY: "Yeah … but it's sometimes like you're not trying hard enough to win."
DOMINIQUE: "What do you mean by that?"
BECKY: "You know, you seem to 'go for it' sometimes and sometimes you don't."
DOMINIQUE: "I don't understand."
BECKY: "Yes you do. Sometimes you just go up for a ball off a missed shot and you tear it down and you play big and you fire the out pass and get into the game. Other times you don't seem to fight for the ball, and if you do get the ball you seem to play a lame pass to a guard."

Dominique was hurt and offended by the coach's words.

DOMINIQUE: "Okay."
BECKY: "What's it going to take for you to play with more aggression, more passion … more fire every second of every game. Are you going to compete for this team every moment you're on the court? This is what I am wondering."
DOMINIQUE: "Are you saying I am not tough enough or not aggressive enough … or both?"
BECKY: "I'm saying both, and you're inconsistent. I want you to be consistent and aggressive. If you're aggressive, I believe you will inspire your team mates, our fans, and me."

Dominique did not know what to say or how she felt at this moment. Her coach's words stung and hurt. She played basketball because she loved it, but what she heard made her feel like her reason for playing the game was different. The stakes seemed higher, the expectations of her felt different, and she was uncomfortable.

BECKY: "Look, I want you to talk to Javier."
DOMINIQUE: "You mean the sport psychology guy who does our meetings sometimes?"
BECKY: "Yes."

DOMINIQUE: "But that's going to cut into my study hall time. I'm already working hard on my grades."
BECKY: "If you want to play and get tougher for this team you're going to have to see him."
DOMINIQUE: "You're making me go?"
BECKY: "It's your choice, but I haven't seen the difference in your play that I need to, so you'll be on the bench until I see something different from you like I was talking about. Tougher. Aggressive. Inspiring."

Dominique had not been benched before, and this was the first time she was hearing about it from the coach.

DOMINIQUE: "So, there's no choice. If I don't go you won't play me; if I do go it will take me away from my studies and you still might not play me until you see what you want?"
BECKY: "I don't want to make this difficult for you. I want the best for the team, and I believe you're capable of inspiring and leading this team by being more physical and aggressive on the court."
DOMINIQUE: "Okay ... so when do I have to see him?"
BECKY: "He said you should call him to set up a meeting in the next day or two. He has fewer clients over the Christmas period and he's flexible with where you meet too."
DOMINIQUE: "Do I have to go to his office?"
BECKY: "No, you can meet somewhere on campus where you're more comfortable."
DOMINIQUE: "Can I go and get cleaned up now Coach?"
BECKY: "Sure. I'll see you tomorrow evening for practice before we leave for our next game."

Dominique turned and walked away. She was tired from practice and feeling reflective. She had not had this kind of conversation before; nor had she been in a situation where her sport conflicted so much with her studies.

Coach Washington went to her office, closed the door, and texted Javier Aguilar. She wrote "You free for a call? I made a commitment for you I hope you can keep." A few minutes later she got her reply: "You did it again! Call me."

BECKY: "Hello Javier, thanks for getting back to me so quickly."
JAVIER: "You know Becky, you have to top doing this! Just because I'm on a retainer doesn't mean I'm available 24/7 every day of the year. You have to stop this."
BECKY: "Yeah, and you have to set better boundaries ... we pay you good money Javier and you need to step up now because I need your help ... what are you doing tomorrow?"

JAVIER: "Tomorrow is my day off. I was going to go out with my family. My kids are home for the school holidays and going to the new Disney movie was our plan."
BECKY: "Well, there's a girl I want you to see this week, she might call you tonight. I told her we had already spoken."
JAVIER: "You've done these things before and you made me look bad. You told the athlete I could meet when I could not. What if I say 'no' to this player?"
BECKY: "Well, I'll remember it the next time the Athletic Director asks me about your value to the team."
JAVIER: "Oh great Becky! You're threatening me and you want me to help you?"
BECKY: "Yes, I want your help because I don't know how to reach this player."
JAVIER: "Who is it?"
BECKY: "Dominique."
JAVIER: "Dominique? … Yes I remember her from the team meetings; studious and thoughtful. Good personality and a good fit with the team."
BECKY: "Yeah that's her. I think she can be a difference maker, but I feel she's got to be tougher and more physical. She can be inspirational but it's been a season and a half and there's no change in her mental make-up. Our coaching is not reaching her."
JAVIER: "Tell me how you set this up between her and me … don't tell me you threatened her too like you did before?"
BECKY: "I said I would bench her."
JAVIER: "Hell Becky! Okay, I'll meet with her, but it will be when I can and the only time will be between 9am and 12pm tomorrow at my office."
BECKY: "I told her you would meet on campus."

Javier was silent for a moment.

JAVIER: "Have her call me."
BECKY: "She will."

Dominique agreed to meet Javier in the main library. She saw him, he did not see her, and sat down opposite him. Javier looked up at Dominique and saw from the clock on the wall behind her she arrived five minutes early.

DOMINIQUE: "Hello Javier. Thank you for seeing me this morning."
JAVIER: "You're welcome."
DOMINIQUE: "Did Coach talk to you?"
JAVIER: "Yes, we spoke briefly. She told me she hoped you would be more physical and aggressive on court."
DOMINIQUE: "Yeah, she said that to me too."
JAVIER: "I imagine today wasn't your first choice for meeting me."
DOMINIQUE: "Coach said I had to see you."
JAVIER: "I heard that."

DOMINIQUE: "Yeah, she said she would bench me if she didn't see me improve."
JAVIER: "Yes I see this is difficult for you. How do you want spend the time given you didn't want to be here?"
DOMINIQUE: "Well I have 40 minutes. I have school work to do. What do you think we should talk about?"
JAVIER: "Okay, let's talk a bit about you for a moment; we don't know each other and I don't know your history very much. How much do you know about sport psychology?"
DOMINIQUE: "Not much, only what we did in the team meetings."
JAVIER: "Okay, so you mean you haven't worked with it before and you don't know how it can help you?"
DOMINIQUE: "Sure."
JAVIER: "How much have you used goal setting and energy channeling to increase focus?"
DOMINIQUE: "Never."
JAVIER: "How much do you know about mental toughness?"
DOMINIQUE: "Not much."
JAVIER: "You really don't want to be here do you?"
DOMINIQUE: "No."
JAVIER: "Okay, we don't have much time, and I know you're smart. What do you want from this meeting?"
DOMINIQUE: "I'm angry I have to be here. I don't feel like I'm being respected for my effort or my school work, and I feel like I'm being punished for things I didn't know before. What Coach told me, the way she did, came out of nowhere."
JAVIER: "I know what you mean."
DOMINIQUE: "Do you?"
JAVIER: "Yes. It's like when someone tells you to do something you don't want to do and they make you do it because they threaten you with something you care about."
DOMINIQUE: "That's right. I love playing basketball and I like studying. I'm not a showy type of person. I don't show my emotions, I get on with things ... since I came here the game's not fun like it used to be. It feels like a job and it seems like you have to yell and act like a bully and then people think you're mentally tough or physical ... whatever."
JAVIER: "There are other ways to be tough and be yourself. Did you know that?"
DOMINIQUE: "What do you mean?"
JAVIER: "Well, there are many athletes who are studious, quiet, almost shy and they play with tremendous intensity, but off the court they almost seem gentle."
DOMINIQUE: "Yeah, that's a bit like me."
JAVIER: "What was it like at high school?"
DOMINIQUE: "My coaches were awesome, it was always fun. Every session we had a goal to achieve, and they helped us achieve it. Practices were fun; we

competed but it wasn't against each other; everything we did felt like it was for the team. I knew my role, what they wanted, and I felt in the zone so many times. They never punished me for not being tough, but they did show me how to be better and took the time to explain things. Here we get drilled and we're always going at each other. It's like Coach is more interested in me focusing on beating my team mates instead of us competing against other teams. It's crazy!"

JAVIER: "You're frustrated ... there are some ways your high school experience could help you with this. Can I tell you how?"

DOMINIQUE: "Sure."

JAVIER: "It sounds like your coaches set you up to be able to channel your intensity into the game by giving you a focus on what they want from you. Do you do that for yourself too?"

DOMINIQUE: "Sometimes, but mostly I look at what the Coach wants."

JAVIER: "Well there are some ways you can be yourself and be tough."

DOMINIQUE: "Like what?"

JAVIER: "Okay, for example, you can set your own goals; you can identify what you need to do and how you need to do it; you can visualize the game you want to play and connect with times when you have been in the zone ... you can use your effort to help you get into the mindset and attitude to play well consistently closer to your zone."

DOMINIQUE: "But how do these things help make me tougher."

JAVIER: "It's not about making you tougher. It's about you getting more out of yourself. The toughness is already in you, it's how you play that matters."

DOMINIQUE: "But I don't want to change who I am."

JAVIER: "You don't have to change. It is about getting more out of yourself and showing the full range of who you are as a player. To do that you can use mental skills to help yourself."

DOMINIQUE: "I don't know how."

JAVIER: "It's my job to help you learn how."

DOMINIQUE: "But what about being more aggressive?"

JAVIER: "Aggression comes from achieving your goals, not by challenging others. In your case, it's not about beating people; it's about being the best player you can be, game in game out."

DOMINIQUE: "So you mean I don't have to compete against others?"

JAVIER: "Yes. I mean by focusing on playing the best basketball you can play things will most likely take care of themselves."

DOMINIQUE: "But what about the physicality and toughness? ... I don't get what Coach will make of it if she doesn't see what she needs to see from me."

JAVIER: "Listen, I don't think Coach is going to bench you if you're making rebounds like you can, passing like you're capable of, and adding points when needed. If you're a coach it makes sense to play someone who is doing that ... right?"

DOMINIQUE: "I suppose so ... but is this going to mean giving even more time to basketball?"

JAVIER: "It depends. I don't know how much time it's going to take for you to develop in the way the Coach needs, and I don't know how heavy your workload is and how you study."

DOMINIQUE: "I have to go soon."

JAVIER: "I know."

DOMINIQUE: "What can I tell Coach this afternoon at practice?"

JAVIER: "Before we get to that, how do you feel about doing a goal-setting exercise for this afternoon's practice?"

DOMINIQUE: "Will it take long?"

JAVIER: "No, about 5 minutes. Do you know what you're going to practice this afternoon?"

DOMINIQUE: "We're going through plays for tomorrow's game."

JAVIER: "Okay, we'll start with that. Let me tell you briefly the key things you need to know about goal-setting."

Discussion questions

1. What are the main issues presented in this case?
2. What challenges does the sport psychology consultant face in this case?
3. What role might anxiety have in Dominique's case?
4. How might you go about implementing a mental toughness training program with Dominique?
5. How might you influence Dominique's mindset concerning the use of instrumental aggression to achieve her and the team's goals?
6. How might you approach counseling Dominique?

Author's notes

This is a difficult case because the student-athlete might have felt manipulated by the coach to attend the session. When a client is mandated to attend a sport psychology-related meeting by a coach this is akin to a medical doctor referring a patient to a specialist for something they did not perceive to be a problem, like weight management. This interaction has to be negotiated first. Often there is tension at the beginning of the interaction and a kind of withdrawal, shown by the client using clipped phrases and unhelpful signposting in the conversation. Knowing how to work with reluctant clients is a skill. In these moments counseling skills that reduce tension while still making progress are important to establish a working alliance between yourself and the client. It is not uncommon for coaches to use sport psychology consultants for situations they do not want to handle and/or are not equipped to cope with, or when a student-athlete needs support and asks for help. Each situation requires a different approach in a variety of ways, including how the relationship with the coach and the student-athlete is processed and how the work is implemented and evaluated. Being aware of the source and context of the referral is important to how work progresses.

Often coaches seem to discuss mental toughness, aggression, and physicality interchangeably. They often know what they mean but do not always communicate the specific definition to their athletes to understand. When asked, coaches will say something like "I know it [mental toughness] when I see it" and common examples they might give are things like diving for a loose ball on the court, playing through pain, taking and giving physical effort at the edge of their capabilities, or making up for mistakes with good play. In this case, the coach is questioning the player's toughness and consistency, and the player is unclear of what they have done wrong and why they are being punished. The sport psychology consultant role is multifaceted: on one hand you might have to interpret the coach's point of view; on the other hand you might have to educate and train the client about what mental toughness is, but also in this case manage your own feelings about how the relationship has been set up by the coach.

It is important to have a clear idea of what mental toughness is, the literature discussing it, and how to implement programs in time-efficient and integrative ways. I typically prefer not to discuss mental toughness; instead I communicate words like intensity, focus, and execution because I can define them more clearly and align mental skills training approaches with the definitions. This gives me greater clarity in my work and I find it easier to talk about the issues because their definitions can be matched with explicit performance behaviors, whereas talking about mental toughness feels too vague and too big for me to work with. But, ultimately, each consultant must adopt an approach that fits their perspective and training, and the demands of the case.

Further reading

Aoyagi, M. W., Poczwardowski, A., Statler, T., Shapiro, J. L., & Cohen, A. B. (2017). The Performance Interview Guide: Recommendations for initial consultations in sport and performance psychology. *Professional Psychology: Research and Practice*, 48(5), 352–360.

Kimble, N. B., Russo, S. A., Bergman, B. G., & Galindo, V. H. (2010). Revealing an empirical understanding of aggression and violent behavior in athletics. *Aggression and Violent Behavior*, 15(6), 446–462.

Krahé, B. (2013). *The social psychology of aggression*. New York, NY: Psychology Press.

Weinberg, R., Freysinger, V., Mellano, K., & Brookhouse, E. (2016). Building mental toughness: Perceptions of sport psychologists. *Sport Psychologist*, 30(3), 231–241.

17

TEAM TOUGHNESS

Introduction

This case introduces students to a variety of factors influencing coach and athlete performance. There are organizational, coach-to-coach relationships and mental toughness issues to contend with. Discussions might go in a number of directions because, on one hand, the issues might seem straightforward but, on the other, considerations of how an applied sport psychology intervention might be employed might be far more complex. Students should consider the needs of the different characters in this case and how each one is seeking something in particular as they deal with the situation they are in.

Content implications

Mental toughness, mental skills training, coach–athlete and coach–coach communication, player leadership, athlete recruitment, and coping with organizational stress are several areas for discussion. This case has different kinds of tensions built into it, much like life, and students are encouraged to examine the broader implications of the issues in this case before narrowing down their decisions about how to operate as a sport psychology practitioner. Consideration might also be given to the type and level of any applied sport psychology intervention and how a program might be evaluated.

Purpose

The purpose of here is to provide students an opportunity to discuss and determine possible solutions to various challenges faced by Robin Marriot, The U's men's head soccer coach.

Student learning outcomes

At this end of this case study learning opportunity, students should be able to:

1. Determine and justify a sport psychology-related solution for the given set of circumstances
2. Explain the key factors influencing Coach Marriot's decision
3. Demonstrate a process of weighing evidence during the decision-making process

Cast of characters in order of appearance

Robin Marriot, Head Coach, Men's Soccer.
Michelle Court, Athletic Director.
Marty Kelly, Assistant Head Coach, Men's Soccer.
Jaime Varedo, Goal Keeping Coach, Men's Soccer.
Mike Brillo, Co-Captain, Men's Soccer.

Coach profile: Robin Marriot, men's soccer

The U's men's soccer team's head coach, Robin Marriot, had led his team to another successful season both by his standards and those of the university. He experienced a number of incidents during the season which have challenged him and his coaching staff. These include: issues around player–coach conflict; a new young goal keeper having to take the starting position; a player needing counseling for alcohol use and drink driving; and a senior player trying to become a professional. The off-field issues were significant, tiring for him and his staff, and compounded a sad loss to The U's biggest rivals too. Sometimes a poor season by any of The U's teams could be forgiven if they beat their biggest rival. But this year was different; the underperformance had gone on too long in the view of The U's Athletic Director.

Robin had grown the program with decent recruitment that brought outstanding player leadership with it. He built the team on players having reliable personal qualities and character, good academic standing, and technical sport ability. In the last three years he gambled on bringing in one or two players he did not know well. He hired a former professional player he believed he could mentor to become an asset to his coaching staff and the team because of his experience in the professional game. Both decisions yielded uneven results for Robin and his team during training, competition, and off the field. Robin was under the most pressure as the men's head coach since he started in the role eight years ago.

The case

Robin Marriot put his cell phone in the top right-hand draw of his office desk. He leaned back in his chair, took a deep breath, and swiveled around to stare out of the window across The U's 5,000-seat varsity soccer stadium. Robin had just finished a 45-minute call with the Athletic Director, Michelle Court. The last part of the conversation Robin remembered:

MICHELLE: "Robin, we've had a good working relationship over the last five years, haven't we? You know we've lost the conference final three times in a row, and two to Barrow!"
ROBIN: "Yeah I know Michelle, I was there."
MICHELLE: "Ticket sales are down and graduating seniors said in their exit surveys there's a loss of confidence in the team. We can't have two more years like this Robin. Deal with it … before I have to … you know … make a decision."
ROBIN: "What does that mean Michelle? You have to fire me. Is that it?"
MICHELLE: "No! I don't want to fire you, but see it from my side Coach. We don't have football or hockey here … Besides basketball, men's and women's soccer are 'IT' and your program is not performing like we expected."

As Robin looked out of the window, he reflected on when he had taken over as head coach eight years earlier. He had settled in during his first year and built relationships with players. He did not change too many things on the field. Results were promising in his first year, but his second year was when he put his mark on the team. He recruited his first class, which contained several hardnosed players with an excellent work ethic. One in particular, a freshman recruit called Tony Djondo, stood out. He loved his team mates, coaches and fans, and they loved him back. With Tony's influence the team got to the conference final in Robin's second year, losing narrowly to the hot favorites and arch rivals Barrow College, but then 'tore' their conference up with a three-peat championship run. With Tony Djondo leading willing team mates, The U had a 60–12 regular season combined record and two NCAA third round appearances during that time. Since Djondo graduated the team had a 40–16 record and no conference championships.

Marty Kelly, the team's long-serving assistant head coach, knocked on Robin's door just as he put the cell phone in his desk.

ROBIN: "Come in!"
MARTY: "Hey Coach, got a minute? I have some ideas about how we should go about getting our next recruiting class. You'll want hear these gems and pearls."

Robin turned in his chair to face Marty. Robin had kept Marty on from the previous coach because he did not want to be head coach. He had been at Unity U as an assistant head coach for 16 years and was 15 years older than Robin. He worked hard and was trustworthy. After working with him for eight years Robin was still unclear what Marty was really good at, but the student-athletes seemed to like having a 65-year-old, retired, middle school teacher and doting grandfather around. Robin counted on Marty as a friend as much as his assistant.

ROBIN: "Okay Marty, let's hear what you've got to say about our next recruiting class …"

Just as Marty was about to speak, Jaime Varedo sauntered through Robin's open office door in his casual way and stood comfortably next to Marty.

JAIME: "Hey Marty, looks like you're about to say something big."

Jaime was 25 years old and in his first coaching job after hanging up his boots following an injury which ended his promising MLS career. He and Marty teased each other gently, but Jaime would never do this with Robin.

MARTY: "Well, I was going to tell Coach how I've been doing some research on ways to get the recruiting class to help us win championships."
JAIME: "Is that so Daddy?" Jaime said to Marty, using his nickname, and then thumping his heart with his fist. "What we need is talent, heart and luck!"

Robin smiled and rocked back in his seat and directed his coaches to his four-seat round table where all their conferences, game reviews and post-game home celebrations took place.

ROBIN: "Guys, find a seat. Tell me all about your ideas for our recruitment strategy for next year's incoming class."

Robin moved over to join them at the table.

ROBIN: "Okay boys, what's the best way to recruit for next year's class?"
MARTY: "Well coach, I've been reading how mental toughness is a big thing. I mean, I always knew about it, but I've been reading about it more since the loss in the conference final this season. It seems like we used to get boys that could get through the tough times, but these days … well … they seem like they're a little soft. I was thinking if we want to beat Barrow, we've got to get some tougher boys. I think juniors, not seniors; boys with experience who have an ego but are still coachable; boys with power and a bit of poise; and boys who can learn our system."

Jaime chuckled.

JAIME: "Good one 'Pops'. Coach, what we need are winners. You know … boys that have 'it'. You know 'em when you see 'em. We just need to scout the major showcases and see the talent. Then we need to make a good money offer, get Coach in front of 'em and they'll be right along. We get to the finals. I mean we're there aren't we?"

Robin stared at Jaime. The young coach had no idea about Robin's recent conversation with the Athletic Director.

ROBIN: "I see where you're coming from Jaime, but things are different now. Being in the final is not enough; we need to win it [the conference] again! We keep doing the same things over and over again and they're not working! Marty, tell me more about this mental toughness idea."

Marty leaned forward on his elbows and opened his iPad. He took a moment to open a web browser showing the classes offered in the kinesiology major this semester.

MARTY: "Coach, I'm not the expert, but I know a group of students that have experience studying mental toughness. I think they might help us."
ROBIN: "Students Marty?"

Marty looked back at Robin, surprised by his reaction. Robin was feeling the pressure. He had tried working with students on projects before but they seldom followed through like he wanted them to. Robin paused and stared at Marty. He knew his assistant coach would not bring him an idea he thought would fail if it was applied.

ROBIN: "Alright Marty, set up a meeting with these students. Don't tell them too much. But ask them, if they were in our shoes how they would use the concept of mental toughness to recruit next year's class."
JAIME: "Coach! Pops, you can't be serious? This sounds like psycho mumbo jumbo. This would never fly in the pros; either a kid has toughness or they don't. Really, students can't help us ... most of them are clueless about soccer."
ROBIN: "Jaime, I am serious. This is not the pros ... Marty, set it up! Tell them they have 10 minutes to convince me to use mental toughness as a way of helping us recruit players to help us win championships. Marty, I hope they're up to it! I don't want any fads or bookstore motivational speaker type stuff."

Robin got up from the table, walked to the window and looked out across the stadium with his back to his coaches. Marty and Jaime looked at each other, sighed gently and left Robin's office together; after all, they were a coaching team.

Robin turned around when Marty and Jaime left his office and looked at the table. He felt he snapped at Jaime and was a little mean to Marty. The pressure he felt from Michelle had upset him. Robin looked out of his window again and thought to himself, "I need another Djondo. Heck … I need three of him, but I'd settle for two. If we find the talent, how will I know they are mentally tough?" He knew he needed a new recruitment strategy and he needed to develop a tough culture.

At that moment Mike Brillo knocked on Robin's office door. "Come in," Robin said without turning around. Mike came in, put his bag on the table and sat facing Robin as he stood in the light of the window. Before Robin spoke, Mike said: "Coach, I'm concerned about next year." "Me too," Robin said gravely as he turned around. He walked over to the table and sat down kitty-corner to Mike.

ROBIN: "What's on your mind Mike?"
MIKE: "Well Coach, I was thinking about the conversation we had at the end of the season when I was disappointed. I remember talking to you about Djondo. He had graduated before I arrived, but I knew he left his mark on this program. The thing is, I want to see this team do better next year. I've put my life into this program and it eats me up not to have beaten Barrow. We should have done better."
ROBIN: "Okay Mike, so you're here to tell me something. Go on …"
MIKE: "Mrs Court asked me how I felt about next season. I told her we have got to get tougher players. I didn't mean the guys we have are weak or anything like that, but they have to be able to play under pressure and they have got to learn how to deal with it, and I'm not sure they can … What does our incoming class for next year look like Coach?"
ROBIN: "We're not sure Mike. We're not sure."
MIKE: "Well Coach, me and some of the others, we've been talking and we wanted to know if it would be alright if we reached out to players we know at other schools and see if they might transfer here to play for us."
ROBIN: "Okay, do you think you know what we really need?"
MIKE: "We do, we know we are two or three guys short, and we need those players to be, you know, leaders. We know we're good players, but we also know we need a bit more, especially in leadership."
ROBIN: "Anything else on your mind?"
MIKE: "Yeah Coach, some of the boys have had enough of Coach Jaime. He kind of brings some of us down. We know he was a top player, but he's a coach now; he's supposed to, you know … be on our side. We feel he's against us and he gets on us too much."
ROBIN: "What do you expect me to do Mike?"
MIKE: "Well Coach, we were hoping for next season you could get Coach Jaime to relax, you know calm down. We know what we have to do but he barks at us like we're dogs sometimes. We know he wants us to be tougher, but it's not working; we prefer you and Coach Marty to work with us. Just yelling at us and telling us to be tougher is not working."

ROBIN: "Okay Mike I hear you, but you got to understand too, we think mental toughness is an issue and sometimes we do have to come down hard on some of the boys, sometimes even you."

MIKE: "Yeah, but Coach Jaime never talks about our goals, we're always tense around him, and he's always reminding us of what we're not doing or can't do. It's not good."

ROBIN: "Okay, I'll talk to him in the summer and we'll see how things go in pre-season training when we get back, okay?"

Discussion questions

1. What are the most important facts in this case?
2. What are the challenges facing Robin Marriot?
3. How might you determine the priorities of an intervention based on the knowledge you have about this case?
4. What tensions exist between the different views coaches have about mental toughness?
5. How might the relationships between the coaches influence a sport psychology intervention to enhance mental toughness?
6. If you were consulting to Robin Marriot what would your recommendations be to help him resolve the problems you feel he is facing?

Author's notes

Robin has his work cut out in this situation because of the organizational pressure from his boss, relationships between his coaches, and his team's performance the previous season. However, the feedback from the player to Robin prompts me to think that team confidence is a key issue. Coach interventions might be necessary too. While I might not influence recruitment for the team or what happens with the student research team that Marty will work with, I would focus on working with Robin to address team goals, team climate, and the training and playing conditions that the coaches can impact like promoting a positive, do your best attitude and providing players with the cues and game understanding for them to perform better under competitive pressure. For example, coaches can set a positive tone with positive feedback to players, they can focus on player strengths, and they reduce the hostility between themselves and their players. They can still give critical feedback, but in ways that focus on the issue not the person, and certainly avoid undermining the confidence of individual players or the team as a whole.

Any necessary intervention is best done in pre-season and, given the nature of the case, this is the ideal time to plan and prepare for the next season. I would have Robin and Marty engage the players in developing a team mission statement aligned with the goals and performance behaviors the team can commit to for the upcoming season. If Jaime is still part of the coaching staff for the new season,

I would work with Robin to regulate his behavior and model positive behaviors for the players.

At an individual player level, a sport psychology intervention which influences cognitive appraisal of the competitive challenges to become more positive through breathing and self-talk strategies would be introduced, supported by goal setting to channel negative nervous energy into task commitment and goal accomplishment. This approach would require a baseline profiling of each player using a tool like the 9 Mental Skills Inventory (Lesyk, 1998) a feedback session, and then player and coach education in 15–20-minute segments over the pre-season ending with 10-minute daily packages players can use for training and competition.

To help reinforce team toughness I would recommend the entire support team—including the coaches, management, sport administrators, and the sport medicine team—be engaged in understanding the playing team's mission and its aims. Positive messages from everyone concerned with the team are important. Robin would be the ideal messenger, but he might use Marty to communicate these messages. I would also invite Robin to have a leadership group for his squad meet with him every other week to address team issues and come up with workable solutions.

Further reading

Connaughton, D., Hanton, S., & Jones, G. (2010). The development and maintenance of mental toughness in the world's best performers. *Sport Psychologist*, 24(2), 168–193.

Jones, G. (2002). What is this thing called mental toughness? An investigation of elite sport performers. *Journal of Applied Sport Psychology*, 14(3), 205–218.

Jones, G., Hanton, S., & Connaughton, D. (2007). A framework of mental toughness in the world's best performers. *Sport Psychologist*, 21(2), 243–264.

Lesyk, J. J. (1998). *Developing sport psychology within your clinical practice: A practical guide for mental health professionals*. San Francisco, CA: Jossey-Bass.

Nicholls, A. R., Morley, D., & Perry, J. L. (2016). Mentally tough athletes are more aware of unsupportive coaching behaviours: Perceptions of coach behaviour, motivational climate, and mental toughness in sport. *International Journal of Sports Science & Coaching*, 11(2), 172–181.

Weinberg, R., Freysinger, V., & Mellano, K. (2016). How can coaches build mental toughness? Views from sport psychologists. *Journal of Sport Psychology in Action*, 9(1), 1–10.

18
TEAM BUILDING

Introduction

This case demonstrates an end-of-season feedback situation requiring a team coach to respond to the players' perspectives and her supervisor's requirements. The case presents performance and organizational issues which expose students to typical contexts in college sport. It is normal in NCAA sports for coaches to have feedback from and interviews with all their athletes at the end of each season. It is also customary for administrators supervising coaches to provide feedback. This case shows this process and the follow-up with a sport psychology consultant.

Content implications

This case invites discussions about coach–athlete relationships, coach education and development, consciousness raising, conflict resolution, professional relationships, team climate and practice design. Readers can determine what the critical team issues are facing the coach, and then decide how they would consult the coach to enhance team performance.

Purpose

The purpose of the case is to present a situation requiring students to break down the factors negatively influencing a tennis team's performance so that they can consider a range of interventions that might improve performance for the following season.

Student learning outcomes

At the end of this case study learning opportunity, students should be able to:

1. Discuss the pros and cons of team building approaches
2. Consider how to work with a coach to develop a team building program
3. Determine the role of coach and player input in a team building program
4. Discuss the strengths and weaknesses of evaluating a team building intervention
5. Recognize the differences between team developments for an intact and a newly formed team

Cast of characters in order of appearance

Celia "Cissy" Drew, Assistant Athletic Director and Women's Sport Administrator.
Tina Morrison, Head Coach, Women's Tennis.
Javier Aguilar, Sport Psychology Consultant.

Coach profile: Tina Morrison, women's tennis

Tina Morrison's team had one of their best seasons ever. They won their conference and got through to the second round of the NCAA tournament, where they met fierce opposition from a top-ranked opponent and lost 4-0. While the team was winning in their regular season the issues in the team between players and their coach simmered. Tina's recruits had played well but they were angry and hostile towards her during practice, but after training the relationship was good; they talked easily—it was just when they were on court that there were difficulties. By late season several players were listening to Tina's instructions but not implementing them. Despite this they kept winning, and their talent and skills were enough to mask their vulnerabilities up to the conference appearance, when two matches were close, and their first round NCAA appearance was decided 4-3 by winning the final doubles match. But their heavy defeat peeled back and uncovered the technical and mental vulnerabilities Tina had tried to have her team eradicate all season. Her lower-seeded players improved, but not at a sufficient rate to make them better than the top players, who in her estimation had not even made marginal games since early season practice.

Her top three players battled each other harshly in training, at times trading barbs, serving and volleying at each other, and working doubly hard to come out on top in drills. They were more competitive with each other than their opponents,' and sometimes could not even bring themselves to cheer for their team mates during matches. Even when support was needed, one or two of the players were half-hearted about things. Tina felt her leading player (who was from Britain) had so much more to offer in terms of leadership and performance, but her behavior in training was harming her ability at this level. The second and third players were the most competitive with each other. Even when they won their matches, they could barely congratulate each other.

In contrast, Tina found the lower-ranked players easier to coach, and they seemed to have more fun too. Her fifth seeded player had the longest unbeaten streak in the team, and loved her tennis. At first she was unhappy with being dropped from fourth to fifth, but after a couple of wins she got used to the idea. Tina wished her top players had the same attitude as her lower-seeded players. She found team meetings especially difficult to manage in the second half of the season. Team goals and standards of conduct were not adhered to. Her lower players seemed to engage in all the activities needed to enhance their performance, but her top players not so much. Her third seeded player had been nicknamed "Coach 2" by a couple of the other players because they would echo the coach's the instructions and demands. At first it felt supportive, but by the end of the season it grated on the team and affected on-court relationships, particularly in doubles. Despite these negative factors Tina enjoyed her season. She was proud of all her team mates; she was optimistic for the next year and looked forward to the challenges ahead.

The case

Cissy Drew knew Tina Morrison well and, like other coaches she recruited, they had a long and trusting relationship. Cissy had seen Tina coach and liked her energy and enthusiasm for training. She also admired how she energized recruits from all over the world to consider The U as a place to study and play tennis. She was heavy-hearted when the results of the season's player survey were returned to her. Despite the team having a great season there were several players who expressed significant disappointment and frustration at how the season had progressed. A little of the criticism was aimed at Tina, but a lot of it was aimed at other team members and Tina for allowing the team climate to get as bad as they perceived it to be. Cissy knew her meeting with Tina could be difficult; after all, Tina was passionate but she could also be defiant.

Cissy met Tina in her office which overlooked the soccer field. No team was practicing and the view was a bright and colorful spring day.

CISSY: "Hi Tina, thanks for coming over today … sit down. How's things?"
TINA: "Good, you know, end of semester stuff. I've been reviewing games, match stats … looking at recruits and signing day's coming up soon. Even though we don't need anyone I like to be in the habit of talent identification. Next year, we'll need two for the roster for sure, maybe three … we'll see. But you know, for now I'm pleased with things and getting ready to review things."
CISSY: "That's great! You sound happy with where things are at. But you might not feel so after you read the end of season reviews."
TINA: "Why? Are they bad?"
CISSY: "Well it's not that they're bad exactly. Read them for yourself and you judge from what your players are saying what the status is."

Cissy handed Tina the player surveys and sat watching her read them. They were fairly short surveys focused on understanding the student-athlete experience and how well things were going for them (or not), and what might be improved for the next season.

Tina read through the anonymous online-administered surveys. She tried not to guess who wrote things, but she saw for herself the level of hostility between the players—with some of it targeted at her. Three quotes caught her attention as they seemed to capture the main points of the whole survey:

> Our best player needs to step up and lead. She needs to take charge and help Coach.
> We are not a team. We don't even like each other.
> I enjoyed winning. We could have gone further if we didn't fight each other so much.

Tina saw conflict in the team was rampant. She knew from team meetings and practices the players were somewhat hostile to each other, but she just tried to coach through it. But to see these quotes really got her attention and focused her mind. She wanted her team to go further in next year's tournament and improve their overall quality of play. Clearly things were worse in the team than she thought. She finished reading the surveys and placed the sheets back on Cissy's desk.

CISSY: "So Coach, what do you think about what you read?"

Tina paused. She felt exasperated.

TINA: "I knew things were not great, but we were winning … and my lower players were doing really great. Just my 2 and 3 players were tough to handle. But I didn't know the others saw one of them as a coach, or wanted my top player to lead more. I mean I saw this, but I didn't know they did too. I didn't know there was so much hassle and nasty things going on between them, and I did not know they didn't see themselves as a team. I preach team every day."
CISSY: "Tina, can you hear yourself? It sounds like you did not know a lot of things were going on. What was going on with you?"
TINA: "You know me Cissy. I was coaching. I was in there doing what you pay me to do and what I enjoy. The bottom players did great and they really helped us win our matches. I relied on them and trusted them to perform."
CISSY: "Did you have the same confidence in your top players?"
TINA: "Sometimes, but, you know, they were difficult to coach. They would not listen … I think for half the season they tuned me out. Even I was beating them at times in practice. I mean come on, that's bad, and when your coach is out hustling you and making you look like you don't belong you should be picking it up and blasting the ball back in play to beat me, right?"
CISSY: "So you played the girls in practice?"
TINA: "Yeah, I always do. We have six to play; one reserve and I rotate in on specific drills and games. I've always done that. Why what's up with that?"

CISSY: "Do you think it's possible that you're beating them has anything to do with how things went in the team?"
TINA: "I don't know, do you?"
CISSY: "Maybe, maybe not. I'm just trying to understand what happened in your team."
TINA: "Look if you mean am I trying to replay my college career or redo my time in coaching in California the answer is 'No', but I make them play hard because that's what I want from them—to play hard for every single point."
CISSY: "Okay Tina I get it, but what about how much they want it? You can't want it more than they do. You can't have more desire than them to play well, otherwise ... well I don't see how your team can perform if your desire for performance is more than theirs."

Tina went quiet and looked sullen.

CISSY: "Let's talk about the coaching in practice. How much did you notice your player coaching the others?"
TINA: "I saw it. I thought she was helping me out."
CISSY: "And you never felt this was a problem to the other girls?"
TINA: "Not really, you know in practice its banter, it's talk, it's athletes and coaches working together."
CISSY: "That's not how the team experienced it Tina. They clearly responded negatively to this and you didn't see its effects on the team."
TINA: "Okay, okay, I did miss some things ... what do you want me to do about it?"
CISSY: "You're not going to fight me on this?"
TINA: "No. Anyway, what's the point, you're my boss right?"
CISSY: "Yes, and we've always worked well. Should I be concerned this is different now?"
TINA: "No. It's just I'm surprised by the feedback and I guess I missed one or two things."
CISSY: "You missed quite a bit."

Tina did not respond. She looked beyond Cissy out of the window to clear her mind.

TINA: "Okay Cissy, what do you want me to do?"
CISSY: "I want you to do a team building piece before your players leave at the end of the semester. I want you to restart your team relationships."
TINA: "Okay ... how do I do that? I haven't done anything like this for a while."
CISSY: "Talk to Javier."
TINA: "The sport psych guy?"
CISSY: "Yes."
TINA: "I haven't seen him for a while."

CISSY: "Call him, get some ideas, and then meet back up with me and walk me through what you intend to do."
TINA: "Are you checking up on me Cissy?"
CISSY: "No. But you need support, and it's my job to help you be successful."

Tina met Javier at his office downtown. She was on her way home for lunch the day after she met with Cissy and it suited her schedule to meet then. Javier had an open time slot and they agreed to meet providing he could eat his lunch during the meeting. Tina had been to Javier's office once before. She liked how his office had big windows looking out onto trees and plants, and felt comfortable in it. Although she did not know Javier too well she approached the meeting positively. She had not told him anything much about her meeting with Cissy.

Javier closed the door and turned to Tina as he made his way to his chair and the sandwiches on a plate on the coffee table next to his spot. "This is a surprise, what brings you here?" Javier said as he sat down and picked up his first cheese and tomato sandwich.

TINA: "Well, Cissy suggested I come and see you and get some ideas about team building. I know you work with a bunch of teams at The U in different ways; maybe you know some things that can help me for the next season."
JAVIER: "Okay, but I don't know what's going on, so why don't you tell me a bit and let's see what we can talk about, okay?"

He munched on his lunch.

TINA: "You look like you're enjoying that sandwich."
JAVIER: "I am, go on."

Tina told Javier about the season, the survey results, and her meeting with Cissy. He ate all the way through her sharing for about 15 minutes, taking small bites and chewing for a long time on each mouthful. He nodded and uttered but did not interrupt Tina. Sometimes he chewed more slowly at key points he seemed to find interesting. He finished eating at the same time Tina finished her last point.

JAVIER: "Well, you focused on yourself and not the team, and now you have a bit of work to do. Based on what you told me you might think more about raising your own level of self-awareness and start there if you want to build your team."
TINA: "What?"
JAVIER: "Clearly you love tennis and your team, but you missed what happened in your team. I suggest start first with yourself and then move to the team."
TINA: "But I have to fix my team too."
JAVIER: "Yes you do, but it starts first with you then them."
TINA: "This makes no sense. I came here to talk about the team not me."

JAVIER: "Listen to me, you set the tone, you are the leader; you are their everything. You are responsible for your behavior. From what you told me you have players who want you to show leadership, so why not role model the behaviors you want from others? Not only lead by example but do by example."

TINA: "I don't like where this is going Javier, you barely know me."

JAVIER: "That's true, but you came here. You and I do not have much of a relationship, and I suspect you came because you were told to. So, given that, I am getting to the point. You have a top player you want more from. So, define what you want from her in behavioral terms; communicate with them and find out if they are willing, if they will let you coach them along how. If you need more help we can talk."

TINA: "You're being strong with me, why?"

JAVIER: "As I said, I think you came here because Cissy told you to and you made this appointment because it was convenient for you. Our commitment to a relationship is not strong, so I give you want you think you want and you leave, and then I don't hear from you until the next time you have a problem."

TINA: "Why are you so angry with me?"

JAVIER: "I'm not. But don't be deceptive with yourself or me. What do you really want?"

TINA: "Man … you're tough on me."

JAVIER: "Really Tina, what do you want? We're here."

TINA: "I don't know how to build a team with the players I have and I need help, and I don't know how much is me and how much is them when it comes down to it. If I need to change things, I'm not even sure what I need to do differently. But I know my team is good; they can be even better if we can move forward. The other issue is I have to get moving on this before they leave after finals. Realistically, I have two weeks to prepare and three weeks to work on things before they leave for summer break."

JAVIER: "Okay, that's a start. I feel like you were being real with me. Please keep doing that. It helps me to know what is going on with you and your situation. If you had three wishes about how your team could improve, what would they be?"

TINA: "I wish all my players would listen and learn from me, get along with each other, and feel like they were a unit."

JAVIER: "Okay, let's start from here. Who is your leading player and how much do they listen to you?"

TINA: "I have a British player, very experienced, a competitor, but ever since early season she has tuned me out. She keeps playing well and adds to the team but she is difficult to coach."

JAVIER: "How much value does she bring to the team?"

TINA: "What do you mean by value?"

JAVIER: "I mean are her performances providing enough value for you and your other players to tolerate what they might feel is prima donna behavior, like challenging team goals and the way things are done?"

TINA: "I haven't really thought about value like that before."
JAVIER: "Okay, think about the value each player brings. Do they know what they bring? Do they know their strengths and weaknesses between the lines and outside them? Have they done an inventory of their strengths?"
TINA: "No. I've never done that. I normally focus on good recruitment and tennis. I try to get players who can perform."
JAVIER: "Your team's issues are interpersonal, which is difficult because doubles is when they are a team as many people understand it. In this case, you have individuals who have to do their bit for the team, train against each other to enhance each other's play. The team climate is very important because on a day-to-day basis it creates the conditions for your team to improve themselves."
TINA: "What is team climate?"

Discussion questions

1. What are the main issues presented in this case?
2. What challenges might a sport psychology consultant face dealing with this case?
3. How might you determine which issues to focus on to start to deal with this case?
4. How might you develop a team intervention for this case?
5. How might you work with an intact (established) team versus a newly forming team?
6. How might you evaluate the impact of your work?

Author's notes

I tend to take a systems view of this kind of case. This means I look at the causal factors and how they relate to each other before going further with any kind of intervention. I want to understand what the relationships are and how they influence the players and the coach. I would prefer to start by knowing what Cissy's position is on things with Tina and her team because she is the boss and Tina reports to her; and if I am working with Tina I might be required to inform Cissy of things too, which blurs the line between client and "recipient" sometimes. In this case, I see Cissy as the ultimate client, and Tina and her team as the recipients of my work. I tend to take an instrumental approach to working with teams. Often the person who pays the bills is not always the person receiving the services, but they are very important in my consideration for future work. It means creating value for both parties and being effective in the delivery of the work.

I also prefer to look at the results and performances at the individual and team level over time, not only this season but the preceding season too. I like to look for patterns, structures, and processes that allow me to identify issues but, more importantly, opportunities for solutions and team development. Doing this gives me a sport performance view and allows me to talk to coaches and athletes about real things that happened for the purposes of understanding. However, understanding on its own is not very valuable if I can't translate it into a process to help the team improve its performance.

I would work with Tina to raise her awareness of the possibilities of finding strength in herself and her team and reframing the issues to team cohesion in two domains—social and task cohesion. This would allow us to identify problems, possibilities, and solutions in a collaborative framework by looking at the issues and not the individuals. By doing this I want to stay away from dealing with perceptions and labels of team members, personality, attitude, or belief issues at this time and stay focused on the issues and concerns initially presented. I would prefer to mirror the process with members of the team too. By getting a two-sided input into the solution I can see the similarities and differences between the two and prepare for the next phase. I would bring Tina and her team together to compare their ideas and facilitate a team development session where all the performance data is available and the feedback is displayed; and I would use high-impact facilitation techniques like ground rules setting for the interactions, visual displays of data and input, weighted decision-making approaches, and role modeling. I would want to create the conditions for the coach and her team to reach a shared understanding of how they can move forward and how they intend to begin the new season as an intact team.

This last point is often overlooked in the literature on coactive team development. There are differences between intact teams and teams that are forming and reforming, and different processes are at work. Many team development processes assume teams are forming from scratch. This is not happening here, and in my mind is a false place to begin. The team itself will be intact and experienced. The team is in development and new personnel are not expected until after the next academic year is completed; therefore, the members of the team are in a dynamic situation of personal development with each other and their coach. Where team systems like this are in place the structural roles of team members, the communication processes, and the performance coaching environment have to be addressed too. Each of these factors would need to be raised to the team members in clear and careful ways for the purposes of understanding, with the goal of recognition and acceptance that business as usual was not what was wanted by team members and that alternative approaches are called for. The case for change needs to be made, and the team itself and their coach should identify the solutions they are ready, willing, and able to commit to that have high impact for the social and task cohesion leading to better performances and a more positive sport experience for all team members and their coach.

Finally, I would use an impact evaluation for the team to complete after the facilitated meeting(s) about the work done, and then again about one month into the new academic year (about fout months) to see the lasting effects of the work. Depending on the results, I might recommend further sessions and follow up at minimum with Tina to check progress on the goals established during the intervention.

Further reading

Davis, L., & Jowett, S. (2014). Coach–athlete attachment and the quality of the coach–athlete relationship: implications for athlete's well-being. *Journal of Sports Sciences*, 32(15), 1454–1464.

Onağ, Z., & Tepeci, M. (2014). Team effectiveness in sport teams: The effects of team cohesion, intra team communication and team norms on team member satisfaction and intent to remain. *Procedia: Social and Behavioral Sciences*, 150, 420–428.

Turman, P. D. (2008). Coaches' immediacy behaviors as predictors of athletes' perceptions of satisfaction and team cohesion. *Western Journal of Communication*, 72(2), 162–179.

Wachsmuth, S., Jowett, S., & Harwood, C. G. (2017). Conflict among athletes and their coaches: What is the theory and research so far? *International Review of Sport and Exercise Psychology*, 10(1), 84–107.

19

TEAM DEVELOPMENT

Introduction

This is a case where the coach does not favor team building and team development. They have a clear frame of reference for the way they lead teams. The coach and players present an intact team, which means a straightforward team development stage model approach might not be the ideal strategy to take to solve the issues facing them. This is a complex case requiring students to think through each issue and develop an approach they feel will meet the competing demands of the situation.

Content implications

This case might be used for discussions centered on coach leadership, team dynamics, team cohesion, athlete leadership, coping under pressure, mental skills training, and coach development. Encourage your students to think broadly about how to develop leadership and team performance.

Purpose

The purpose of this case is for students to consider ways to help build teams that are introducing new players but are mostly intact, and to work with coaches who might have contrary ideas about how teams are built and developed.

Student learning outcomes

At the end of this case study learning opportunity, students should be able to:

1. Discuss the pros and cons or team building
2. Respond to the common criticisms discussed in the case

3. Consider how to work with a coach to develop a team building program
4. Determine who the client is and how they are served by team building

Cast of characters in order of appearance

Cissy Drew, Assistant Athletic Director and Women's Sport Administrator.
Viktor Varga, Head Coach, Men's Water Polo.
Cindy Varga, Viktor's wife.

Coach profile: Viktor Varga, water polo

The U's water polo program has grown steadily over the last decade. The head coach, Viktor Varga, developed it from nothing and eventually coached the men to two national championships. A class of players graduated and took their capabilities and leadership with them, leaving behind a group of freshman and sophomores. In the tenth year of the program Viktor's program developed a habit it had never had before: his team built up one and two goal leads which they gave up frequently. Their frailties were exposed ruthlessly by arch rivals Barrow in the final game of the regular conference season, who bounced back from a three-goal deficit to win the game by two goals. The U's players were crushed. They had split the season series with Barrow, but this game meant they slipped to third seed for their conference playoffs and finished with a three-game losing streak against the top three opponents in their conference. The team was low in confidence when they entered the conference playoffs and lost in the first round. This was the earliest they had been knocked out of the playoffs for seven years. They were reeling from the loss of form and the result tarnishing the team's record in recent times.

During the final weeks of the regular season and into the playoffs the young squad lost confidence in their playing system and, to some extent, their coach and team captains. They felt a bit disconnected. Key players went "hiding" during games, and communication between some players had been toxic. Several times in the locker room after a game players had been in conflict with each other, but not in front of the coach. Players questioned who should be captain, and the players that had been made co-captains did not have a strong desire to be in the role. The most outspoken player with the strongest personality and greatest desire to win was the goal keeper. Unlike other players, he wanted to lead and he wanted to improve; the problem for him was that he was a freshman in his first season, and he was from California. He was still settling into a new way of life, a new team, and a new coach.

At the end of each season the Assistant Athletic Director, Cissy Drew, surveyed all the athletes about their experience during the season. This was customary, and all coaches expected the survey and the results to be shared with them before the end of the season so that they could talk with their players before they left for the summer.

The case

Cissy and Viktor met in the Champions Conference room in The U's Athletic Department administrative building overlooking the sport complex and facilities. The women's soccer team were training on the field below them.

CISSY: "Thanks for coming Viktor. I prepared the athlete survey feedback for you and summarized my thoughts and recommendations based on what I read. I know you have not had a chance to see the results, so how about you take 10–15 minutes to read them. I will come back with coffee for us; how do you like your coffee?"

VIKTOR: "Black with three sugars. Will we discuss the results when you get back or do I take what you say and do what the recommendations tell me to do?"

CISSY: "We'll discuss the results Viktor. You're not in trouble. I'll be back with the coffee."

Cissy left the room and Viktor read through the summary and recommendations first, then pawed at the survey results. He could feel himself simmering with frustration as he read through the anonymous surveys. He did not care who said what, but he cared a lot about what was said.

Cissy returned to the room. The women's team were still training, and Viktor was sitting staring out of the window at them.

CISSY: "Here's your coffee."
VIKTOR: "Thank you."
CISSY: "So, you had a chance to review the survey results."
VIKTOR: "Yes."
CISSY: "And …"
VIKTOR: "And … and I am pissed off! These are the words of children not men. Their behavior and attitude is disappointing … clearly they gave up, they were not tough, and they allowed their emotions to get in the way of our team's goals. It's not what I expected. Yes, we had a tough end to the season, but I didn't know the reasons for it were so silly and childish. Why didn't they say something to me? Why only be brave after the season? Why not focus on winning first and dealing with these things second? This would never happen in Hungary."

CISSY: "Okay Viktor, take a breath. What did you think of my recommendations? … I take it you didn't like what I suggested."

Viktor stared at Cissy.

CISSY: "I'm on your side Viktor. This is the first time in years this has happened. You're a great coach but you have a different group this year. You might have to operate differently."

VIKTOR: "I used similar approaches as the previous years when we have been successful. I don't understand what went wrong. I recruited these students, they knew what to expect and they knew the standards we have here."

CISSY: "That might be the case but they are inexperienced in some things, and clearly are not capable of sorting themselves out. You had a situation where you lost their focus in the middle of the season and did not change things up, and you were unaware the team was attacking itself. I mean we all know your players are hyper-aggressive and you recruit players who play up to the edge of the physical rules of your sport. You're lucky there were no brawls in your locker room because, based on the results, that kind of behavior was not far away. Imagine if that had happened. We would be having a different conversation about that, and maybe about your role here at The U."

VIKTOR: "So what are you saying? I did not know what I was doing? It was them who did not communicate with me. They are the ones to sort themselves out, just like previous teams have done. They are responsible for their behavior not me."

CISSY: "Viktor you are missing the point. This team has no leadership and it is confused. You are expecting things from them they don't know how to do. They know and play good water polo, but they are not yet equipped to lead themselves as your recent teams have, and this year's recruits will make your team even younger in experience at the level you play. You are going to have to adapt what you do and how you do it. If this is not dealt with you could face another season of underperformance and, even worse, a team that damages itself from the inside—and I don't think you or anyone here wants that."

VIKTOR: "I'm stunned."

CISSY: "No doubt you are. This has not happened to you before."

Viktor shifted focus to a recommendation Cissy made about team building.

VIKTOR: "I see that you recommended I do team building with the group. Why?"

CISSY: "I think it is an approach that could bring your players together and help them sort through some of their challenges."

VIKTOR: "I hate team building. It does not work ... meetings and concepts without transfer, no change in behavior, consultants and so on who don't know the sport, the team, or them telling us how to work together ... oh yes and I have seen the touchy-feely stuff that builds anger toward team mates and stupid obstacle courses and lifting people through spider webs of string and rope ... silly things with no transfer to water polo."

CISSY: "Well it sounds like you don't think this will work."

VIKTOR: "How can it? I mean, can you show me any evidence for any elite water polo team where this kind of thing has an impact and makes a difference in play? Besides, I don't want to pay outsiders from my budget to do these things for my team."

CISSY: "You mean you don't think getting players to talk is a good thing? You're team's communication broke down because they could not communicate with each other. I mean you can see from the survey they were at each other. Your team has no leadership and they say you didn't know this."

VIKTOR: "Don't tell me what I know and don't know about my team. They are the ones who should look to themselves."

CISSY: "Okay Viktor, did you see there were problems with your team or not this season?"

VIKTOR: "My seniors left, they took their leadership with them. I put captains in who I thought would do the job the team and me needed."

CISSY: "Were you wrong about this year's captains?"

VIKTOR: "Not exactly. In games we won they did well; in games we lost they did not do so well."

CISSY: "But we both know it's the games you struggle in that leaders should step up and build the team's energy and focus, and you didn't have that this year. I saw the game versus Barrow. That was a tough loss and it hurt."

Viktor knew the loss to Barrow was a turning point in the whole season, especially after losing the previous two matches. There was no bigger game for any team at The U than against Barrow.

CISSY: "You know the women's squad do all kinds of team building activities throughout the year."

VIKTOR: "That's different. They're girls. I treat them differently."

CISSY: "Yes, but you can still learn from their experience and use it for your men's teams."

VIKTOR: "It's a different sport with different ideas. It's not men's water polo."

CISSY: "Yes but their performance is consistent, their coaches adapt year on year to the players, and they address issues as they emerge."

VIKTOR: "Our performance has been excellent. We have won national titles and been conference champions. We are feared."

CISSY: "Yes, that was before this year. After this season everyone in your sport will know you have problems, and so will your recruits if they come to visit this campus and your team is unhappy. There is a bigger picture Viktor. This season might impact who you recruit, who transfers from The U to another school, who steps out, and maybe your walk-on players might stop playing too. You have to get your head around the problems you face and find solutions now. Times have changed and you have to adapt with them."

Viktor looked down at Cissy's notes and read a recommendation about team captains.

VIKTOR: "Cissy, why do you say here that I should make the freshman goal keeper the team captain?"

CISSY: "Because it seems like he is the person who fits your way of thinking the most. He is a great goal keeper, very aggressive and disciplined. I have seen him train and he is totally committed to his preparation. He is a good student. I checked his academic record he has an A-grade point average and, most importantly, most of his team mates want him as captain."

VIKTOR: "I choose the captains not them, and I don't like freshmen or sophomores leading teams. It creates disharmony. Older players should lead."

CISSY: "You have a different group and you need to look at what you have here and not get hung up on ideas you used to use. It seems like this student is capable of leading. Why not give him the chance?"

VIKTOR: "Tell me, who else does this here? … Anyone? … No! So why are you making me even think about this?"

CISSY: "Because your team is not in the same place it was last year, or the year before that, or the year before that! Don't be mule-headed on this Viktor. Things need to improve and there are solutions you can use if you want to."

VIKTOR: "You are telling me how to run my team."

CISSY: "No I am not. I am telling you nothing. I am showing you the results of the survey and I made recommendations. In the end Viktor, this is your decision, but if things do not improve this year you might get one more year, but then … you know how this works. We can allow two years of up and down performance, but a third year? No way! This is not how we work and you know that. As long as any of our coaches are doing everything in their power to improve the student-athlete experience on and off the field of play we will support them. But it is clear from what the students said about themselves and you that we can expect next year to be poor too. We want to support you, so give these ideas a chance."

VIKTOR: "Wow! You mean my job's on the line if I do not follow your recommendations. I am here because of my qualities and my experience. You don't trust them anymore?"

CISSY: "I am not threatening you. I am asking you to consider the options in front of you and develop an approach that solves the problems you and your team faces. You know how we operate here. We will support you, but these results tell a story we have to listen to."

VIKTOR: "How long do I have to think about things?"

CISSY: "Well, we expect your team to have their exit interviews with you before the end of the semester starting in three weeks."

VIKTOR: "Have you done this with anyone else here since I have been here?"

CISSY: "You mean had this kind of conversation?"

VIKTOR: "Yes. How come you did not tell me earlier?"

CISSY: "You were not ready to hear me."

VIKTOR: "Who is it?"

CISSY: "Tina."

VIKTOR: "The tennis coach?"

CISSY: "Yup."

VIKTOR: "What happened?"

CISSY: "I can't go into details, but what I can say is that Tina was receptive and acted in the interests of her team."

VIKTOR: "They had a great season. What happened?"

CISSY: "Teams are difficult. You never know what the right mix of things between the coach and players is to make things work. Things change from year to year, personalities develop, and injuries happen, coaches get into bad moods …"

Viktor smiled as he listened to the last things Cissy said. She saw this.

CISSY: "Is some of this making sense now?"

VIKTOR: "I don't like it."

CISSY: "No coach would like this situation Viktor. Listen, think about things, give it a chance, and let's talk next week. Call me and set something up. How's your coffee?"

VIKTOR: "It's cold."

CISSY: "Sorry … can I suggest one more thing?"

VIKTOR: "If you want to."

CISSY: "Talk to Cindy. Tell her about this and see what she says. You can't show her the survey because of confidentiality, but you can give her a general sense of the situation. I know you will listen to her."

There was a long pause. They both took a breath and looked at the women's soccer team finish their session and come in for a team cheer before dispersing.

VIKTOR: "Thanks Cissy. I didn't like to hear this but I'm glad you told me and we can talk more about it."

CISSY: "We're on the same team Viktor. Go U!"

Cissy raised her hand and Viktor high-fived her back, got up and left the room, leaving his mug on the conference table.

Viktor got home before his kids, Laura and Lucas, arrived. Cindy had finished her nursing shift at a local outpatient clinic, which allowed her to get home by 6pm and dinner with the family. Viktor's kids did their homework from their second grade teacher in the kitchen before dinner as he prepared his usual Tuesday night meal of spaghetti Bolognese. Cindy came home and they all sat down to eat at the table the kids had been working on.

CINDY: "How was your day, honey?"

VIKTOR: "Interesting."

CINDY: "Uh oh, what happened?"

VIKTOR: "Cissy gave me some feedback from the team. It wasn't good."

CINDY: "You mean you didn't like it but it was true and you're upset."
VIKTOR: "I hate that ... you always know me."
CINDY: "It's about how bad the season was, right?"
VIKTOR: "Yes. How did you know?"
CINDY: "You complained all season about things. How the boys were not united or responding well to each other."
VIKTOR: "I did?"
CINDY: "Yeah. Short memory."
VIKTOR: "Ahh, okay. Yes it was about that. I just did want to hear it today and see it written down."
CINDY: "Cissy was fair with you, right?"
VIKTOR: "Yes, you know her—professional and supportive. She made it difficult for me to be angry."
CINDY: "Well, she supported you and helped you establish the program. She is invested in you. What did she say?"
VIKTOR: "I have to do team building and leadership things with the players. I have to think about improvements and make them and be seen to be doing what I can."
CINDY: "Well, that's your job as a coach, right?"
VIKTOR: "Yeah."
CINDY: "So what are you going to do, Coach?"
VIKTOR: "I don't know, but I know I have to do something. I just never been in this situation before and never been given this feedback by players before. It's not a good feeling."
CINDY: "You know, since we met there have been ups and downs in water polo. This is just a down moment. You've had so much success and your players came to The U because of the program you built, the players who helped the program succeed. This is a thing that's all. Talk to Cissy about what you are supposed to do. Don't be proud about this."
VIKTOR: "I don't know how to do so many new things."
CINDY: "Can you ask Cissy for help?"
VIKTOR: "Yes."
CINDY: "Then ask her. Is there anyone else?"
VIKTOR: "Yeah another coach, and maybe Javier the sport psychology guy I worked with. But I don't know if he does team building stuff."
CINDY: "Okay, but you have support and these people like you and respect you, right?"
VIKTOR: "They do."

Discussion questions

1. What do you think is going on in this case?
2. How might you present team building as a solution to a coach if you perceived their team needed it?

3. How might you respond to the objections to team building raised by the coach in this case?
4. How might team building be introduced to the water polo squad?
5. What kind of coach and player education might be necessary in this case?
6. What role might you take as the sport psychology consultant if a team building solution was implemented for this squad?

Author's notes

It is not uncommon that a coach will strongly respond to perceived criticism of their coaching methods from their players or from administration. At the time it can feel quite unfair and hurtful to them, so the process of providing a coach feedback has to be addressed carefully. I prefer a three-person set-up when giving a coach feedback that might require some kind of facilitation to soothe the situation, provide support for both parties, and focus on the issues while acknowledging the emotional difficulties that can arise. I usually find myself as the facilitator, so ensure I have a full grasp of the facts and the expectations of the feedback meeting before it takes place. I also make sure my role is explicitly understood by both parties in the meeting.

Once the feedback has been shared, discussed, and an agreement reached to follow up, my role typically shifts to one of adviser to the coach. I am careful not to tell them what I think they should do; instead, I come alongside them and share possibilities. Communication and operation rapidly become collaboration between us. I am mindful to remember the coach I am partnering with wants to be successful too but might not have the knowledge, capability, or tools to achieve their goals. It helps when they are open-minded about solutions they can imagine being effective and transferable to their team. This phase of my role might be a couple of hours to several days long, depending on the issues presented and how the coach feels about the solutions available to them.

If I am retained to conduct a team building program I typically ensure goals, team roles and responsibilities, leadership, and communication matters are attended to. I address these things by gaining as much input from team leadership and coaching staff as possible before the program begins. Commitment to the process from formal and informal leadership connected to the team is critical. Finally, if the head coach is not committed I typically prefer not to do this work because unless they are supportive, resourcing the process and suitably engaged, the work often fails to deliver the results it promises in the planning.

Further reading

Bloom, G., Stevens, D., & Wickwire, T. (2003). Expert coaches' perceptions of team building. *Journal of Applied Sport Psychology*, 15(2), 129–143.

Paradis, K. F., & Martin, L. J. (2012). Team building in sport: Linking theory and research to practical application. *Journal of Sport Psychology in Action*, 3(3), 159–170.

Yukelson, D. (1997). Principles of effective team building interventions in sport: A direct services approach at Penn State University. *Journal of Applied Sport Psychology*, 9(1), 73–96.

Yukelson, D., & Rose, R. (2014). The psychology of ongoing excellence: An NCAA coach's perspective on winning consecutive multiple national championships. *Journal of Sport Psychology in Action*, 5(1), 44–58.

20

SPORT ADMINISTRATOR-DIRECTED IMPROVEMENT: PART 1

Introduction

This is a complex case involving three coaches, a sport administrator, and a sport psychology practitioner. Sport psychology practitioners are often invited to work with administrators and coaches around key issues affecting the organization and the team. It is possible emerging sport psychology consultants might not be exposed to workings and dealings of organizational life as part of their training, or be in roles requiring them to work through a range of dilemmas connected to a single case. This is the first of a two-part case related to others in this text. (See "Cast of characters: chapters" for other cases involving the protagonists in this case.)

Content implications

This case might be used for discussions about organizational stressors and the perspectives of sport administrators toward their coaches and staff. Further discussions might take place concerning the role of the sport psychology practitioner and the range of possible challenges they face when they are in a position to have dual roles. Finally, sport psychology consultants might sometimes be entrusted with information from the person who is paying for the service and the person receiving the service. Sorting through the complexity of relationships and appropriate professional responses makes for rich discussion.

Purpose

The purpose here is to help students consider how to work in a complex organizational setting with enduring relationships between all the participants, and to recognize the challenges of being in a dual role.

Student learning outcomes

At the end of this case students should be able to:

1. Discuss different ways to conceptualize coach–athlete relationships
2. Respond to common issues arising in coach–athlete relationships
3. Consider how to work with coaches to enhance relationships with their athletes
4. Determine the scope of a sport psychology practitioner working to enhance coach–athlete relationships

Cast of characters in order of appearance

Celia "Cissy" Drew, Assistant Athletic Director and Women's Sport Administrator.
Viktor Varga, Head Coach, Men's Water Polo.
Robin Marriot, Head Coach, Men's Soccer.
Tina Morrison, Head Coach, Women's Tennis.
Vivian Moreno, Sport Psychology Consultant.

Coach: profile: Viktor Varga, Robin Marriot, and Tina Morrison

Viktor Varga (men's water polo coach), Robin Marriot (men's soccer head coach), and Tina Morrison (women's tennis coach) were at the end of the academic year. They had completed player feedback meetings and exit interviews, and received a lot of input from a variety of sources connected with their sports. Each had had meetings with Cissy Drew, the Assistant Athletic Director and Senior Women's Administrator. Cissy knew the coaches well, having helped recruit them, and provided support over the years. For various reasons the most recent season had challenged them all in different ways.

They had faced poor results, underperformance, choking under pressure, players challenging their coaching and leadership, and personal issues in their own lives influencing their behavior as coaches. Now was the best time to take stock—when the students had left campus, new recruits had been confirmed, and there was space in their schedules to work on things for the new season without the pressure of the regular school year to contend with.

Cissy Drew called a meeting two weeks after finals week with the coaches, to give them a break after finals week and time to reflect and prepare for their meeting. She informed them the sport psychology consultant, Vivian Moreno (whom they all knew in different ways), would be attending to help facilitate the meeting. Cissy also sent them an agenda with one item on it for discussion and a timeline for when decisions and plans would be submitted for review. The next meeting's date was already set too. Cissy had checked the vacation schedule before calling the meeting, and knew when the coaches would be on campus during the summer. The item Cissy wanted to discuss in the meeting was: coach–athlete relationships.

The meeting was scheduled for a Friday morning to last for 3.5 hours, with breakfast and coffee served. It was going to be a working meeting involving problem identification, solution generation, and action planning. She allowed the coaches two weeks to work on things before the next meeting. She described Vivian's role with the coaches as facilitator and content expert, but this did not involve telling them what to do or how to do it. Cissy asked Vivian to facilitate the meeting because the latter was less well known to the coaches and she had experience in her counseling practice mediating different types of conflict.

The main reason behind Cissy calling the meeting was that she was concerned the feedback from the student-athlete revealed weaknesses in these coaches. The coaches seemed unaware of the severity of the issues that had surfaced. This meant that if the issues were not resolved Cissy might need to warn them about their performance or, worse, terminate their employment if the new season did not yield improvements in the student-athlete experience. She did not want to be in this position, and only she and the Athletic Director knew that these options were possible. Making her position even more difficult was that each coach had different needs; but she thought that in bringing them together they might form a support group to help each other. After all, Robin, Tina, and Viktor had talked with her about their teams and some of the issues they had in common. Additionally, Robin and Tina were more open to developing their coaching, and might influence Viktor.

The case

The group met in the Champions Conference Room at The U. The long, polished, mahogany conference table had space for 20 seats. The room was filled with poster-size photographs of athletes from every team in action and showing various emotions. On the wall at the far end from the group were plaques listing hall of fame athletes, coaches, and teams. Taking pride of place were academic and volunteer service contributions. Quotes from athletic alumni were printed around the room too. It was an inspirational place, with a wall of floor to ceiling windows overlooking the indoor training facilities for all The U's teams. The group of five sat in a semicircle at one end of the table, leaving space behind them for a flip chart next to a counter laid out with markers, sticky notes, pens, and plain paper. As it was Friday, dress for all of them was casual and, being in this room made all the coaches feel relaxed and good humored.

CISSY: "Good morning everyone, thank you for being here this morning. I know sometimes you might not have meetings like this on Fridays, but I am sure this is important and necessary for us to meet. As you know, there is only one item for us to deal with—and, I should say, I will not be present when you discuss it. You will be in Vivian's hands for that part of the discussion.

The reason I felt this was necessary is because you all have had student-athletes express their concerns about the quality of their experience in your teams. You have all seen your own survey data from your teams and you have had time to think about it. I feel you have an opportunity now to begin to develop fresh and possibly new approaches to how you work with your athletes. I know you all well, and I know you work hard and in your heart want your teams to play well and have a good experience, but things have to improve. Change is necessary and I want you to lead your own improvement."

VIKTOR: "So we're in trouble and you want us to figure this out?"

ROBIN: "Yes, we are in trouble and we need to figure this out, otherwise worse things might happen to us?"

TINA: "Worse things? Like what?"

CISSY: "Look, I called this meeting so each of you could work on your own team, and work together and support each other. I want you to focus on how to improve your relationships with your players and improve the student-athlete experience. You have all had successful teams, good times, and positive moments. I am asking you to get back to those things and stop some of the behaviors you have all used this season which have clearly been detrimental to your teams' experiences."

VIKTOR: "So you're saying, get better at these things or bad things will happen?"

CISSY: "Viktor, I am saying I want you to enhance your relationships and work to ensure your teams have positive experiences in your sport."

VIKTOR: "Okay, I get it."

TINA: "So we're not in trouble?"

ROBIN: "Not yet."

CISSY: "Vivian, can you talk about your role here this morning and throughout this process?"

VIVIAN: "Sure. Well, thanks for having me here today. I know all of you in a few ways, but I do not know very much. I typically work with The U when Javier Aguilar is unavailable. I am clinical psychologist and I work with organizations and families when there is conflict present. My understanding of my role is to facilitate this meeting and make sure each of you leaves with an action plan to return with in two weeks to share with the group and present to Cissy too. I am not here to tell you how to do things or how to be; but if you ask me about things that might be helpful to you as you think about your teams and how you want to do things, I am happy to share. You should know I have no vested interest here. I have not had any conversations with Cissy about your teams, I don't know the issues, I don't know the data you know about, and I don't know what happens after this two-step meeting process. I am able to talk individually with you between meetings, but my role officially ends after the second meeting. I am here purely in the role of facilitator."

CISSY: "Thank you Vivian."

She looked around at each coach.

CISSY: "Do any of you have any further questions for me before I leave?"

The coaches said nothing.

CISSY: "Okay, I'm going to leave. But the last thing I want you to know is that I do not want to discuss your ideas with any of you between now and the next meeting. Work among yourselves and with Vivian."
VIKTOR: "Why is that? You're involved in this, and we might have questions."
CISSY: "Yes you might have questions, Viktor, but all I have to say on these issues has been said. We know the same information about your teams, so the only new things to discuss will be your solutions, and that is what I want you to focus on. Concentrate on enhancing your team not talking to me about it. I'm looking forward to returning in two weeks to this group."

With that, Cissy got up and left the room. The coaches sat and looked at each other like they realized they were expected to work hard and were feeling a little anxious. Vivian spoke up.

VIVIAN: "Okay, let's get some coffee, eat something, or maybe go to the bathroom before we start."
TINA: "Good idea."
VIVIAN: "Let's start in 10 minutes."

The coaches nodded.

Vivian organized herself and wrote a t-chart with a heading above the left column stating "Issue" and the right column stating "Perception." Ten minutes went by; Tina and Robin (with coffee and a bagel) were in their seats ready to go on time. Vivian began: "Okay, what I would like us to start with is you listing the issues you have in your team and your perception of it. Tina, would you go first please?"

TINA: "Sure, I just say what I think?"
VIVIAN: "Yes, and I will write down what you say as you say it on the flip chart."

She picked up a black marker and prepared to write.

TINA: "Okay, well, basically some of my squad say their team mates are dominating the team and I am allowing it to happen. They also claim my coaching is not good during matches—I give too much information. They say I am a great coach off the court, but on the court not so good. But then half of them say I am really good and they love me on and off the court ... but they tend to be my lower seeded players. It's the top players that seem to have a problem with me."

VIVIAN: "Okay, can you give me some more details?"
TINA: "Well, what I mean is, my top players feel I compete with them in training, which affects their performance; but, on the other hand, they feel like they can talk to me off the court. My other players feel they can talk to me off the court and get good things out of me on the court. There is one player who feels like she started off having a positive relationship with me but now things have changed and she feels there's tension and conflict in our relationship. She also says that this has affected her performance. The sad thing is, she's my top player. She could be a real champion for our team."

Vivian wrote down all the key points, then addressed Robin.

VIVIAN: "When we do feedback to each other Robin, you are going to reflect what you have heard from Tina, okay?"
ROBIN: "Sure."

Viktor entered the conference room and went to sit down.

VIKTOR: "Sorry I'm late. I lost track of time."

Vivian watched him all the way. She put her marker down and asked Viktor to step outside with her for a moment. The two stood outside the room, leaving Robin and Tina wondering what was being said.

VIVIAN: "Viktor, we agreed to a 10-minute break. You are late."
VIKTOR: "It's no big deal. I made it back didn't I?"
VIVIAN: "I find it disrespectful to your peers and to me. In future, if you are going to be late please say so before we break."
VIKTOR: "Wow! Really ... okay. I'll announce my behavior to you and everyone before I act, okay? Can we go back in now if you are so focused on this meeting?"

The two entered the room and Viktor took his seat. Tina and Robin saw by the look on his face that something had been said that irritated him. He wore a deep frown and brooded in his chair. Vivian returned to her role and took up her markers.

VIVIAN: "Okay Robin, please share what is going on with your team and I will list the issues and perceptions you have."
ROBIN: "Well, things have been difficult. We didn't have the season we wanted. One of my players, my assistant, and me got into a terrible mess; and, if I'm honest, I have no idea why I responded the way I did. Basically, I've been taking a dominant position and upsetting my players. I've been intimidating them, and I'm embarrassed by what I've done and how I've been this year.

Cissy knows all about this, and my wife told me I was totally heavy-handed this season. I can't reach several of my players. I like recruiting independent-minded and talented players, but it seems like the players I wanted on this team are the ones I have the hardest time with. I also have a team leadership issue, and I'm thinking my behavior has something to do with it. I think I've been getting too anxious because our results have not been good, and putting pressure on myself and then in turn on the players. I think I've made my team's climate one where they depend on me for more things than themselves and we are not interdependent. We have good players and I helped them get to higher levels of play, but this last year I think we got distanced and my players lost trust in me. The situation I mentioned earlier had a big impact on me. I have to think whether I'm going to keep or fire an assistant coach because I didn't realize how negative their role in my team was. I suppose I'm a bit lost. I acted with good intentions, but can see I really had a bad year as a coach, and I don't want to have next year go the same way or things will be awful for all of us. Things have to change."

VIVIAN: "Thanks Robin. Seems like you have thought about this a lot and taken responsibility for some things you can improve."

ROBIN: "Yeah, but it's not been easy. I have another assistant who I could listen to even more often. I kind of went off the rails."

VIKTOR: "What is this? Therapy? You're a coach, your players should respond to you."

ROBIN: "That's true, but it's my team and how things go reflect on me and my leadership. If my team loses trust in me I have nothing. I'm just being honest. I'm not frightened of admitting my mistakes or my weaknesses. I helped build this program, and I want my team and all my athletes and everyone associated with my team to have a great experience and perform better. But I am the head coach, and it starts with me. Are you scared, Viktor? I mean what's your problem? You returned late and now you're kind of calling me out. What's your deal?"

TINA: "Whoa! Let's all calm down here."

VIKTOR: "I am not scared of anything. I just don't feel like sharing anything here. It's not my way."

TINA: "But Cissy wants us here, and she thinks this can be positive. Let's face it, we all need to improve, so better to try together than apart. Anyway, why were you late coming back to the meeting?"

Viktor looked at Robin and Tina. He looked sullen.

VIKTOR: "Agh! I'm frustrated. I never been in this situation before. My team fell apart in the playoffs. I recruit the most aggressive players I can find. I want my team to play fast and physical and terrorize our opponents in the water, but this year me and them failed. I don't feel close to my players and I don't feel like them and me are committed to each other. I think they should be more committed to me than me to them. But I am not sure. I never faced these problems before."

TINA: "I heard you had some personal problems too. Do you?"

VIKTOR: "How did you hear about that?"

TINA: "Just through the grapevine, you know."

VIKTOR: "Yes, okay. It's been a tough year. I have not been myself, but I don't want to talk about it here."

TINA: "No problem Viktor, but sometimes just saying stuff helps others understand where you're at."

Vivian had stepped back almost behind the flip chart to observe the interactions between the coaches. When Tina finished, she stepped forward.

VIVIAN: "Thank you for sharing your views, Viktor, and building on what Robin shared. Give me a moment to capture everything you said on the flip chart."

The coaches sat watching Vivian complete her notes on the chart. Each coach had filled two poster sheets with notes with their feedback. She used her phone to photograph each sheet to share with the coaches.

VIVIAN: "Thank you for providing your viewpoints and naming your issues out loud. Now you know what each of you is facing, I want you to take 15 minutes to work on a plan to address the needs in your team. You can ask me questions if you want to during your time. Now, let's take a 10-minute break."

VIKTOR: "I will be back in time. Sorry to everyone for earlier."

The group looked back at him, acknowledging his apology. Ten minutes later, everyone was in their seat and the meeting restarted on time.

VIVIAN: "Okay, before you take 15 minutes here to work on your plan, what do you take away from the conversation we have so far?"

The coaches reflected on the question and wrote notes on paper they had placed in front of them earlier in the meeting.

TINA: "Well, I think I need to build relationships with my top players and figure out how to do that. Based on what I hear, I'm different with them than with the others and I need to do something different."

VIKTOR: "I hate this stuff. I don't know how to change what I am doing. I've never been in this situation before and I am going to need some help. My issue is me, not them. They are kids, what the hell do they know? Nothing! That's my problem. It's all on me to sort this out."

ROBIN: "I feel like this is going to be hard work. I know we all have to work on things, but I need help too. I don't know where to begin. I kind of think I have to work on my management skills and my communication skills, and I might have to fire my goal keeping coach. But where do I start?"

Vivian sat down and set her markers on the table.

VIVIAN: "Thanks for sharing. As Cissy said, I'm here to help you. Let's take 15 minutes and then reconvene to give each other some highlights from our season and then meet in two weeks. Remember, you can ask me for help."

Discussion questions

1. What do you think the issues presented suggest about the coaches' approaches to leadership?
2. What do you think are the main points of coach–athlete conflict presented in this case?
3. How might you determine which coach-athlete behaviors should be addressed first?
4. What do you think the role of Dr Moreno is in this case?
5. How might you work with the coaches between meetings?
6. What challenges does this case present the sport psychology practitioner?
7. What counseling approaches might you use if you were presented with this case?

Author's notes

I have facilitated meetings like this, and sat in on others when a colleague has led them. The case presented here is an example of a meeting where the coaches involved had advance notice and access to their own data for feedback. Often meetings take place and things are revealed to coaches only at the time, which often provokes negative and unhelpful responses. In my experience, administrative leaders like Cissy operate as here in the interests of the coaches and players because they desire a long-term solution and want to support coaches they invested in. Irrespective of how I feel about the way a situation like this is created, I see my role as making sure it is a positive and helpful experience for all involved.

To do this kind of work I attended meeting facilitation workshops and an intensive course to facilitate meetings for decision making. I gained confidence and competency in this area of work by training outside of psychology and gaining skills for a range of contexts. Many psychology programs train counselors and the like on group processes and interpersonal interaction. While this might be helpful, those meetings often do not end up with decisions being made. Meeting facilitation to achieve results is very different. In this case, decisions are required, action plans generated, implementation expected, and evaluation likely to happen. These are behavioral processes which require displays of observable actions and commitments from the individuals involved. Because of the set-up of this kind of meeting, individuals understand that their choices are limited and that they are expected to comply. This mandated behavior can cause reluctance and disappointment, which means you have to be ready to deal with conflict as it arises. Recognizing how to process and mitigate conflict so that it does not block progress is important. Having the skills to deescalate, engage and foster positive communication behaviors is important in cases like this.

Acting as a facilitator with expert contribution can be tricky because you have to balance roles and responsibilities. Be clear on what you are doing and have a rationale for your contribution. It is important to do this because individuals might attach their gain or loss from the process to your contribution, thereby diffusing their responsibility from the outcomes achieved. An action plan should contain the intellectual work of the coach responsible for implementing it. Plans should match the coach's confidence and ability; and, where they need support to deliver their plan, resources should be allocated to help them reach their goals.

Further reading

Connole, I. J., Watson, J. C., Shannon, V. R., Wrisberg, C., Etzel, E., & Schimmel, C. (2014). NCAA athletic administrators' preferred characteristics for sport psychology positions: A consumer market analysis. *Sport Psychologist*, 28(4), 406–417.

Fletcher, D., & Scott, M. (2010). Psychological stress in sports coaches: A review of concepts, research, and practice. *Journal of Sports Sciences*, 28(2), 127–137.

Knight, C. J., Rodgers, W. M., Reade, I. L., Mrak, J. M., & Hall, C. R. (2015). Coach transitions: Influence of interpersonal and work environment factors. *Sport, Exercise, and Performance Psychology*, 4(3), 170–187.

Watson, J. C., Way, W. C., & Hilliard, R. C. (2017). Ethical issues in sport psychology. *Current Opinion in Psychology*, 16, 143–147.

21

SPORT ADMINISTRATOR-DIRECTED IMPROVEMENT: PART 2

Introduction

This completes the two-part case introduced in Chapter 20. This part shows how the coaches responded to challenges posed there, and how they represented themselves to the sport administrator and each other.

Content implications

This scenario increases the complexity of information for students to sort through. The role of the sport psychology professional in this story (Vivian Moreno) is provocative and powerful. She is being used as an instrument of the sport administrator (Cissy Drew) to achieve the latter's ends. They are also in a mediating, facilitation, and counseling role with varying degrees of openness given they have information from the sport administrator that the coaches involved do not possess. Encourage students to consider the demands they might place on themselves if they are in this position and how they might self-manage in the future if they were faced with the challenges posed in this case. Students should be encouraged to determine who is and who is not their client, and explain how they might cope with the potentially conflicting demands of their multiple roles in this situation.

Purpose

The purpose here extends the learning from the first part of the case to help students consider scope of their role in an enduring work setting with added organizational burden and responsibilities to the purchaser and the recipients of service.

Student learning outcomes

At the end of this case students should be able to:

1. Recognize the organizational stressors affecting coach–athlete relationships
2. Consider the role of a sport psychology practitioner in a situation where a coach's livelihood is on the line
3. Discuss the ethical challenges of a sport psychology practitioner in a multi-purpose role
4. Consider a range of possible interventions enhancing positive coach–athlete relationships

Cast of characters in order of appearance

Vivian Moreno, Sport Psychology Consultant.
Celia "Cissy" Drew, Assistant Athletic Director and Women's Sport Administrator.
Tina Morrison, Head Coach, Women's Tennis.
Robin Marriot, Head Coach, Men's Soccer.
Viktor Varga, Head Coach, Men's Water Polo.

Coach profile: Robin Marriot, Tina Morrison, Viktor Varga

Two weeks have passed since the first meeting where Cissy Drew, the Assistant Athletic Director, explained to coaches Tina Morrison, Viktor Varga, and Robin Marriot that she expected them to develop plans for improving the sport experience for their athletes. She placed the responsibility for the action plans on the coaches. The coaches left the first meeting disturbed they could not speak to Cissy about their collective or individual situation between meetings. But they accepted this was her decision and there was nothing they could do about it. They recognized they were on their own but that they could ask for help from psychologist Vivian Moreno, who stepped in when Javier Aguilar, The U's usual sport psychology provider, was unavailable.

    Shortly after the first meeting Cissy called Vivian and told her in confidence that each coach would be observed following the second meeting to see if they had implemented their plans and to what extent they would be successful. Cissy had been thinking about the process and keeping Javier's and Vivian's contributions to The U's athletic teams separate. She invited Vivian to be part of the observation and feedback process, thereby extending her role to the whole of the next academic year. Cissy disclosed to Vivian that the coaches might lose their jobs if the student survey experience data did not improve and that results were also poor. Cissy did not inform the coaches of her communication or invitation to Vivian during the two weeks between meetings. Vivian agreed to the expanded role and agreed to provide feedback, but the details would have to be worked out closer to the beginning of the new academic year, which was about 11 weeks away.

During the two-week period, each coach had called or met with Vivian to discuss their ideas. Interactions were kept to 30-minute periods, either by phone or video conferencing. Vivian was out of town during this time and the coaches were around campus but with light duties. Robin spoke with Vivian twice. The first time Robin discussed the pros and cons of firing his goal keeper coach and having his veterans over to dinner at his house before pre-season preparation to start off on the right note. He wanted the players to see he had a family and that he was not a terror to work with. The second call to Vivian was about Robin fearing he could lose his job at the end of the next academic year. He was scared his plans to improve the student experience might not go well and that he could be let go. He only knew how to coach soccer, and did not really have any other skills. Cissy had told him he needed to get himself sorted out and results had to improve. He was frightened.

Tina called Vivian once to present her ideas, which centered on building a strong coach–player relationship base and doing some different things with her coaching, such as the use of technology, having a graduate assistant, and undergoing personal development. She was upbeat and excited to put things right.

The final calls were three from Viktor. The first was to discuss his proposed team-building program, which sounded like a military boot camp experience. Vivian urged Viktor to rethink his approach, but his ideas were promising and going in the right direction. His intent was to build a team, but his inexperience in program development came through. The second call concerned mental toughness and how to develop a program that all the boys could benefit from; and the third call was to ask Vivian to help him become a better coach. Viktor's wife had suggested this. Vivian did not answer either way about this idea because she wanted to wait until the next meeting took place and Cissy Drew was present.

The case

Once again the group met in the Champions Conference Room at The U, set up as before. Vivian arrived early to make sure things were ready to go on time, and Cissy Drew arrived about 30 minutes before the coaches were expected.

VIVIAN: "Hello Cissy, how are you?"
CISSY: "Fine thank you, and you?"
VIVIAN: "Yes, I'm well. I wondered if you were going to tell the coaches about our conversation during the break."
CISSY: "Yes, I plan to tell them once I've heard their plans. I want to see what they say and do without knowing they have support first, then we'll talk a bit and I'll let them know you agreed to work with them."
VIVIAN: "You should know that Viktor asked me to work with him one-on-one to help him through this. My sense is that he wants to do well; he wants to make improvements but he doesn't how. He even told me his wife suggested he work with me."

CISSY: "That sounds about right. His wife is the brains in the family. He's a good person but he can be rough and a bit harsh. What else did he talk about?"
VIVIAN: "Mental toughness."
CISSY: "Oh, okay, you mean for his team?"
VIVIAN: "Yes, for his team. He thinks it's a good strategy."
CISSY: "What do you think?"
VIVIAN: "I think it depends on what's done and how it's done. In itself it can be very helpful. But it depends."
CISSY: "I don't like it. If he does more of the same again this year, he's going to put me in a difficult situation."
VIVIAN: "Yes, so what can you tell me about my role, and what you want from me exactly when observing and working with the coaches?"
CISSY: "I want you to monitor them, coach them if you have to. I want you to be directive. Keep them going in the right direction. At the end of the season I don't want to fire anyone, but I will if I have to. I'm looking to you to help them improve and keep them in their job. Losing a coach is tough; there's so much hassle with the new hiring, the students get mixed up, and some get upset, some leave. The best thing is to improve the experience, but if he gives me no choice, he'll be out."
VIVIAN: "Are you going to tell them what your expectations are and what the consequences of this year might be for them?"
CISSY: "I'm not telling them, and I don't want you to either. But I want you to know I support you. I support them and I'm behind what we do. I'll make sure they don't know you and I talk, and I want you to do the same. If we talk it's only between us, okay?"
VIVIAN: "But what if I'm put in a situation where I might need to say something to them about their conditions?"
CISSY: "Then we will talk first and then, once I'm clear on things and what you're going to say, you can talk to them. Otherwise, don't say anything. Just help them and coach them up."
VIVIAN: "Do you want to know about the others?"
CISSY: "Sure, how's Robin?"
VIVIAN: "He's worried you're going to fire him."
CISSY: "Yes, I might have to do that. It's up to him. I warned him about his position and he has to respond if he wants to be here after this year. He knows what he has to do. I heard about what happened with Mark Champion, one of his players. That was outrageous, and exactly the kind of bone-headed behavior I hate from any coach, especially him. He's a good coach. I have no idea why he lost his head this season. That incident was terrible. We are lucky Mark and Javier sorted things out and it didn't get out how that situation blew up." [See Chapter 6.]
VIVIAN: "Will you say something to cool him down and give him confidence through this process?"
CISSY: "I'm going to tell him that he needs to work closely with you and listen to you. If he has any doubts about his direction he should contact you and sort

them through. I'm staying out of this situation. I want you to take the lead with him and the other two. I'm too deeply involved. Besides, I don't like being too close to people if I have to let them go."

The three coaches showed up together, greeted Cissy and Vivian, and took the same seats in the same positions around the conference table as they had done for the first meeting. They each took folders out of their bags and placed them on the table in front of them. The coaches seemed choreographed in their movements, which Vivian seemed to catch on too.

VIVIAN: "Good morning everyone, it's good to see you again and I'm excited to hear about your plans. Before we begin hearing the specifics of your intentions, does anyone want to share anything?"

TINA: "Yes, I have something on my mind. What happens if things don't go well? Are we being set up to fail ... I mean is this really about improving or are we just doing an exercise and we'll lose our jobs anyway?"

VIKTOR: "Yeah, I was wondering about that too."

ROBIN: "Me too." The room was immediately filled with tension. Vivian looked at Cissy, who seemed incensed by Tina's questions. She felt she was being ganged up on by the coaches. There was a period of silence while Cissy looked each coach in the eye.

CISSY: "Right now your jobs are not on the line. I have spoken to you individually, and you know you have to improve. Any decisions that are going to be made will be made next March after all your seasons are completed. It seems like you've been talking and you ambushed me. Do you think that is a high-quality way to treat me given all I've done for each of you?"

TINA: "We were worried that we would get fired if this doesn't work out. I mean, we're not sure if you need wins or just for the students to like us."

CISSY: "You know what you have to do. Don't look at me. I am not coaching your teams, you are. I am your boss, and I'm giving you a chance to improve your teams and yourselves. I mean, come on! You all used to be confident go-getters. What happened to you?"

ROBIN: "When you hired me, it was to build a program. I did that. I won championships. I got results. But that doesn't seem to matter anymore around here. The same for Viktor. He's won national championships. Where's the respect for the past?"

CISSY: "You got a whole lot of respect back then Robin. But now is different, and you better have a new way of approaching the new year and the new future because your athletes are different, their expectations of coaches are different, and if you feel like what you've been doing is working, then I'm telling you, you will coach yourself out of a job ... and you know it."

The room fell silent as everyone took in what Cissy said and let it sink in. Vivian waited about 20 seconds, then began.

VIVIAN: "Okay, it seems like there's some fear here. Let me put this in context. We all knew two weeks ago why we were doing this. We have talked and I have experienced a lot of energy from each coach about the future. I feel it is a stronger choice for you and for Cissy to discuss your ideas. Let's take a break and reconvene to share ideas and goals. I have an idea about each of your plans, and I am optimistic all of us will take positive things from this sharing. Come back in 5 minutes."

The coaches stayed in the room, and Cissy and Vivian went to the bathroom.

VIVIAN: "Are you okay?"
CISSY: "Sure. I really did not want that conversation this morning."
VIVIAN: "Well it's done. Let's move forward."

As Cissy and Vivian closed the door behind them on the way to the bathroom Viktor spoke to Robin and Tina.

VICTOR: "I am glad you said it Tina. Cissy has to know. It's not personal. She's a good person, but she had to know what we were feeling. Now she knows, we should forget about it and move on."
ROBIN: "Thanks for doing that Tina. Well … I guess I know where I stand. Get better or get out."

Tina said nothing back. She wished she had not been the one to raise the subject, but her colleagues seemed scared to voice their concerns, so she volunteered. Vivian and Cissy returned to the room.

VIVIAN: "Good, everyone is here. Viktor, would you mind starting off and telling us about your ideas?"

Cissy sat down. She looked more relaxed and calm. The short break had been useful to get her focus back. After all, she wanted what the coaches wanted, which was their success.

VIKTOR: "Okay, the big ideas are these. My first idea is to have all my top players over to my house for a BBQ before school starts, and I want them to think about goals they think we should set as a team. Vivian agreed to help me run the meeting. Then, I wanted to get one or two of our alumni players from the national championship teams to return to talk to the players about mental toughness and being strong. The next thing I want to do is redesign training. I talked to Vivian and I think I want my goal keeper to be the captain. He is a young player, a sophomore this year, but I realized all the players connect with him, some more than others, and he is the player I see most like myself. Perhaps he can lead where I can't. The next thing I am doing is going to see

Javier regularly. I have to work on myself and get better. I realize this year has not been good for me. I want to get better ... So what do you think about my ideas?"
CISSY: "Wow! How did you come to those conclusions?"
VIKTOR: "Well, I talked to my wife, and me and Vivian talked. I figured I need to shift responsibility to the students and not be so angry and frustrated. I suppose I have to relearn they are not me."
VIVIAN: "Thank you Viktor. Robin, can you go next?"
ROBIN: "No, I'll go last if it's okay with Tina."
TINA: "Sure, I'll go ... what ... you shy of sharing your plan?"

Robin looked away sheepishly.

TINA: "Well my plan is like this. First, I want to say Vivian was a big help when we talked. It was just good to talk through process things, but I called two of my old team mates who coach now and asked them how they do things. They're good coaches and I know they'd be helpful, so I decided to take some of their ideas and put them with mine, and this is what I came up with. I wrote them down in steps, so bear with me as I read them out.

Step one—I need an assistant coach. I can't do this all on my own because I need to individualize every bit of training and match play coaching this year. I need Cissy to look at the budget and see if she can get me a part-time practice coach for this year who can help me run practice, take videos, and make clip packages of the things the girls do well and where they can improve; and then and me and the girls can provide individualized feedback packages. I will get video on the road and they can cut it for feedback. I want to design practice based on the evidence, not my opinion. Sometimes I feel the top players don't believe me and blow me off because it's my opinion.

Step two—I want to meet all my players one-on-one at the beginning of the year off campus to talk about our personal relationships and find out where they are at and how they can improve. Then I want to meet with my top players and have them input into how practice is designed. And something else I want to do this year is build mini game plans for each doubles partnership. I can do this if I have an assistant coach.

The last thing I want to do is keep all the good things going we already do. If things go wrong it won't be because I threw everything out. Besides, Vivian will be on hand and I want to introduce her to the team and let them know I'm working with her to make myself better. She is part of the team."
CISSY: "Would a 20-hour, full-time graduate assistant be enough for you? Your budget won't stretch to an outside coach."
TINA: "Yeah, but the grad student needs to be able to hit balls and play. I didn't mention it, but I don't want to play against the girls this year unless they invite me. One of my friends said it's not good when I play hard and smash them. I want my assistant coach to hit with them. Then I can step back and lead."

CISSY: "Okay, you recruit the graduate student you want between now and when the team returns. Work with our human resource staff to make it happen. I'll check your budget, and if it's tight I'll find a way to make it work for you."
VIVIAN: "Great! Thank you Tina. Thank you Cissy. Robin, you're up."
ROBIN: "Well, I don't have much really. I mean I thought about things, and I had a good talk with Vivian, but I need more time."
CISSY: "You need more time. For what?"
ROBIN: "Well, I need more time because I'm going to fire the goal keeping coach."
CISSY: "What then? What else are you intending to do to improve your situation?"
ROBIN: "I hadn't thought that far. This is a big decision for me. He's good, but he's raw and young ..."
CISSY: "Robin, I told you you would coach yourself out of a job. This is unacceptable. You had two weeks. You had Vivian. All you have come here with is a decision you should have made during the season. Do you want to be a coach here? Do you know what is expected of you? Do you understand what you were asked to do to be here? The answer to all of these questions is 'yes'. You're a disappointment this morning Robin."
ROBIN: "I need more time."
VIVIAN: "Perhaps we can work on things after this meeting, Robin, and you can present them to Cissy before the end of the day?"
CISSY: "No Vivian. I see exactly where this is going. Robin, you do what you think is right. I have given you a chance for next year. If you want to stay here after the meeting and work with Vivian, fine. But if you don't, I'll know you don't see your future here after next year, and neither do I."
VIVIAN: "Let's take a break and return in 10 minutes. Robin, can I speak with you?"

Robin stayed behind while the others left the room. Vivian approached him.

VIVIAN: "What do you need my help with?"
ROBIN: "I didn't want to say in front of the others. I am the one that needs counseling and help, not the players. I don't know why or how I got in this position. I feel confused and I don't know why. Like I told you in our phone call, I don't know why I did most of the things I did this year the way I did. I don't think I'm mentally ill. But I don't want to talk about it with Cissy or in front of the others."
VIVIAN: "Okay, I understand where you're at. But you need to give Cissy something. It sounded like your job is on the line."
ROBIN: "Yeah. Can you help me tell her, but after we have finished. I've had a terrible year. I need a fresh start."
VIVIAN: "Sure."

Discussion questions

1. What issues are presented in this case?
2. How might the solutions the coaches presented enhance their next season's performance?
3. What challenges does this case present for the sport psychology practitioner serving the coaches and the Assistant Athletic Director?
4. How might organizational pressure be placed on a sport psychology practitioner in this case?
5. How might Vivian Moreno consider operating to maintain trust with all parties and be effective?
6. How might Vivian's work be evaluated at the end of the next season?

Author's notes

I find situations like the one shown in this case to be extremely tiring, difficult, and complex to manage because there is so much information, and sometimes you get squeezed between the organizational representative who employed you and the employees; in this case, the coaches are the employees. Most times I do not intend to be in the middle and in a position to know both sides of the story, but I knew I was responsible and accountable for all the communication I engaged in, which meant maintaining high levels of confidentiality. I found it common to have the scope and duration of the work expand too. I know I have established value when a client asks for further work when I have not invited them to do so.

In cases where an individual's employment is at stake, providing there are no unethical, abusive, or harmful behaviors demonstrated which I would bring up with them and the person who hired me, I see my role as helping keep them in their job. The interventions the coaches bring forward are a place to start. When coaches bring plans forward, they have goals and intentions, and I assume first they want to improve things and be positive; but I know plans look good on paper but they only get tested when they meet reality. When this happens coaches need support. Often good plans achieve poor outcomes, and taking early action to avoid disappointment is essential. I give attention to how plans roll out and how they are received, and take action as early as possible to build on the positive things and mitigate the negative aspects. I prefer to guide; but if I see a coach missing something I will rapidly bring it to their attention. I feel it is more important to be the coach's guide on the side with feedback and insight helping them shape and deliver coaching that fits their skills and personal qualities. If they are open to feedback and willing to improve, I believe a coach *can* improve and should be given the opportunity to do do.

When a coach like Robin needs personal support, I find my role being much less about what happens in the context of sport and more about the life the coach is experiencing. I focus on coaching the coach in this area; but if the issues presented by the coach are beyond my scope of practice, I refer them to a licensed mental health professional. In contrast, a clinical psychologist like Vivian Moreno can work on the personal and performance aspects without delay. Therefore, I advocate for all sport psychology professionals working with NCAA athletes to hold a clinical mental health license.

Further reading

Baltzell, A., Schinke, R. J., & Watson, J. (2010). Who is my client? *Association for the Advancement of Applied Sport Psychology Newsletter*, 25(2), 32–34.

Etzel, E. F., & Watson, J. C. (2007). Ethical challenges for psychological consultations in intercollegiate athletics. *Journal of Clinical Sport Psychology*, 1(3), 304–317.

Stewart, C. (2014). Failure to rehire: Why coaches get fired. *Physical Educator*, 71(4), 699–710.

Stapleton, A. B., Hankes, D. M., Hays, K. F., & Parham, W. D. (2010). Ethical dilemmas in sport psychology: A dialogue on the unique aspects impacting practice. *Professional Psychology: Research and Practice*, 41(2), 143–152.

INDEX

Abell, Derek xiii–xiv
academic mentors 70, 73
academic studies and sport priorities: academic mentors 70, 73; burnout and self-handicapping 6–8; career path, missed opportunities 93, 97–99, 100; career path, parental pressures 93–95, 141; student expectation challenges 105–106, 109, 110–111, 142
Aguilar, Javier: burnout/self-handicapping 3–8; coach-athlete relationship conflict 18, 52, 53–55; coach development 88; coach personal development 113–120; college sport, transition out 96–99; coming out, suggested advisor 62–63; high school to college transition 67–72; injury rehabilitation 78; on-court aggression 144–148; professional soccer, transition issues 22–28; team building 162–165
anterior cruciate ligament (ACL) injury rehabilitation: athlete profile, women's soccer 30–35; cast of characters 30; discussion points 29; discussion questions 35; imagery program implementation 31–35; student learning outcomes 30

Ball, Michelle 135–138
Banks, Carolyn 93–95
Banks, Shawndra 92–99
basketball, men's: athlete underperformance 103–109; high school to college transition 66–72

basketball, women's: college sport, transition out 92–100; on-court aggression, athlete's opposition 141–148
Beck, Mike 66–73
binge drinking: athlete profile, men's soccer 132–133; athlete's attitude to alcohol, coach's anger 133–135; cast of characters 132; counseling, uncomfortable questioning 135–138; discussion points 131; discussion questions 138; professional judgements and practices 138–139; student learning outcomes 131–132
Brillo, Mike 155–156
bullying, behavior patterns 13–18, 82, 144–145
burnout/self-handicapping: athlete profile, women's swimming 2–3; cast of characters 2; discussion points 1; discussion questions 8; sensitive approach in athlete meeting 3–8; student learning outcomes 2; symptoms and treatments 8–9

cast of characters xxiii–xxiv
Champion, Mark 50–55
coach-athlete, interpersonal conflict: athlete profile, women's tennis 11–12; cast of characters 11; coach behavior patterns 17–18; conflict event and reactions 12–17; discussion points 10; discussion questions 18; peer coaching and guidance 83–87; post-conflict talks and goal setting 18; student learning outcomes 10–11

coach-athlete relations: athlete's attitude to alcohol, coach's anger 133–135; coach's frustration over injury 76–77; coach status unchallengeable 51–53; communication gaps and solutions 110–111; fair treatment and encouragement 51–52, 67, 96, 113–114; negative competition, team discord 159–165; negativity and isolation problems 69–71, 108; organizational review, selected coaches 179–186, 189–195; psychologist as facilitator 46–48, 55–57, 89, 139; sensitive subject, discussion challenges 125–129; team confidence issues 155–156; team discord, coach unawareness 169–172; transfer and team coordination difficulties 104–107, 108–109
coach-athlete relationship conflict: athlete profile, men's soccer 50–51; cast of characters 50; coach challenged, player reprimanded 51–53; discussion points 49; discussion questions 55; psychologist, intervention guidance 55–57; psychologist, player consultation 53–55; student learning outcomes 49–50
coach-coach relations: peer appraisal 42–43; peer coaching and guidance 83–87, 156–157; player recruitment, tense discussions 152–155; sensitive subject, advice sort 125, 128; team inclusion differences 104–105
coach-consultant relations: athlete's personal development plan 73; behavior awareness and education 130, 162–165; coaching reviews, psychologist's roles 179–186, 189–193, 195, 196–197; coach's aggressiveness 144–145; coach's doubts over usefulness 114–117, 176; confidentiality issues 71; critical feedback, supportive solutions 176; leadership and support strategies 157; life transitions, identification and therapies 119–121; referral, reasons behind 148–149
coach development: cast of characters 82; coach profile, women's tennis 82–83; discussion points 81; discussion questions 88; education opportunities 87, 89; peer coaching and guidance 83–87; sports psychologist, role for 87–89; student learning outcomes 81–82
coaching style: bullying, behavior patterns 13–18, 82, 144–145; demeaning and negative 155–156; encouragement and responsive learning 67, 141–142, 146–147; influencing junior coaches 82–83; set standards/expectations 42–43, 51–53, 69, 142–144, 170–173; transition expectations 22, 24–27
coach personal development: cast of characters 113; coach profile, water polo 113–114; discussion points 112; discussion questions 120; personal mindset and life transitions 119–120; psychologist, doubts over usefulness 114–117; psychologist's multi-therapy approach 121; student learning outcomes 112–113
cognitive appraisal model 110
college sport, transition out: advice, mistaken expectations 95–96; athlete profile, women's basketball 92–93; career path, parental pressures 93–95; cast of characters 92; discussion points 91; discussion questions 99, 100; stress-related aggression 96; student-athletes, shared attributes 100; student feedback scarce 100; student learning outcomes 92; transition concerns, consultant discussion 96–99
coming out: athlete profile, women's tennis 59–60; cast of characters 59; discussion points 58; discussion questions 63; peer support and guidance 60–63; person-centered counseling 63–64; student learning outcomes 59
consultant confidentiality: athlete trust, gaining of 68; background information and permission 4, 9, 63; coaching reviews 191, 196; feedback to coaches 71, 89, 97–98, 139
consultant referral, athlete's reluctance 67–68, 78, 148–149
Cooper, Sara 59–64
counselor, professional: managing client responses 135–138
Court, Michelle 152

Davis, Diana 2–8
Dean, David 124–130
debrief technique 46–47
Diaz, Esmerelda 12, 13, 14–16
diving, women's 124–130
Drew, Celia 'Cissy': athlete underperformance 105–106, 107; coach-athlete, interpersonal conflict 16–18, 53; coach-athlete relations, organizational review 179–182, 189, 190–195; coach development 83, 85, 86, 87–88; team building 160–163, 165; team development 169–174

eating disorder: athlete profile, women's diving 124; body weight pressures 127–128, 129; case, approach variations 122–123; cast of characters 123; coach's knowledge and actions 124–125, 128–129; coach's sensitive questioning 125–128; discussion points 123; discussion questions 129; psychologist's approach 129–130; student learning outcomes 123

family relationships: athlete character and family values 50, 54, 141; athlete sexuality, response concerns 61–62; career path, parental pressures 93–95; community-centered 66; financial support 103–104; parent in coaching role 11–12; parents as sounding board 39–40, 41–42, 71–72; sibling illness, major distraction 76–78; unstable parents, athlete's coping strategies 132–133

goal keeping errors (soccer): athlete profile, men's soccer 38–39; cast of characters 38; coaching style, peer appraisal 42–43; discussion points 37; discussion questions 46; player-coach relations 40–41, 43–46; player improvement, psychological solutions 46–48; sports psychologist, wariness of 45–46; student learning outcomes 38; unconfident player and team expectations 39–43, 46

goal setting, coach/athlete relationship: hand injury, recovery process 79–80; mental skills, training to meet expectations 145–148; post-conflict talks 19; underuse by coaches 109

hand injury, recovery process: athlete profile, men's water polo 75–76; cast of characters 75; coach's frustration, misjudged injury 76–78; coach's goal setting 78–79, 80; discussion points 74; discussion questions 79; psychologist involvement 78, 79–80; sport medicine professional's plan 76–77, 79; student learning outcomes 74–75

high school to college transition: academic mentors 70, 73; athlete profile, men's basketball 66–67; cast of characters 66; consultant confidentiality 68, 71; discussion points 65; discussion questions 72; interpersonal skills development 72–73; negativity and isolation problems 68–72; student learning outcomes 66

Hollander, Jocelyn A. xvii

imagery programs: coaches' underuse 109; sport medicine professional's use 29, 31–36

injury and athlete behavior: goal setbacks 21–22; self-handicapping 1, 3, 5–7, 8–9

injury rehabilitation: imagery programs and trained use 31–36

Johnson, Jake 104–107
Johnston, Jenny 76, 79–80

Kelly, Marty: goal keeping errors (soccer) 42–46, 47; team toughness 152–154, 156–157

Landing, Mike 104–105
life and career transitions 21–28

Marriott, Robin: athlete's binge drinking 132, 133–135, 139; coach-athlete relationship conflict 51–53; coach-athlete relations, organizational review 179–186, 190, 191–193, 195; coach development 82–89; goal keeping errors (soccer) 42–43, 47; professional soccer, transition issues 22–27; team toughness 151–157
meeting facilitation skills 186–187
mental health professional, referrals to 139
mental skills training: coaches' underuse 109; integrated practices 111; mental toughness, approaches to 145–148, 149, 157; sport medicine professional's use 29, 31–36
Moreno, Vivian: athlete underperformance 107–109; coach-athlete relations, organizational review 179–186, 189–195
Morrison, Tina: coach-athlete, interpersonal conflict 11, 12–19; coach-athlete relations, organizational review 179–185, 190, 192–193, 194–195; coach development 82–89; team building 159–166

on-court aggression: athlete profile, women's basketball 141–142; athlete's toughness, coach expectations 142–144; cast of characters 141; coach's aggressiveness to psychologist 144–145; discussion points 140; discussion questions 148; mental skills training and goal setting 145–148; student learning outcomes 140–141

Papadopoulos, Yannis 103–111
Payton, Drake 132–139

personal relationships: athlete goals and partner tensions 21, 22–26, 28; coming out, shared experiences 60–63; local gym, shared outlook 75; team mate as coach messenger 14–16

professional soccer, transition issues: athlete profile, men's soccer 21–22; cast of characters 21; commitments, sporting and personal 22–26, 28; consultant/coach relationship 26–27, 28; discussion points 20; discussion questions 27; goal and achievement schedules 27–28; student learning outcomes 20–21

Radic, Sime 75–80
rapid technique correction 46–47
rational emotive behavioral therapy (REBT) 63–64
Redmond, Mark 21–28, 38–39
Reinwagner, Otto 39–40, 41–42
Reinwagner, Rob 38–47
Rowland, Micah 30–35

Schmid, Isabel 60–63
self-handicapping: coping with burnout 1, 3, 5–7; symptoms and treatments 8–9
soccer, men's: athlete's binge drinking 132–139; coach-athlete relations, coaching review 179–186, 191–193, 195; coach-athlete relationship conflict 51–57; college to professional, transition issues 21–28; player errors, impact on self, team and coaches 38–48; team toughness 151–157; transition, coach expectations 22, 24–27
soccer, women's: ACL injury rehabilitation, imagery programs 31–36
Sparks, Lily 'Sparksy': ACL injury rehabilitation 31–33, 35; burnout/self-handicapping 3, 5–8
sport medicine professional: imagery programs and trained use 29, 31–36; injury rehabilitation 76–77, 79–80
sports administrator: athlete underperformance 105–106, 107, 110; coach-athlete, interpersonal conflict 16–18, 56; coach recruitment 83; organizational review, selected coaches 179–182, 189, 190–195; peer talk for coach development 85, 86, 87–88; psychologist and client relations 165; psychologist's role, expansion of 191, 196; team building 160–163, 165; team development, supportive solutions 169–174; team mission, support role 157

sports administrator-directed improvement: part 1: administrator objectives 179–180, 186; cast of characters 179; coach-athlete relations, coaching review 180–186; coach profiles 179–180; discussion points 178, 186; discussion questions 186; meeting facilitation, psychologist's role 186–187; student learning outcomes 179

sports administrator-directed improvement: part 2: administrator objectives 189; cast of characters 189; coach-athlete relations, review conclusions 190–195; coach profiles 189–190; discussion points 188; discussion questions 196; psychologist in advisory/observational role 189–193, 195; student learning outcomes 189

swimming, women's: burnout and self-handicapping trade-off 2–8; student-athlete schedules 1

teacher's role and responsibilities: assessment methods xix–xx; cases, writing process and use xx–xxii; communication through facilitation xvi–xvii; critical thinking skills xv; discussions, preparation activities xvii–xviii; ground rules xviii; inclusive learning xviii–xix; participation policy xix; questions for effective discussion xv–xvi; time management xviii

teaching case method: approach to learning and responsibilities xiii–xv; assessment, participation and performance xix–xx; cases, selection criteria xiii–xiv; cases, writing process and use xx–xxii; communication skills xvi–xvii; discussions, preparation activities xvii–xviii; ground rules xviii; inclusive learning xviii–xix; role of the teacher xv; time management xviii; training and self-help programs xx

team building: cast of characters 159; coach profile, women's tennis 159–160; coactive team development 166; discussion points 158; discussion questions 165; leadership and evaluation skills 164–165; player's negative competitiveness 159–162; poor coach awareness, denial of 161–164; psychologist as facilitator 165–166; student learning outcomes 158–159

team development: cast of characters 169; coach profile, men's water polo 169; discussion points 168; discussion questions 175–176; negativity, supportive solutions 174–175; psychologist as facilitator 176;

results related recommendations 172–174; student learning outcomes 168–169; team building, coach's dismissal 171–172; team discord, coach unawareness 169–172
team mates: demeaning coach, impact of 155–156; false friendship 75; interaction experience, impact on play 39, 40–42, 45, 105–106; negative competitiveness 159–161; negativity and isolation problems 69–70, 71, 108; support role, player-coach conflict 14–16, 55; team confidence issues 155–156, 163–165, 169, 170–172
team toughness: cast of characters 151; coach profile, men's soccer 151; discussion points 150; discussion questions 156; mental skills training 157; player recruitment, tense discussions 152–155; poor results, coach pressurized 151–152; student learning outcomes 151; team confidence issues 155–156
tennis, women's: athletic development 11–12; coach-athlete conflict, event and reactions 12–17; coach-athlete relations, coaching review 179–185, 192–193, 194–195; coaching style, impact on students 17–18, 82–83; coming out and relationships 60–64; team building 159–166
Tham, Quang 95–96
Thompson, Mike 'Thompo': ACL injury rehabilitation 31–35; student's eating disorder 125, 128

underperformance: athlete profile, men's basketball 103–104; cast of characters 103; discussion points 102–103; discussion questions 110; mental skills training 109, 111; student learning outcomes 103; transfer and team coordination difficulties 104–107; transition concerns, consultant discussion 107–109; transition concerns, solutions 110–111

Varedo, Jaime: coach-athlete relationship conflict 51–53; goal keeping errors (soccer) 40–41, 42–43, 47; team toughness 153–154, 155–157
Varga, Cindy: coach personal development 113–114, 119, 121; team development 174–175
Varga, Viktor: coach-athlete relations, organizational review 179–185, 190–191, 193–194; coach personal development 113–120; injury rehabilitation 75, 76–80; team development 169–176

Washington, Becky: mentor role 92; on-court aggression, athlete's opposition 143–148
water polo: coach-athlete relations, coaching review 179–185, 190–191, 193–194; coach personal development 113–120; hand injury, recovery process 75–80; team development 169–176

Xavier, Dominique 141–148

Yang, Jenny 124–130
Young, Louisa 11–19

PGMO 06/06/2018